**DEMOCRATS
OF OREGON:**
The Pattern of
Minority Politics
1900-1956

University of Oregon **Books**

EUGENE, OREGON

1970

Robert E. Burton

DEMOCRATS OF OREGON:
The Pattern of Minority Politics,
1900-1956

FOR TEDDY

Contents

Preface   ix

I   The Political Setting of Oregon   1

II   The Politics of Reform   17

III   Division and Debacle:
          A Party in Shambles   39

IV   The Great Depression:
          Political Challenge and Lost Opportunities   61

V   The Democratic Party in Transition   91

VI   The Liberal Challenge:
          Building A New Party   103

VII   The Democratic Party at Flood Tide   125

Epilogue   141

Note on Sources   147

Appendices   150

Index   153

Tables

1   Modified One-Party Republican States   8-9

2   Oregon Republican Gubernatorial Primary
      Vote in Relation to Other Votes Cast, 1906-1956   8-9

3   Summary of Voting Figures for President
      in Oregon, 1900-1948   94-95

4   Summary of Voting Figures for Governor
      in Oregon, 1902-1948   94-95

5   Summary of Voting Figures for Senator
      in Oregon, 1906-1948   98-99

Preface

This book is an account of the history of the Democratic Party in Oregon between 1900 and 1956. The major objective has been to sketch the history of the Democratic Party, but I have also sought to describe the tenor of Oregon politics in the twentieth century and the impact of national political trends on the state. The study concludes with a few remarks on the nature of Democratic Party politics in the decade following 1956, but a complete explanation of this period must await the day when the papers of Senator Wayne L. Morse and others are available.

In an attempt to give this study some relevance beyond the confines of Oregon politics, I have proceeded on the general assumption that national politics is based on state politics and that the history of one political party in one state can contribute to a better understanding of the political life of the nation. Consequently, parallels are drawn between the pattern of Democratic politics in Oregon and the pattern of national Democratic politics. Where possible, the experience of the Oregon Democratic Party is measured against that of other state Democratic parties. In addition, a tentative explanation is offered for voting behavior in Oregon based on the concept of political culture, but a detailed statistical analysis of voting behavior has not been the primary concern.

In writing a book, an author invariably puts himself into the debt of many people. No written acknowledgement, however, can adequately express my debt of gratitude to Professors Earl Pomeroy and Martin Schmitt of the University of Oregon. Both have given generously of their time in matters of criticism and advice, and helped in many other ways.

The political cartoons which appear in the book are the work of Quincy Scott who was staff artist for the Portland *Oregonian* in the 1930s and the 1940s. They are adapted here with the permission of the University of Oregon Library, where the original drawings have been placed.

I thank Monroe Sweetland, Howard Morgan, James Goodsell, and Edward F. Bailey for sharing with me their recollections of Democratic Party history before and after the Second World War. A special word of thanks is given to Senator Maurine Neuberger for granting permission to consult the papers of Senator Richard L. Neuberger. Finally, I acknowledge the assistance of Professor George T. Morgan, Jr., of the University of Houston who read portions of this manuscript and offered many valuable suggestions. My wife, Teddy, to whom this book is dedicated, contributed more than she knows.

San Luis Obispo, California   R.E.B.
August 1970

I THE POLITICAL SETTING OF OREGON

When Will Rogers was asked about his politics he said, "I belong to no organized party: I'm a Democrat." Democrats in Oregon would have recognized Rogers' reply as an apt description of their own party for much of its history. The lack of Democratic unity, complicated by an overwhelming disadvantage in registration, gave Republicans control of Oregon politics most of the time from the late nineteenth to the mid-twentieth century.[1]

After the Second World War, however, a determined group of liberal Democrats set out to renovate and rebuild the party. They faced a twofold task: to seize control of the party from old-guard conservatives, who by contrast made many Oregon Republicans appear liberal, and to initiate a grass-roots movement to rebuild party organization and entice bright young men to join their cause. A major victory came in 1950 when Democratic registration, for the first time in the twentieth centry, exceeded Republican. In 1952, the office of attorney general, held by Republicans for sixty years, fell to the Democrats; two years later, Democrats elected a United States senator for the first time since 1914, one representative, and the first Democratic commissioner of labor in state history. This series of victories reached a climax in 1956, when the party won the governorship, a second seat in the United States Senate, three of the four congressional positions, and control of the state legislature. Since then, a competitive two-party system has prevailed in Oregon.[2]

---

[1] Between 1858 and 1950, Oregonians elected twenty-five governors: fifteen Republicans, nine Democrats, and one independent. From 1859 to 1950, thirty-seven United States senators were selected: twenty-six Republicans and eleven Democrats. In the same period, 106 congressmen were elected: eighty-eight Republicans, and eighteen Democrats. In presidential elections, Democrats captured the state on six occasions (1868, 1912, 1932, 1936, 1940, and 1944). See Leonie N. Brooke, "Voting Behavior In Oregon: An Analysis," *Oregon Historical Quarterly* 52 (Mar. 1952), pp. 3-22.

[2] For a general description of Oregon politics which centers on the period

Nevertheless, during the long period of Republican hegemony, the Democratic Party, without adequate organization or registration majorities, managed to elect some candidates to high state and federal posts. These victories suggest that factors other than number and organization influence the outcome of elections and the status of a party.

The pattern of politics in any state reflects the social, economic, and political variables which from time to time, and in varying degrees, impinge upon and determine the behavior of the politicians and the voters. Oregon is by no means unique in its broad socio-economic characteristics—the state in fact shares much in common with certain other states—but it differs significantly in detail.

An absence of minority groups, ethnic or racial, large enough to play a decisive role in state politics is a marked characteristic of Oregon's past and present social composition. Several European nations have contributed to Oregon's population, but there exists no important ethnic community with a separate political identity. Nonwhite residents of the state have never totaled more than five per cent of the population, and usually comprised less than two per cent. For the first ninety years of statehood, Negroes accounted for less than one half of one per cent of the population, and not until 1960 did the figure reach one per cent.

The territorial census of 1850 reveals that immigrants from the eight states of the Mississippi and Ohio river valleys predominated in the first wave of migration to Oregon. Important contingents also came from New England, the South, and the Middle Atlantic states. Immigrants from Germany, England, Ireland, Canada, and the Scandinavian countries constituted the majority of foreign-born who made Oregon their home.[3] Although early Oregonians were of diverse origins, the state's physical isolation and slow but steady rate of growth for three decades after 1850 enabled the inhabitants to blend into a homogeneous group. Later migration and economic growth had their impact, of course, but these changes did not upset the gradual social evolution of the state. Indeed, several historians of the Pacific Northwest identify social and economic continuity as the key fact of Oregon history.[4]

since 1956, see John M. Swarthout and Kenneth R. Gervais, "Oregon: Political Experiment Station," *Politics in the American West*, ed. Frank H. Jonas (Salt Lake City, 1969), pp. 297-325.

[3] Jesse S. Douglas, "Origins of the Population of Oregon in 1850," *Pacific Northwest Quarterly* 41 (Apr. 1950), pp. 95-108.

[4] See Dorothy O. Johansen, "Oregon's Role in American History: An Old Theme Recast," *Pacific Northwest Quarterly* 40 (Apr. 1949), pp. 85-92; James R. Robertson, "The Social Evolution of Oregon," *Oregon Historical*

It is true that successive waves of immigration did not greatly alter the early established social patterns, but it is important to note that at two periods in Oregon history emigration had a profound effect on the political balance of the state. The residents of Oregon prior to 1860 came, in the main, from the Midwestern states, and had carried with them the ideals of Jeffersonian agrarian democracy. A firm allegiance to the Union prompted them to "steer a middle course," as one historian has put it, "to avoid the extremes of both North and South."[5] The Democratic Party mirrored this political persuasion, and for twenty years after Oregon's admission to the Union in 1859, that party dominated the politics of the state. Between 1859 and 1879, Oregonians elected twice as many Democrats as Republicans in statewide elections for governor, secretary of state, state treasurer, and congressman. Democratic control of the state legislature during this period resulted in the selection of eight Democrats as United States senator while only three Republicans were chosen.[6] But beginning in the 1880s, the Democrats became a minority party when immigrants from Wisconsin, Michigan, and Minnesota, as well as increased numbers from Sweden, Norway, and Germany, migrated to Oregon and made the Republican Party their political spokesman.[7]

Even though Oregon experienced later surges in population, not until the boom in employment associated with the Second World War did newcomers to the state appreciably alter the political picture. In this instance, the Democratic Party benefited most. The workers who came to Portland's shipyards and to the forests of southwest Oregon provided bases upon which to rebuild the Democratic Party.

In religion, the state has been dominated by various Protestant

---

Quarterly 3 (Mar. 1902), pp. 1-37; Lancaster Pollard, *Oregon and the Pacific Northwest* (Portland, 1946), chaps. 9-12.

[5] Robert W. Johannsen, "Spectators of Disunion: The Pacific Northwest and the Civil War," *Pacific Northwest Quarterly* 44 (July 1953), p. 108.

[6] William D. Fenton, "Political History of Oregon from 1865 to 1876," *Oregon Historical Quarterly* 3 (Mar. 1902), pp. 38-70; M. C. George, "Political History of Oregon from 1876-1896 Inclusive," *Oregon Historical Quarterly* 3 (June 1902), pp. 107-122.

[7] During the first wave of migration to Oregon, heads of families were more from the Northeast than the general population. The large number of Mississippi Valley immigrants was composed to a large extent of children who left Missouri at early ages. Thus the apparent political change stemming from the migration of the 1880s, when many families of New England and Middle-Atlantic stock moved from the Old Northwest to Oregon, was perhaps not so great as it seemed. See Douglas, "Origins of the Population of Oregon in 1850," pp. 95-108. For a discussion of migration in the 1880s, see Pollard, "The Pacific Northwest," *Regionalism in America*, ed. Merrill Jensen (Madison, 1951), pp. 206-209.

denominations. The last published religious census (1936) and supplementary findings of the National Council of Churches report the Methodist Episcopal Church as the largest Protestant denomination, followed by Presbyterians, Lutherans, and the Protestant Episcopalians. In 1936, Roman Catholics constituted 25.5 per cent of all church members in the state and the combined Protestant congregations totaled 71 per cent; in 1950, the Roman Catholics accounted for 26.4 per cent and Protestants for 72 per cent. Jewish congregations, centered almost exclusively in Portland, never totaled more than two per cent of church membership. In reported church memberships, as a percentage of total population, Oregon ranks lowest among all states.[8]

For the greater part of its history, Oregon's economy has depended on its natural resources. Agricultural products, timber, and the fishing industry traditionally have provided the primary means of livelihood. The fertile Willamette River Valley, bounded on the west by the Coast Range and on the east by the Cascade Mountains, serves as the heartland of the state. Among the farms and orchards of the valley are the major urban areas and nearly two-thirds of the population of the state.

The Cascades form a natural barrier between the moist, mild climate of western Oregon and the dry plateau country of the east. The northern and central areas of eastern Oregon, traversed by streams, are good country for wheat and cattle. The southern portion of this region, by contrast, is barren and dry, capable of supporting only scattered and isolated sheep ranches.

The narrow coastal plain on the west quickly became the center of shipping and fishing activity. At the northern terminus of this plain, the Columbia River forms the boundary between Oregon and Washington. Inland, across the Coast Range in the north, lies Portland, the state's largest city, commercial center, and port. Throughout most of Oregon, but mainly in the south and on the slopes of the Cascades and Coast Range, forestlands abound.[9]

The first permanent settlers to Oregon were attracted by the rich farmland in the Willamette Valley. From the mid-nineteenth century until the Second World War, farm produce led the Oregon economy. Beginning in the late 1930s, however, the base of the Oregon economy began to change. Farm products yielded first place to lumber and wood products, and by 1940 Oregon surpassed

---

[8] U.S. Bureau of the Census, *Religious Bodies: 1936* (Washington, D.C., 1941), I, pp. 807-808; *Churches and Church Membership in the United States: An Enumeration and Analysis by Counties, States and Regions* (New York: National Council of the Churches of Christ in the U.S.A., 1957), Series C, No. 56 Oregon.

[9] Pollard, *Oregon and the Pacific Northwest*, pp. 33-48.

all other states in timber production, besides supplying approximately one half of the nation's plywood. The war brought workers to new Oregon industries, and union membership increased nearly 300 per cent between 1935 and 1953. The lumber industry has maintained its position as the mainstay of the economy, employing 63 per cent of the industrial workers of the state and accounting for two-thirds of the industrial payroll.[10] The per capita income in Oregon, like the per capita income of the Far West, consistently has been higher than the national average.[11]

The persistence of an agricultural way of life is reflected in both the urban/rural distribution of the population and representation in the state legislature. Not until the decade of the 1920s did urban dwellers in Oregon number approximately 50 per cent of the population. The ratio remained nearly static until the late 1950s. In 1960, the percentages stood at 62.2 per cent urban to 37.8 per cent rural. Before reapportionment of the Oregon state legislature in 1952, the rural regions of the state were grossly over-represented. Since 1910, Multnomah County, containing approximately a third of the state's population, elected less than a fourth of the Oregon house and senate. Until 1952, the rural minority elected a majority in both houses of the state legislature.[12]

Oregon's measured rate of growth, the religious, ethnic, and racial homogeneity of its small population, and an economy dominated by resources within the boundary of the state have combined to produce a high degree of intrastate cohesiveness. This, in turn, prompted a relatively stable attitude toward politics, a contrast to some states where cultural diversity and a rapid industrial pace nurtured continuing political divisions in the electorate. This is not to say that politics in Oregon existed without acrimonious debate or, on certain occasions, militant third-party movements; what is suggested is that the uniform socio-economic background of Ore-

---

10 Lester G. Seligman, "Political Change: Legislative Elites and Parties in Oregon," *Western Political Quarterly* 17 (June 1964), pp. 177-179; *Oregon Blue Book 1967-1968* (Salem, 1968), pp. 147-148.

11 Earl Pomeroy, *The Pacific Slope: A History of California, Oregon, Washington, Idaho, Utah, and Nevada* (New York, 1965), p. 373.

12 Gordon E. Baker, "Reapportionment by Initiative in Oregon," *Western Political Quarterly* 12 (June 1960), pp. 508-515. Occupations of state representatives reflect the rural domination of the legislature. Before 1937, farmers constituted more than one-third of the house and senate, but increased urbanization and industrialization since then has resulted in a decline of farmers in the state legislature. Beween 1937 and 1956, this occupational group totaled but one-fifth of the house and senate. See Waldo Schumacher, "Oregon Legislators," *Commonwealth Review* 20 (Jan. 1939), pp. 675-682; Michael Munk, "The Oregon Political Elite: A Study of State Legislators' Social Characteristics, 1939-1957" (unpublished master's thesis, University of Oregon, 1959), pp. 24-26.

gon politics has influenced the role of its political parties and the behavior of its voters.

In party registration and voting, Oregonians over the years favored the Republican Party. Between 1900 and 1932 the Republicans always enjoyed a two-to-one registration ratio over Democrats and several times a majority of three to one. Even during the administration of President Franklin D. Roosevelt (1933-1945), Republican registration never dropped below 50 per cent of all registered voters in the state.[13] And, while there is little agreement among political scientists on the best measure of party competitiveness,[14] the results of two widely used formulas indicate that until recently the state could be classified as "modified one-party Republican."

Selecting the four decades between 1914 and 1954, Austin Ranney and Willmoore Kendall tabulated the results of all elections for three offices having a statewide constituency: president, governor, and United States senator. On the basis of the percentage of victory for each party in forty-eight states, Ranney and Kendall designated Oregon and several other states "modified one-party Republican" because the Democratic Party won no more than 25 per cent of all the elections, but received over 30 per cent of the vote in over 70 per cent of elections.[15] The figures for Oregon and seven other "modified one-party Republican" states are given in Table 1.

In a classic study of Southern politics, V. O. Key, Jr., employed a second quantitative test for gauging party competition which is related to primary elections. A characteristic of one-party states is the large participation of the majority party in the primaries as compared to the general election. It is in the primary that the various factions of the dominant party battle for nominations, because with large advantages in registration, candidates nominated in the primary are likely to be successful in the general election.[16]

---

[13] Registration statistics are from the *Oregon Blue Books*.

[14] For different approaches in measuring party competitiveness see Joseph A. Schlesinger, "A Two-Dimensional Scheme for Classifying the States According to Degrees of Inter-Party Competition," *American Political Science Review* 49 (Dec. 1955), pp. 1120-1128; Robert T. Golembiewski, "A Taxonomic Approach to State Political Party Strength," *Western Political Quarterly* 12 (Sept. 1958), pp. 494-513; Richard I. Hofferbert, "Classification of American State Party Systems," *Journal of Politics* 26 (Aug. 1964), pp. 550-567; V. O. Key, Jr., *American State Politics: An Introduction* (New York, 1956), pp. 98ff; Joseph A. Schlesinger, *Ambition and Politics: Political Careers in the United States* (Chicago, 1966).

[15] Austin Ranney and Willmoore Kendall, *Democracy and the American Party System* (New York, 1956), pp. 158-166.

[16] V. O. Key, Jr., *Southern Politics in State and Nation* (New York, 1949), pp. 406-416.

Statistics for the Republican gubernatorial primary vote in relation to all other votes cast were tabulated for Oregon and appear in Table 2.

Table 2 illustrates that on occasion Oregon exhibits one-party tendencies, as in the period from 1914 to 1930, but on the whole it does not conform to the familiar Southern pattern. In no gubernatorial election between 1906 and 1956 did the Republican percentage of the total primary vote exceed the all-party vote in the general election as is common in one-party states.[17] In only five of the fifteen gubernatorial elections did the number of Republican primary votes actually exceed the Republican votes in the general election. But in eleven of the fifteen gubernatorial elections the Republican percentage of the total primary vote surpassed its percentage of the total general election vote. In tests of party competitiveness, the decrease between the Republican primary and general election vote is an indication of strength—provided the Republican candidate wins the general election.

Statistical measurements of party strength are, of course, only imperfect indicators of trends and often obscure more than they explain. Although Oregon may be considered "modified one-party Republican" until the decade of the 1950s,[18] there was seldom ideological or organizational unity within either Republican or Democratic ranks beyond the party label. This lack of party regularity can be attributed to several nuances of the Oregon political scene.

Party organization in Oregon is defined and prescribed in detail by statute. A political party is legally recognized if its presidential electors receive at least 20 per cent of the vote at the time of presidential elections. Parties are organized primarily on a hierarchical base. Each of Oregon's thirty-six counties is subdivided into precincts which elect precinct committeemen and committeewomen. These officers choose county chairmen and vice-chairmen, who then select the chairman of the state central committees. Precinct, county, and state chairmen are selected biennially. Since 1913, na-

---

[17] Compare the Oregon patterns to the uniformly higher Democratic primary totals in southern states as given in table 13 of V. O. Key, Jr., *Politics, Parties and Pressure Groups* (New York, 1952), p. 427. A second useful comparison can be made with the Republican primary vote in Wisconsin, where that party maintained a somewhat stronger position than did the Republican Party of Oregon. See Leon D. Epstein, *Politics in Wisconsin* (Madison, 1958), table 2, p. 40.

[18] This type of classification does not take into account the virtual monopoly Republicans had on other state offices in Oregon. For example, although the Democrats elected a state treasurer in 1948, the first since 1886, no Democrat has been elected secretary of state since 1874. Similarly, the state legislature was in the hands of Republicans over most of the twentieth century before 1956. During the New Deal, Democrats captured the lower house in 1934 and 1936.

TABLE 1		Republican Wins	Democrati Win
Modified One-Party Republican States	Oregon	27	
	Iowa	36	1
	Kansas	38	
	Maine	41	
	North Dakota	37	
	New Hampshire	40	
	Pennsylvania	28	
	South Dakota	36	

TABLE 2

Oregon Republican Gubernatorial Primary Vote In Relation To Other Votes Cast, 1906-1956	1909	1910	1914	1918	192
Republican primary vote as per cent of total primary vote:	77%	81%	70%	83%	82%
Republican general election vote as per cent of total general election vote:	77%	40%	49%	53%	43%
Republican primary vote as per cent of Republican vote in general election:	99%[a]	89%[a]	73%	109%	116%

[a] Indicates Democratic victory.

[b] Indicates three way race between Republican, Democrat, and Independent; in 1930 the Independent candidate won.

SOURCE: Table 1. Austin Ranney and Willmore Kendall, *Democracy and the American Party System* (New York: Harcourt, Brace, and Company, Inc., 1956), Tale 1, p. 164. Reprinted with the permission of Harcourt, Brace, Jovanovich, Inc. Table 2. *Trends in Oregon Voting, 1858-1960* (Salem: Secretary of State, 1962).

Third Party Wins	Per Cent of Democratic Wins	Per Cent of Elections with Democratic Vote over 30%	Per Cent of Elections with Democratic Vote over 40%
1	25.0	89.1	56.8
0	21.7	89.1	71.7
0	15.5	97.8	68.9
0	8.9	91.1	55.5
0	17.8	75.5	57.8
0	13.0	100.0	86.9
0	22.2	91.7	66.7
0	20.0	97.8	73.3

1926	1930	1934	1938	1942	1946	1948	1950	1954	1956
78%	82%	65%	52%	64%	66%	65%	52%	61%	53%
53%	19%	29%	57%	78%	69%	53%	66%	57%	49%
102%	309%[b]	160%[ab]	61%	62%	41%	84%	54%	62%	69%[a]

tional committeemen and committeewomen have been elected for four-year terms in statewide primaries held in nonpresidential-election years.[19]

Statutory provisions for organization notwithstanding, the adoption of political reforms during the first decade of the twentieth century weakened parties in the state. Enactment of the direct primary in 1904 most noticeably corroded effective party unity. Prior to adoption of the law, party conventions selected candidates for office, but the new statute required party neutrality while individuals or coalitions vied for nominations. As a result, potential candidates created personal organizations in campaigns for nomination, and because factional divisions frequently extended beyond the primary, personal followings supported by business, civic, or agricultural groups often took the place of party machinery in the general election. Two Republican governors, Earl Snell (1943-1947) and Douglas McKay (1949-1952), who were automobile dealers before their election, effectively used the Oregon Automobile Dealers Association as a base of political support. So successful was this support that Charles A. Sprague, an incumbent Republican governor who was defeated by Snell in the gubernatorial primary of 1942, said of his opponent's alliance with automobile dealers: "I was up against the strongest personal political machine that has been organized in this state for a great many years."[20]

The Republican Party most clearly demonstrated the debilitating effects of the direct primary, a condition complicated by ideological differences within that party. At times an obvious bifactional division between conservatives and progressives prevailed, particularly in the period between 1900 and the First World War and in the decade of the 1930s when social, economic, and political reforms were at issue. On other occasions, multifactional coalitions based on personality or local rivalries characterized the party. Without the party as a unifying agency, candidates rarely cooperated with one another in the general election. Even during those periods when progressives and conservatives formed loose bifactional groups, mutual suspicions within each camp sometimes destroyed potential cooperation. A veteran reporter of Oregon politics described the typical election campaign as one in which "Each candidate picks his own surfboard and rides the waves on it."[21]

[19] *Outlines of the Government of Oregon: Summary of Constitution and Statutes,* ed. James D. Barnett (Corvallis, 1940), pp. 2-6; Barnett, "The Presidential Primary in Oregon," *Political Science Quarterly* 31 (Mar. 1916), p. 92.

[20] Harold Swayze, "Party Politics in Oregon" (unpublished bachelor's thesis, Reed College, 1952), pp. 37-43; Sprague to Robert W. Sawyer, May 18, 1942, Robert W. Sawyer Papers (University of Oregon, Eugene).

[21] Ralph Watson, political editor of the *Oregon Journal,* as quoted in Swayze, "Party Politics in Oregon," p. 61.

Eventually the direct primary not only destroyed the integrity of political parties but also weakened loyalty among individual voters. The observation of one Oregonian, writing to a gubernatorial aspirant, is not unique: "I have always registered as a republican and voted for republicans, but . . . there are so many self starters that we have to choose the man, not the party."[22] Similarly, the Salem *Capital Journal* concluded that after three decades the direct primary had so weakened party responsibility that public confidence in parties had been destroyed. "The public has come to look to individuals of character, vision, integrity, and courage for their leadership," not to political parties.[23] The Portland *Oregonian*, the most powerful and influential Republican newspaper in the state, agreed: "Major contests are decided on the basis of personal fitness or personal popularity of the candidate. Practically the only party significance any more to an election of governor is that success enthuses the party with which he affiliates."[24]

If the direct primary weakened unity in both parties, primary factionalism was not to blame for the lack of organization among Democrats. Rather, the small number of party faithful, repeated failures at the polls, and wholly inadequate finances,[25] caused the party apparatus to wither early in the century. Out of necessity, and without any hope of effective party support in winning elections, Democrats established the same kind of extra-party organizations as did the Republicans. Furthermore, quite aware that a successful campaign depended upon Republican votes, Democrats appealed to the electorate on the basis of nonpartisanship and personality, not party doctrine. In fact, those Democrats who successfully won office before the Second World War, except for a few years during the 1930s, skillfully emphasized the ecumenical approach to politics. One of the few Democrats elected to the Oregon state legislature before the revival of the party following the Second World War gave this account of his campaign: "The party was in a hopeless position and I was on my own in each election. In campaigning I never mentioned partisan politics but played up the fact that I was of an old pioneer family and a good athlete while in

---

22 Frank Patton to Sam H. Brown, Oct. 23, 1934, Sam Henry Brown Papers (University of Oregon, Eugene).

23 Salem *Capital Journal*, July 3, 1937, p. 4.

24 Portland *Oregonian*, May 25, 1934, p. 8. Between 1870 and 1950, 29 per cent of Oregon's elected governors had held no previous political office. This figure is greater than for any other state in the nation. See Joseph A. Schlesinger, *How They Became Governor: A Study of Comparative State Politics 1870-1950* (Lansing, 1957), p. 19.

25 In 1928, for example, the Democratic National Committeeman reported that the party was nearly bankrupt, even lacking funds for postage stamps. Corvallis *Gazette Times*, Mar. 14, 1928, p. 1.

college. My neighbors and university friends, many of them Republicans, helped me in my campaign."[26] Noting an unusual exception to this strategy, C. C. Chapman, conservative Republican editor of the *Oregon Voter*, remarked of a Democratic senatorial candidate, "In his platform he admits he is a democrat, which is extraordinarily honest for a candidate of that party. Most of them masquerade as non-partisans."[27]

Because Democrats elected under these circumstances owed a greater debt to Republican voters than to their own party they often assumed a nonpartisan approach in matters of patronage and made but little effort to build a viable party organization.[28] While he served as governor and United States senator, Democrat George E. Chamberlain so frequently ignored the party in these matters that several prominent Oregon Democrats refused to support him in elections. "I know of my own personal knowledge that during his entire career as Governor, he suppressed all discussion of democratic doctrines for fear of alienating republican votes," wrote one disgruntled Democrat. "My opposition to him is largely because . . . he fails to support the party and maintains that so-called independence of action that will surely bring the whole [party] structure about our ears."[29] As to patronage, another Democratic critic asked, "What has Senator Chamberlain done for the democrats of Oregon or the democratic party?"[30]

Chamberlain was by no means the only elected Democrat who ignored his party. The attitude among Democratic office holders became so typical that in 1928 a party newspaper declared: "For the past 30 years there has been no Democratic party in Oregon . . . The few Democrats that have been elected owed their success to their personality and political skill. They were individualists and did nothing to build up organization."[31]

Neither the ill effect of the direct primary on Republican unity nor the nonpartisan strategy of the Democrats fully accounts for

[26] Interview with Edward F. Bailey, Apr. 1, 1968. Bailey was elected to the lower house of the state legislature in 1922 and to the state senate in 1926. He was the Democratic gubernatorial candidate in 1930.

[27] *Oregon Voter* 45 (May 15, 1926), p. 14.

[28] In their attitude toward patronage, Democratic office holders, at least during the first decades of the twentieth century, tended to confirm the thesis that when patronage is limited elected officials utilize it to strengthen their own position rather than to increase the party's vote to a maximum. See James Q. Wilson, "The Economy of Patronage," *Journal of Political Economy* 69 (Aug. 1961), pp. 369-380.

[29] C. E. S. Wood to Harry Lane, Mar. 31, 1914; *ibid.*, June 1, 1914, Richard Lewis Neuberger Papers (University of Oregon, Eugene).

[30] Portland *Evening Telegram*, Feb. 21, 1920, p. 1. Portland *Oregonian*, Feb. 22, 1920, p. 15.

[31] Salem *Capital Journal*, Sept. 1, 1928, p. 4.

the minor role of parties in Oregon politics. In some states the party performs one of its most significant roles by manipulating heterogeneous groups into a coalition. But in Oregon, politics remained comparatively free of pluralism because the ethnic, racial, religious, and socio-economic homogeneity of the population provided no real basis or opportunity for the type of coalition politics that produced celebrated political machines elsewhere.[32] As late as 1955, one commentator described the Oregon political arena as "part of the last frontier of the small businessman and his agrarian competitor, the relatively independent farmer."[33] Disputes between these two groups often led to political conflict, but because the farmer and the businessman were both registered Republicans their differences took the form of intraparty bickering. The Democratic Party in Oregon, with no opportunity for appeal to ethnic or racial minorities and an insignificant industrial labor force to attract, could not create the kind of collage that supported the New Deal. Ideological differences in Oregon politics, therefore, seldom broke along party lines; more often than not the major political differences found expression in contests between the Grange and the Chamber of Commerce, with Democrats dividing their support between the two.

Possessing numbers, but lacking party discipline or ideological unity, the Republican majority always faced the danger that internal factional differences might result in the election of a Democrat. Election results often exposed the party's weakness. Democrats triumphed in the gubernatorial elections of 1902, 1906, 1910, and 1922, although registration ran approximately three to one against them. The Republican nominee in the gubernatorial contests of 1930 and 1934 ran last behind two other candidates despite a registration advantage of two to one; in 1930 an independent won, and in 1934 a Democrat.

In the senatorial elections of 1912 and 1914, Democrats, while outnumbered more than two to one by registered Republicans, scored upset victories. A Democratic candidate for Congress won in 1922 in a district 64 per cent Republican. In the eighteen elections for congressman between 1930 and 1940, Democrats triumphed

---

[32] Lester G. Seligman, "A Prefatory Study of Leadership Selection in Oregon," *Western Political Quarterly* 12 (Mar. 1959), pp. 159-161. Two investigators who analyzed the difference in voting behavior among social classes in Oregon on 103 initiative and referendum measures between 1910 and 1914 concluded that " the agreement between the classes is surprisingly striking." William F. Ogburn and Delvin Peterson, "Political Thought of Social Classes," *Political Science Quarterly* 31 (June 1916), p. 313.

[33] William Appleman Williams, "Historical Romance of Senator Neuberger's Election," *Oregon Historical Quarterly* 56 (June 1955), pp. 101-102.

eight times, and only once was the winning Democrat elected from a district that had a majority of Democrats.

Although the outcome of any election must be considered in terms of the specific issues and partisan forces at work, these illustrations indicate that Oregonians have not been so wedded to the Republican Party as to preclude voting for other candidates. The more complex question, of course, is what general kinds of issues led Oregon Republicans to desert their party.

In recent years, political scientists and sociologists have focused on the concept of political culture to explain electoral behavior and comparative politics. A political culture, at the highest level of generalization, is the system of orientations and attitudes toward a political system and its various parts. The components of such a culture are diverse and include such factors as migration, demographic characteristics of the population, historical patterns, customs, laws and other elements that, when combined, produce an approach or style of politics illustrative of the general cultural milieu.[34] Gabriel A. Almond and Sidney Verba, for example, point out that the United States has a general political culture distinct from other nations.[35] But within the United States there exists much diversity, and the national political culture is but a synthesis of various subcultures.

In a study of American federalism, Daniel Elazar suggests that Oregon, in addition to eight other states, possesses a moralistic political culture. Politics in such a setting is viewed as a "public activity centered on some notion of the public good and properly devoted to the advancement of the public interest."[36] Both the electorate and politicians conceive of democratic government as a commonwealth wherein politics becomes the means to improve society. And, in assuming that government service is essentially public service, the chosen representatives of the people have a moral obligation to promote the public good.

Since government in the moralistic culture is predicated on the idea of selfless community service, politicians are expected to fulfill this expectation at the expense of party regularity, if necessary. Party allegiance, therefore, takes second place to the public interest.

---

[34] For a general discussion of political culture see H. V. Wiseman, *Political Systems: Some Sociological Approaches* (New York, 1966), pp. 21-42; Samuel C. Patterson, "The Political Cultures of the American States," *Journal of Politics* 30 (Sept. 1968), pp. 187-209.

[35] Gabriel A. Almond and Sidney Verba, *The Civic Culture: Political Attitudes and Democracy in Five Nations* (Princeton, 1963).

[36] Daniel J. Elazar, *American Federalism: A View from the States* (New York, 1966), p. 90. In addition to Oregon, the states are Maine, Vermont, Michigan, Wisconsin, Utah, Minnesota, North Dakota, and Colorado. See pp. 89-92.

Politicians and the voters may switch regular party ties with impunity when conditions justify such action to attain the community's goals. Elazar makes clear that the concept of a moralistic culture is intended to be an ideal type and "not fully extant in the real world;" nonetheless, his model does serve, in a tentative way, to help explain voting behavior in Oregon.

On repeated occasions, a majority of Oregon voters affirmed the principal values of a moralistic political culture. In most elections when Republicans crossed party lines to elect a Democrat or independent, the primary issue, whether political reform, conservation, prohibition, or public development of hydroelectric power, was advanced by the winning candidate in the rhetoric of social improvement or community betterment, aimed at all the people. The nonpartisan approach of Democratic politicians was especially effective in its appeal to the dominant values of the moralistic culture.

In 1908, the victorious Democratic candidate for United States senator declared to a Republican, "I place my country above party and . . . you can rest assured that the needs of the people will always be a first consideration with me. I can afford to be and will be a free lance . . . and stand only for those things which are calculated to do the greatest good to the greatest number."[37] Likewise, the basic question in the gubernatorial contest of 1910, according to one newspaper, was "an issue, not of Republicans and Democrats, but of measures, not of parties and partisanship but of principles and public order."[38] The successful Democrat declared after his election, "I was a victorious candidate in a righteous cause."[39] In 1926 a leading Republican who crossed party lines to support the Democratic senatorial candidate asserted, "Party victory means nothing to the great mass of common people unless by party victory the general welfare is promoted . . . Let me plead that each citizen vote not for party spoils but for the good of his country."[40] The Democrat, who emphasized nonpartisanship in the campaign, narrowly failed of election.

Democrats had no monopoly on nonpartisan appeals. In 1930, the independent candidate for governor called upon Oregonians to eschew party loyalty and "put on the armor of right and battle for the cause of the people . . . against men, corporations and special interests . . . protected by political machinery."[41] Echoing these

37 George E. Chamberlain to Alvin Jones, Apr. 20, 1908, George Earl Chamberlain Papers (Oregon Historical Society, Portland, Oregon).

38 *Oregon Journal*, Nov. 7, 1940, p. 8.

39 Quoted in Chester Harold Case, Jr., "The Oregon System and Oswald West" (unpublished bachelor's thesis, Reed College, 1952), p. 117.

40 *Oregon Journal*, Oct. 31, 1926, p. 4.

41 Julius Meier to Rufus C. Holman, Aug. 6, 1930, Henry M. Hanzen Papers (University of Oregon, Eugene).

views, his campaign manager explained: "When a political party, through the intrigues of the politicians . . . fails to function in the interests of the people it is time for the people themselves to organize in their own interests."[42] The independent candidate won the election with bipartisan support.

In 1934, a prominent Republican, urging the voters to cast their support for a second independent candidate for governor, said, "Loyalty to party, right or wrong, harkens [sic] back to the days when party bosses wore their trousers stuffed in their high boots, chewd [sic] tobacco and could spit through a knot hole clear across the room . . . I place loyalty to the state and its people ahead of loyalty to party," he exclaimed, and suggested Oregonians do the same.[43] In 1955, Senator Wayne L. Morse, after bolting the Republican Party, declared, "No Republican party officials, state or national, ever had the right to assume that in the name of party regularity I would sacrifice my responsibility to the people of Oregon by voting a party line whenever I thought a so-called party policy was not in the public interest."[44] It was in this spirit that one Oregon newspaper advised its readers:

> When the election of one man would obviously promote the public welfare, and the election of another wouldn't, vote for the former, regardless of whether he wears one party label or another. The only hope for better government, nationally or locally, is a determination on the part of the people as a whole, not to be hoodwinked by the cuckoo cry of 'vote the ticket straight.'[45]

Throughout the twentieth century, Oregon politics has been shaped by such independent attitudes and sentiments. Yet at no time did Democrats more successfully articulate the premier values of the moralistic culture than in the decade and a half before the First World War.

---

[42] Portland *Oregonian*, July 29, 1930, p. 3.

[43] "State or Party?" Manuscript copy of radio address by Sam H. Brown, Nov. 1, 1934, Brown Papers.

[44] *Oregon Democrat* 23 (Feb. 1955), p. 9.

[45] Medford *Mail Tribune*, Dec. 24, 1921, p. 4.

II THE POLITICS OF REFORM

The progressive movement in Oregon is said to have transformed the state "into sort of a political camp meeting" where the air was filled "with 'hallelujah' and 'amens' and general thanksgiving for a new political light that is leading the people on."[1] Through adoption of the initiative, referendum, recall, direct primary, and other legislation, the people of Oregon embraced a philosophy of direct democracy, rendering the established patterns of political authority a severe blow. For the Democratic Party, a decided minority since the 1880s, these new forms of institutional democracy created opportunities for political advancement. With the disruption of Republican Party unity, and in an era of political turbulence, Democrats gained the confidence of reform-minded voters and overturned the Republican control of state politics.

If the "progressive potential of Democrats in the Far West [ran] high, higher than in most other parts of the country,"[2] it is perhaps because in Oregon, at least, Democrats were converted to reform before the turn of the century. Though the revolution in technology, industry, transportation, and agriculture following the Civil War reshaped America as a major world power, it also created what many considered grievous political and economic abuses. In Oregon, as in other parts of the nation, the concentration of wealth, political corruption, and the plundering of natural resources gave rise to a reform movement which spanned two decades. Keenly aware of the value of winning the votes of dissidents, and recognizing their own minority status, Democrats at first attempted a strategy of alliance with third parties during the 1890s; later, in the first decade of the twentieth century, they reversed this tack and ran independently of the party label as nonpartisans.

---

[1] Burton J. Hendricks, "Statement No. 1, How the Oregon Democracy Working Under the Direct Primary Has Destroyed the Political Machine," *McClure's Magazine* 37 (Sept. 1911), p. 508.

[2] Pomeroy, *The Pacific Slope*, p. 233.

Democrats were among the first in Oregon to respond to the agricultural discontent of the late nineteenth century. When a group of Grangers, Prohibitionists, and Knights of Labor met at Salem in 1889 to form the Union Party to agitate for antitrust legislation, the Australian ballot, and stricter banking laws, Democratic Governor Sylvester Pennoyer endorsed their cause. Running for reelection in 1890, Pennoyer not only received the unanimous nomination of his party but also engineered a coalition with the Union Party and independent Republicans in Portland, thereby winning their backing for the governorship. Anticipating the Populist panacea of free silver, the Democratic state platform of 1890 called for the free coinage of gold and silver. Remembered as an exceptionally able campaigner, Pennoyer stumped the small towns of Oregon, decrying the evils of monopoly, accumulated wealth, and the oppression of the masses by the industrial order. With approximately twice as many Republicans as Democrats voting in June 1890, Pennoyer won with a plurality of 5,155 votes. After the election, D. P. Thompson, the Republican gubernatorial candidate, reported that Pennoyer succeeded because "every possible 'ism' in the state was combined and united in his support."[3]

Pennoyer's success in 1890 provided convincing evidence that skillful Democrats, in alliance with other reform groups, could overcome the Republican majority. At the same time, the results of the election demonstrated that Democrats could not count on liberal platforms or the coattails of a popular candidate to bring success to the rest of the ticket. Aside from the governorship and a few seats in the state legislature, Republicans swept all other state and federal offices.

The Democratic coalition with the Union Party in 1890 proved much easier than cooperation with the Populists. From February 1892, when the People's Party was formally organized in Oregon, until February 1901, when the party disbanded, support between Populists and Democrats existed only sporadically and seldom on a statewide basis. Both groups recognized that Republicans could be turned out of office by joining in a popular front, but factions within each did not want to surrender political identity through fusion. Consequently, Democrats and Populists more often than

---

[3] Very little has been written on Oregon politics of the 1890s. Unless otherwise noted, the following account of Pennoyer, the position of the Democratic Party on reform, and the activities of the Populists is drawn from three sources: Maude D. Chapman, "Sylvester Pennoyer, Governor of Oregon, 1887-1895" (unpublished master's thesis, University of Oregon, 1943); Marion Harrington, "The Populist Movement in Oregon, 1889-1896" (unpublished master's thesis, University of Oregon, 1935); and George, "Political History of Oregon from 1876-1896 Inclusive." D. P. Thompson is quoted in Chapman, p. 48.

not split the votes of the disenchanted during the 1890s, while Republicans continued in office.[4]

After his reelection in 1890, Governor Pennoyer warned that unless the national leadership of the Democratic and Republican parties acknowledged the serious social, economic, and political problems of the day, a third party would be organized. The governor's prophecy became fact in 1891 with the organization of the Populist Party at Omaha, Nebraska. Angered by the national platforms of the Democratic and Republican parties in 1892, Pennoyer bolted his party and announced allegiance to Populism in October 1892. Oregon Democrats found themselves split between supporting Grover Cleveland in the coming presidential election or following Pennoyer out of the party to the standard of James B. Weaver. As a compromise, most Oregon Democrats supported Cleveland in the presidential election but adopted a state platform calling for free silver and the direct election of senators. Daniel Murphy, chairman of the Democratic State Central Committee, urged Populists to support Democrats in elections to Congress and the state legislature, but his appeal was ignored; "middle-of-the road" Populists, in control of the new party, insisted on their own candidates and wrote a platform nearly identical to that of the Democrats. With the two parties divided, the only victories for the forces of reform were the election of Democrat Nathan Pierce as presidential elector for James B. Weaver and the elevation of a few Democrats and Populists to the state legislature.

In 1894, the Democratic state platform went beyond the espousal of free silver and the popular election of senators; it favored the initiative, referendum, a graduated income tax, and stricter regulation of banking practices, all of which echoed the Populist platform of that year. Although Harvey W. Scott, editor of the Portland *Oregonian*, declared that "the democratic party in Oregon [was] virtually submerged in populism,"[5] a statewide alliance between Democrats and Populists did not materialize. Even though members of both parties joined to support candidates on the local level, fusion was not complete. In Portland, such prominent Democrats as C. E. S. Wood and Joseph N. Teal worked with Populists for the election of a reform slate for mayor and other city offices; in Baker, Clatsop, and Clackamas counties fusion tickets for the state legislature and other state offices were advanced. But in Wal-

---

[4] Through the 1890s, Populist strength was centered in Southwest Oregon; in Jackson, Josephine, and Coos counties the Democratic Party lost strength to the Populists, and in Multnomah County Republicans defected to the People's Party.

[5] Quoted in Harrington, "The Populist Movement in Oregon, 1889-1896," p. 63.

Iowa and Coos counties, Republicans and Democrats united against Populist candidates. In most counties, the voters chose between separate Republican, Democratic, and Populist tickets. Except for the election of seven Populists and one Democrat to the state legislature, Republicans swept all other offices.

As the presidential election of 1896 approached, the Democratic and Populist parties in the state engaged in heated factional debate over the question of fusion. When the national nominating conventions of both parties agreed on William J. Bryan as their presidential candidate, Oregon Democrats and Populists only reluctantly fell into line. To support the national effort, the reluctant allies offered a fusion ticket of two Populists, one Democrat, and one silver Republican for presidential electors but could not agree on a fusion slate for state offices or congressional elections. Moreover, harmony did not prevail among Democrats in the November elections. Though the Democratic state platforms of 1890, 1892, and 1894 endorsed free silver, disunity plagued the party on this issue. In the fall of 1896, C. E. S. Wood, Democratic National Committeeman, and W. E. Carll, chairman of the Democratic State Central Committee, refused to support Bryan because of the silver plank in the Democratic platform.[6] In addition, the Pendleton *East Oregonian* and the Portland *Evening Telegram*, the two leading Democratic newspapers of the state, advised Democrats against fusion in other state contests.[7]

Widespread party division and factionalism made the results of the election of 1896 predictable: Republicans carried Oregon in both the presidential and congressional elections. In contests for the state legislature, Populists ran well ahead of Democrats, capturing eighteen seats to seven for Democrats. Sylvester Pennoyer scored the only significant Democratic victory when, having returned to the Democratic fold, he successfully overcame the Populist-Democratic antagonisms in Portland and won the mayoralty of that city with the backing of both parties. While Democrats found the election disappointing, they could take comfort from the fact that Oregon voters responded in greater numbers to the call of reform. The presidential election marked a shift of twelve Republican counties to the Democratic column.

Not until 1898, well after the groundswell of Populism reached its peak, did Democrats and Populists agree on fusion in state elections. At party conventions in the spring of 1898, Will R. King,

---

[6] Democratic State Central Committee, "An Address by the National Democratic Electors to the Voters of Oregon" (n.p., 1896).

[7] Richard C. Frey, Jr., "The Oregon Press and the Beginnings of the Oregon System, 1890-1903" (unpublished master's thesis, University of Oregon, 1963), pp. 65, 68.

former Democrat, was named as the Populist gubernatorial candidate to head a fusion ticket. Other nominees included Democrat R. M. Veatch, for congressman in the first district, C. M. Donaldson, silver Republican for congressman in the second district, and Populist J. L. Story for attorney general. Still, the opposition of "middle-of-the-road" Populists and anti-silver Democrats hampered unity. In the elections that June, the fusion ticket failed to win a single state or national office. In 1900, the silver factions of the two parties joined for the last time in backing William J. Bryan for the presidency.

The failure of the Democratic Party to register important political victories in the 1890s did not dampen the party's ardor for reform. But after 1900, unlike in the preceding decade, Democrats of progressive persuasion relied less on party machinery, platforms, or fusion, and more on personal nonpartisan appeals to the electorate. Perhaps some Democrats, mindful of Sylvester Pennoyer's success, were educated to the proposition that the Republican majority in Oregon was willing to vote for individual Democratic candidates but, regardless of liberal platforms, would not back the party itself as a vehicle for reform. On the other hand, by 1900 the Republican Party finally showed signs of awakening to the necessity for reform. Given the overwhelming Republican bias of Oregonians, it would be futile for Democrats to campaign on the party label and expect to defeat Republicans identified as advocates of reform.

In a more general sense, however, the new style of Democratic politics was indicative of an era in which political issues superseded party lines. Democrats and Republicans alike exercised an independence of party and nonpartisanship in an attempt to secure reform. "I am going to get the initiative and referendum in Oregon if it costs me my soul," declared William S. U'Ren, chief architect of the Oregon System. "I'll do nothing selfish, dishonest, or dishonorable, but I'll trade off parties, offices, bills—or anything for that."[8] In a similar vein, a Democrat observed: "Party ties are not strong [because] the electors are looking rather for a man who stands for something than for a man who stands simply as the representative of party."[9] Equally important in negating party regularity was the fact that political parties themselves came under attack as autocratic organizations that abridged the right of the voters to participate effectively in the electoral process. Much of the legislation sponsored by both Populists and progressives was aimed specifically at weakening, if not totally disabling, the tradi-

---

[8] Lincoln Steffens, "U'Ren, the Law-Giver," *American Magazine* 65 (Mar. 1908), pp. 536-537.

[9] George E. Chamberlain to Joseph W. Folk, Oct. 24, 1907, Chamberlain Papers.

tional role of parties. "I have no faith in party organization or party government," asserted one champion of reform, and undoubtedly many voters held the same conviction.[10]

If these considerations did not provide reason enough for Democrats to act independently of the party, further inducements could be found in the state of party finances and organization. Throughout the progressive era, indeed over much of the twentieth century, the party lacked funds for both state elections and presidential campaigns. Democrats in Oregon reported regularly that the party tottered on the brink of bankruptcy. One high ranking party member observed, "Our State Committee is always as poor as a church mouse, and the only money it ever has for campaign purposes is contributed by candidates on the state ticket and in amounts so small that it is impossible to assist candidates further than to write letters and get out a small amount of literature."[11]

Furthermore, no financial assistance came from the national Democratic organization. In the presidential campaigns of 1900, 1904, and 1908, the Democratic State Central Committee confided that no aid would be forthcoming from the national committee.[12] With only four electoral votes, Oregon was scarcely considered a worthwhile investment. "We don't think we should ask [for funds]," declared the secretary of the State Central Committee on one occasion, "because there are several other states sure to go Democratic which have far more electoral votes."[13] Moreover, astute Democrats quickly recognized that in order to obtain Republican support in the state they could not risk playing a partisan role in presidential elections. Consequently, in the presidential contests of 1904 and 1908, Democratic Governor George Chamberlain assiduously avoided identifying himself with the party's presidential

---

[10] Quoted in Robert C. Woodward, "William Simon U'Ren: In An Age of Protest" (unpublished master's thesis, University of Oregon, 1956), p. 45.

[11] Chamberlain to Thomas E. McKnight, Mar. 5, 1908, Chamberlain Papers.

[12] W. E. Burke to Robert A. Miller, Aug. 23, 1900, Robert A. Miller Papers (University of Oregon, Eugene). See also Chamberlain to Joseph T. Fanning, May 5, 1904; John E. Lathrop to Chamberlain, Apr. 29, 1903; Chamberlain to Sam White, Apr. 29, 1908; Chamberlain to Sam White, Sept. 29, 1908; Chamberlain to Norman E. Mack, Sept. 30, 1908, Chamberlain Papers.

[13] W. E. Burke to Robert A. Miller, Aug. 25, 1900, Miller Papers. "Oregon and those states which cannot possibly be placed in the Democratic column ought to leave the naming of [presidential] candidates to those states which are solidly Democratic," wrote Governor Chamberlain to a Democratic delegate to the national convention in 1904. See Chamberlain to T. J. Howell, Apr. 11, 1904; Chamberlain to August Belmont, Apr. 25, 1904; Chamberlain to M. F. Tarpey, May 4, 1904, Chamberlain Papers.

candidate, although he did agree to carry on a "quiet campaign" in 1908.[14]

Aside from financial difficulties, the Democratic Party was unable to provide effective organizational support for its candidates. In 1900, the chairman of the State Central Committee charitably described party unity as "not what it should be"; in 1908 a Democratic senatorial candidate found "no organization in the state at all"; and in 1914 a Democratic gubernatorial hopeful declared that "chaos" best typified party organization.[15] In part at least, elected Democrats who used patronage to insure continued Republican support exacerbated this unhealthy situation.

Bereft of finances, organization, and numbers, and laboring in a period influenced by a political ideology which called for bipartisan cooperation in advancing reform legislation, Democrats pursued an independent course. Accordingly, as one of the most successful practitioners of progressive politics put it, Democrats followed a strategy of "every man for himself and the devil for the hindmost."[16]

For such a method to be fruitful, Democrats had to win Republican votes. Emphasis on nonpartisanship facilitated Republican support, but chronic and prolonged disagreement within the Republican Party over the merits of reform provided greater aid to Democratic candidates. Rank and file Republicans had defected to the Populist crusade throughout the 1890s, but not until 1895 did differences over free silver cause dissension in the high echelons of the party and inaugurate a decade of factionalism in Republican politics.

In the legislative session of 1895, Jonathan Bourne, Jr., prosperous mine owner, attorney, and acknowledged leader of the Republican silverites, joined with Populists and silver Democrats to oppose the election of Joseph N. Dolph to the United States Senate. A one-time law partner of Bourne and strong advocate of the gold standard, Dolph received the backing of Joseph Simon and Henry Corbett, two principal powers in the Republican Party. After successfully blocking the election of Dolph, Bourne sought to further the cause of free silver in 1896 when he declared for William J. Bryan and attempted to enlist Republicans in support of the Democratic presidential candidate.[17]

---

14 Chamberlain to O. P. Choshow, Oct. 5, 1908; Chamberlain to W. H. Cannon, Oct. 5, 1908; Chamberlain to B. F. Irvine, Oct. 6, 1908, Chamberlain Papers.

15 W. E. Burke to Robert A. Miller, Aug. 23, 1900; Miller to Chamberlain, Oct. 31, 1913, Miller Papers; Chamberlain to John E. Lathrop, Feb. 19, 1908, Chamberlain Papers.

16 Chamberlain to Sam White, Feb. 26, 1908, Chamberlain Papers.

17 When officials of the Democratic Party refused to back Bryan because

The dispute over silver gradually expanded into party division over sponsoring political reforms. In the legislative session of 1897, Bourne opposed Republican Senator John H. Mitchell, a former ally, when Mitchell abandoned free silver and accepted the backing of the Simon-Corbett group in a bid for reelection. With the party now split into two, sometimes three, factions, Bourne struck a bargain with Populist William S. U'Ren in the famous "hold-up" session of 1897. U'Ren, who joined the Populist Party in 1893 because Republicans refused to sponsor direct legislation, agreed to organize the Populists in opposition to the election of Mitchell in exchange for Bourne's support of constitutional amendments for the initiative and referendum, as well as other political reforms. The Bourne-U'Ren combination, with support from Democrats, effectively prevented a quorum in the lower house of the state legislature and thereby prevented the election of Mitchell.[18]

Until internecine warfare erupted in the Republican Party over bimetalism and reform, Republican state platforms remained silent on such proposed legislation as the initiative and referendum. Now, the Bourne-U'Ren *entente* in the state legislature prodded the Republican Party in a new direction. In the legislative session of 1899, this alliance secured the passage of a voter registration bill and approved a constitutional amendment to introduce the initiative and referendum. The Oregon constitution required the affirmative action of two legislative sessions before a constitutional amendment could be presented to the electorate for ratification. Aware of growing support for direct legislation, the Republican Party officially, though not unanimously, endorsed the measure for the first time in April 1900. The session of 1901 performed as expected: the initiative and referendum won approval for a second time, and additional legislation passed, tightening election procedures and strengthening the authority of election boards.[19]

Still far from united, many Republicans now perceived the drift of opinion and sought to don the mantle of reform. When the People's Party disbanded in 1901, Democrats found themselves outnumbered four to one in registration. Democrats could compete against such odds only if recalcitrant Republicans opposed continued reform and caused division in the party. The Republicans

---

of their opposition to free silver, Bourne filled in as a distributor of funds sent to the state by the national campaign committee. Albert H. Pike, Jr., "Jonathan Bourne, Jr., Progressive" (unpublished doctoral thesis, University of Oregon, 1957), pp. 11-22.

[18] *Ibid.*, pp. 24-29; Woodward, "William Simon U'Ren: In An Age of Protest," pp. 25-38.

[19] Russel Gordon Hendricks, "The Effect of the Direct Primary Upon Senatorial Elections in Oregon, 1900-1909" (unpublished master's thesis, University of Oregon, 1951), pp. 15-21.

never achieved consensus on a broad program of reform, and in the decade and a half before the First World War some Democrats deftly exploited the situation.

The pattern of Democratic politics throughout the progressive period is anomalous. Between 1902 and 1914, Democrats won three of the four gubernatorial elections and three of the five senatorial contests, but they failed to capture a single congressional district or any other executive post in state government. A Democrat twice served as mayor of Portland in this period, but in other local elections the party fared badly. Except for the selection of eleven Democrats to the lower house of the legislature in 1902 and ten in 1904, the party maintained an average of but four representatives in both houses of the legislature.

Although Democrats held a near monopoly on the governorship and showed surprising strength in senatorial elections, these achievements cannot be considered party victories. Not only were the issues in all these elections of a bipartisan nature, but those who won office did so largely on the basis of reputation and personality. The highly personal nature of these successes is underscored by the fact that three men dominated the offices captured by Democrats. George E. Chamberlain won two of the three gubernatorial elections and two of the three senatorial elections. Harry Lane, grandson of Oregon's first territorial governor, was twice elected mayor of Portland before being elevated to the United States Senate. Only Oswald West, elected governor in 1910, had not won an earlier victory.

A consummate politician, Chamberlain projected an appeal to both Republicans and Democrats. A student of his early career in Oregon politics attributes his bipartisan following to the fact that "he represented his ideas with a minimum of partisanship and a maximum of appeal to the masses."[20] Moreover, he possessed shrewd political judgment. Never the early agitator for what later became a popular cause, Chamberlain nevertheless quickly championed reform when the voice of the electorate became clear. He first won office as a prosecuting attorney for Oregon's Third Judicial District in 1884, and in 1891, when the state legislature created the post of attorney general, Governor Pennoyer appointed him to the position. In 1892, Chamberlain won election for a full term as attorney general largely because of his good fellowship among Republicans. Chamberlain never associated himself with Populism in the 1890s, but he did assume the leadership of several local reform organizations that attempted to improve schools, secure the enactment of

---

[20] Gene Harper McIntyre, "The Pre-Senatorial Career of George E. Chamberlain: Victorious Democrat" (unpublished master's thesis, University of Oregon, 1965), p. 54.

prohibition, and bring about more equitable tax schedules. His activities in local politics allowed him to maintain close contact with the grass roots while avoiding the stigma of radicalism sometimes associated with Populism.[21] Thus, he stood on the sidelines until, in 1902, he received his party's nomination for governor at a time when sentiment for reform permeated nearly all areas of the state.

In the elections of 1902, the Democrats, united behind a state ticket headed by the popular George Chamberlain, faced a numerically strong but faction-torn opposition. Politics in Multnomah County, the locus of power for the Republican Party and the state's most heavily populated area, was a tangled skein. Here bitter political and personal disputes among the leaders of the party robbed the party's gubernatorial candidate, William J. Furnish, of full support and encouraged rank and file Republicans to defect to the Democratic candidate.[22]

Prior to the election, the Democratic Party adopted a platform that endorsed several reforms. Ignoring the party's broad program of reform, Chamberlain made adoption of the initiative and referendum the chief plank of his campaign. In declaring for the proposed constitutional amendments, he characterized direct legislation as "the only salvation for the mass of people" and called upon Oregonians to vote for it regardless of party affiliation. As if to set his own candidacy aside from other offices contested by Democrats, Chamberlain explained the nonpolitical character of the governorship and asserted that he, as a citizen and not a politician, could best serve as the chief executive of the state.[23]

In June the voters of Oregon, convinced of the necessity of reform, adopted the initiative and referendum by the overwhelming margin of 62,024 to 5,668. Having identified his candidacy with the issue of direct legislation, Chamberlain defeated Furnish by 246 votes out of nearly 91,000 cast for governor. In races for the lower house of the state legislature, the Democratic Party scored its most impressive victory of the entire progressive era by increasing its representation from two to eleven. The majority of these gains came from Multnomah County, where Republicans and Democrats joined in a bipartisan effort to elect candidates who endorsed the initiative and referendum. Democrats, however, once again failed to capture a single federal office or any other high executive post in state government.[24]

21 *Ibid.*, pp. 44-47, 57, 76.

22 Hendricks, "The Effect of the Direct Primary Upon Senatorial Elections in Oregon, 1900-1909," pp. 59-67.

23 McIntyre, "The Pre-Senatorial Career of George E. Chamberlain: Victorious Democrat," pp. 97-105.

24 *Ibid.*; Hendricks, "The Effect of the Direct Primary Upon Senatorial Elections in Oregon, 1900-1909," pp. 67-69.

The circumstances surrounding the election of 1902 in most respects typified the conditions by which Democrats would successfully seek office during the following decade. Although Republicans maintained enough unity to ensure control of congressional districts, the state legislature, and most executive posts in state government,[25] party factionalism became endemic over the selection of gubernatorial and senatorial candidates. Sometimes, personal ambition among Republican Party leaders prompted division; more frequently, elections for senator and governor coincided with intraparty battles over extending the Oregon System. As nonpartisans, Democrats focused their campaigns around the single issue of either furthering reform or defending the Oregon System against the attacks of conservative Republicans.

As governor, Chamberlain fulfilled his campaign pledge of nonpartisanship in administering state government. When Democrats complained about his selection of two Republicans for judicial positions, he replied that politics had no place in such appointments.[26] In 1903, he declined to campaign openly for a Democratic candidate in a special election for Congress.[27] Chamberlain also defended the initiative and referendum from legislative attacks designed to weaken the laws, and urged on the legislature programs of prison reform, tighter railroad regulation, and statutes favorable to labor. By these actions, and after four years as governor, he had dramatically increased his popularity and reputation as a bipartisan. In seeking reelection in 1906, Chamberlain defeated his Republican opponent, James Withycombe, by a plurality of over 3,000 votes and carried two-thirds of the state's counties.

While Chamberlain advanced progressive programs as governor, the voters of the state sought to strengthen the Oregon System. Those who wished to reorder the state's political system persistently agitated for a direct primary law, especially in the selection of senatorial candidates. In 1901, the state legislature enacted the Mays Law, which allowed rank and file party members, through primary election, to indicate their choice for senator. The Mays Law underwent its first test in 1903 when Democrat C. E. S. Wood and former Republican Governor T. T. Geer received the nominations of their respective parties. Subsequently, Geer defeated Wood in the general election, but Republican Party bosses subverted the intent

---

[25] Republicans frequently ran unopposed or received the nomination of both Democratic and Republican parties. In 1910, when Oswald West was elected governor, the party failed to run candidates for attorney general and state treasurer. Although Democrats challenged Republicans in all elections for Congress, they were repeatedly defeatd by large margins.

[26] Chamberlain to J. D. Matlock, Mar. 1, 1905, Chamberlain Papers.

[27] John E. Lathrop to Chamberlain, Apr. 23, 1903; *ibid.*, May 12, 1903, Chamberlain Papers.

of the law by engineering the election of a Republican stalwart, Charles W. Fulton, in the legislature. The election of Fulton by party regulars aroused the electorate, and in 1904, through the use of an initiative petition, the voters forced adoption of a Direct Primary Law.[28]

Even though the federal Constitution entrusted the election of senators to the various state legislatures, a provision in the Oregon primary law attempted to make the legislature responsive to the dictates of the electorate in senatorial primaries. Candidates for the legislature could pledge themselves to "Statement Number One," which bound them to vote for the choice of the voters in the primary, or "Statement Number Two," an affirmation of party regularity. Neither statement was mandatory, but reformers applied pressure on legislative candidates through a publicity campaign designed to make the signing of Statement Number One a prerequisite to nomination and election. Republican candidates were generally reluctant to endorse Statement Number One, but Democrats immediately declared in favor of the proposal. In Eugene, Democrats warned that any member of the party who ran for any office and failed to subscribe to Statement Number One would be opposed by the party. The Democratic Central Committees of Multnomah, Clackamas, and Umatilla counties made similar threats.[29]

That Statement Number One would deny party leaders control of senatorial elections was immediately evident. In 1906, when the primary was first used in a senatorial contest, insurgent Republicans secured the nomination of a candidate who favored the statement. Jonathan Bourne, Jr., running as a self-proclaimed "Popular Government" candidate, defeated party regular H. M. Cake by making Statement Number One the single issue of the primary. The nomination of forty-two Republicans who eventually signed Statement Number One in races for the state legislature paralleled Bourne's primary victory. After defeating Democrat John M. Gearin in the general election, and in spite of opposition from Republican Party leaders, Bourne was elected to the Senate by the state legislature in 1907.[30]

[28] Allen H. Eaton, *The Oregon System: The Story of Direct Legislation in Oregon* (Chicago, 1912), pp. 92-98.

[29] Hendricks, "Statement No. 1, How the Oregon Democracy Working under the Direct Primary Has Destroyed the Political Machine," pp. 505-519; Woodward, "William Simon U'Ren: In An Age of Protest," pp. 80, 102; Hendricks, "The Effect of the Direct Primary Upon Senatorial Elections in Oregon, 1900-1909," pp. 176-181, 184-186. In 1924, a Portland newspaper recalled that "even constables were elected or defeated on the declaration of their attitude toward Statement No. 1." Portland *Oregonian*, Oct. 2, 1924, p. 12.

[30] Pike, "Jonathan Bourne, Jr., Progressive," pp. 56-69.

Democrats quickly appreciated the lesson to be learned from Bourne's success. At the time of Bourne's election, Democratic Governor George Chamberlain, always mindful of the grass roots, observed that Republican division over Statement Number One provided an opportunity for Democrats to win the senatorial election of 1908.[31] Having urged the legislature to elect Bourne on the strength of public sentiment for Statement Number One, Chamberlain identified his administration with the new primary device.[32] In 1908, he announced as a senatorial candidate.

Chamberlain conducted his campaign for the Senate, like his previous campaigns for governor, without the benefit of any meaningful party assistance. Nor did Chamberlain wish the party label to be associated with his candidacy. Shortly before he entered the primary, the Governor confided to a friend that if he ran it would be "as a free lance, fighting along those lines which seem best calculated to further the interests of Oregon."[33]

After winning the Democratic senatorial nomination, Chamberlain, like Bourne, built his campaign around a defense of Statement Number One. "The only way to purge the Senate of the United States of the representatives of special interest," Chamberlain asserted, "is to bring about the election of senators by the direct vote of the people."[34] Because Statement Number One provided an opportunity for the popular selection of senators in Oregon, Chamberlain argued that the statement should be signed by all dedicated supporters of good government and the rule of the people. The importance of the issue demanded that party loyalty be set aside. To a political confidant, Chamberlain wrote, "It is a question in the minds of many of us here whether we should nominate a ticket in those counties where good substantial Republicans are willing to sign Statement No. 1. I do not like to see our party unrepresented on a ticket," the Governor stated, "but the question at issue is so vital that it seems to me it ought to be the first consideration rather than party."[35]

Chamberlain's sensitivity to the mood of the voters again proved accurate. With Republicans outnumbering Democrats three to one, Chamberlain defeated the regular Republican senatorial candidate.[36] Not particularly sanguine about a Republican legislature

---

31 Chamberlain to John E. Lathrop, Aug. 6, 1907, Chamberlain Papers.

32 Pike, "Jonathan Bourne, Jr., Progressive," p. 72.

33 Chamberlain to John E. Lathrop, Aug. 6, 1907, Chamberlain Papers.

34 Chamberlain to William Morfitt, Mar. 25, 1908, Chamberlain Papers.

35 Chamberlain to John E. Lathrop, Feb. 19, 1908. Chamberlain outlined the same strategy to others. See Chamberlain to Olof Anderson, Apr. 27, 1908; Chamberlain to Thomas E. McKnight, Mar. 2, 1908; Chamberlain to Sam White, Apr. 29, 1908, Chamberlain Papers.

36 Chamberlain defeated Republican H. M. Cake 52,421 to 50,899. For a

electing him to the Senate, Chamberlain subsequently advised Lincoln Steffens that if the legislature repudiated Statement Number One "there [would] be a political revolution in Oregon."[37] If, indeed, a political revolution was in the offing, the legislature averted it by elevating him to the Senate in 1909.[38]

The election of Bourne and Chamberlain naturally aroused those committed to party rule. "The Republican Party of Oregon behaves as if it had made up its mind to do nothing rational anymore,"[39] complained the Portland *Oregonian* after Chamberlain's victory. The direct primary especially dismayed party regulars. Not only did the law deny party control of nominations, but Democrats, as members of the minority party, often turned the primary to their advantage by registering and voting in the Republican primary to select the weakest candidate.[40] One Republican summed up the case against the Oregon System in general, and the primary specifically, when he observed, "Under the System the brains of neither party will be called in convention to select a suitable candidate, but someone will have cheek enough to announce himself as either the democratic or republican candidate. It may occur that neither are fit for the place, but by chance they get on the ticket, and then the intelligent voter must choose between two evils."[41]

By 1910, the simmering resentment among party stalwarts reached the boiling point. Conservative Republicans, under the editorial leadership of Harvey Scott, sought to circumvent the direct primary in the gubernatorial election that year. Scott proposed that the Republican Party hold "assemblies" to nominate candidates for the primary elections. Delegates to the assembly

---

discussion of the election see Russel G. Hendricks, "Election of Senator Chamberlain, the People's Choice," *Oregon Historical Quarterly* 53 (June 1952), pp. 63-88; Warren M. Blankenship, "Progressives and the Progressive Party in Oregon, 1906-1916" (unpublished doctoral thesis, University of Oregon, 1966), pp. 22-42.

[37] Chamberlain to Lincoln Steffens, June 11, 1908, Chamberlain Papers.

[38] Republican President Theodore Roosevelt urged the Oregon legislature to elect Chamberlain. The friendship between Roosevelt and Chamberlain stemmed from Governor Chamberlain's support of the President's conservation policy. "I am one of his admirers," wrote Chamberlain of Roosevelt, "for on things which affect the vital interests of the people most, he is as good a Democrat as Jefferson or Jackson, and in carrying out his views he is as fearless as the latter." See Chamberlain to John M. Gearin, Jan. 2, 1906, Chamberlain Papers; Blankenship, "Progressives and the Progressive Party in Oregon, 1906-1916," p. 39; Oswald West, "Reminiscences and Anecdotes: Mostly About Politics," *Oregon Historical Quarterly* 51 (June 1950).

[39] Portland *Oregonian*, June 2, 1908, p. 8.

[40] For an analysis of Democratic participation in Republican primaries see Eaton, *The Oregon System: The Story of Direct Legislation in Oregon*, pp. 86-89.

[41] James E. Martin to Robert A. Miller, Oct. 8, 1909, Miller Papers.

would be selected by party members over the state, and, in this way, Scott reasoned, party organization would be restored. Accordingly, a Republican assembly nominated Jay Bowerman for governor and several candidates for the state legislature. For those Republicans who opposed the assembly scheme, Scott promised, " 'the knife' will be used with utmost vigor and the knife to the hilt."[42]

The primary election of 1910 both muted the threat by Scott and presaged the results of the general election. Although Bowerman won the Republican nomination for governor, twenty-four assembly-named candidates for the state legislature were defeated. In the Democratic primary, Oswald West easily won nomination for governor over Jefferson Myers, a Multnomah County Democrat, who sought nomination as a party regular.[43]

In his campaign for governor, West developed the fine art of nonpartisanship to its most effective expression. In campaign literature and speeches, the Democratic candidate seldom made reference to his membership in the Democratic Party. Instead, he cast himself in the role of defender of the Oregon System and an opponent of the Republican assembly. West sought to enhance his reputation as a reformer by including in the *Voter's Pamphlet* long newspaper quotations praising his effectiveness as state land agent in ferreting out corruption in the famous land fraud trials of 1905 and his later career as Railroad Commissioner.

Calling on all Oregonians to rally to his standard, West declared in campaign letters that the time was at hand when "Independent voters and members of minority parties in the State should present a united front against the assault of the Assembly and Corporation crowd on the Direct Primary and other popular measures adopted by the people." If elected, he promised, "no corporation nor individuals, nor machine nor combination of men, will have the slightest claim on me."[44]

---

[42] Portland *Oregonian*, July 14, 1910, p. 10.

[43] Myers made no reference to the issues of assemblyism or reform in the primary contest. See *Voter's Pamphlet at the Primary Nominating Election 1910* (Salem: Secretary of State, 1910), p. 2. West later recalled that he only reluctantly entered the race. Failing to persuade Harry Lane to run, West reminisced: "It was midnight when I reached my hotel. I ate a banana and crawled into bed. Lay awake hoping for a call from Dr. Lane, but none came. I again surveyed the field for a suitable candidate. As the time neared 2 A.M., I decided to become a candidate myself ... In the morning, I caught an early train for Salem; borrowed the required filing fee from my fellow commissioner Tom Campbell, and thus became a Democratic candidate for Governor and—strange as it may seem—was elected." Oswald West, "Reminiscences and Anecdotes: McNarys and Lanes," *Oregon Historical Quarterly* 52 (Sept. 1951), p. 153.

[44] West Campaign Letters, Oct. 15, 1910, Oct. 19, 1910, Oswald West Papers (University of Oregon, Eugene).

West was aided in his campaign against Bowerman by the active support of prominent Democrats, an unprecedented departure from previous Democratic practice. George Chamberlain, who had earlier avoided identification with Democratic candidates, enthusiastically campaigned for West. "The life of the Oregon System is now the issue," declared Chamberlain, "it is trembling in the balance." Harry Lane, whom West had initially urged to run for governor, added: "In a fight for popular rule and right rule we must forget party lines—we must stand for ourselves."[45] When progressive Republicans, led by Jonathan Bourne, threw their support to West the election was no longer in doubt. In the fall of 1910, Oregonians elected their third successive Democratic governor by a margin of over 6,000 votes despite a registered Republican superiority of three to one.[46]

Until 1912, those Democrats elected to high state and federal posts in Oregon faced single opponents in their campaigns for office. Progressive Republicans, in open revolt against party nominees, worked for and made possible the election of George Chamberlain and Oswald West. But in the election of 1912, this informal coalition dissolved when the liberal wing of the Republican Party formally organized a Progressive Party to support the presidential aspirations of Theodore Roosevelt.

Aside from the presidential contest, the voters of Oregon were to elect a United States senator in 1912. The incumbent, Jonathan Bourne, Jr., could expect no aid from regular Republicans who scorned his political independence and mistrusted him personally. According to the most influential Republican newspaper in the state, Bourne had "disorganized and debauched party; he has been the voice of faction and the spirit of strife and political manslaughter."[47] Undeterred, Bourne entered the Republican primary against three other candidates, but lost to party regular, Ben Selling, by 7,000 votes. At the same time, the Progressive Party nominated Alfred E. Clark as their senatorial candidate and the Democrats chose Harry Lane. The senatorial race developed into a four-way contest when Bourne declared as an independent candidate two months before the general election.

---

[45] *Oregon Journal*, Oct. 24, 1910, p. 1; Oct. 26, 1910, p. 1.

[46] Bourne's support of West was not overlooked by Bowerman, who complained, "Mr. Bourne is openly supporting Mr. West and hoped to secure Mr. West's election in order that he may perfect a political machine in the state." See Jay Bowerman to H. L. Browning, Nov. 3, 1910, West Papers. Republican Ben W. Olcott, an old friend of West, financed much of West's campaign in 1910. In 1911, when Republican Secretary of State Frank W. Benson died, West appointed Olcott to that position. See George S. Turnbull, *Governors of Oregon* (Portland, 1959), p. 64.

[47] Portland *Oregonian*, Apr. 21, 1912, p. 6.

Harry Lane's credentials as a progressive equaled or surpassed those of Clark and Bourne. He was, more than Chamberlain, an ideological nonpartisan. Born in Corvallis, Oregon, in 1855, Lane first attended Willamette University and later the College of Physicians and Surgeons of New York, where he received an M.D. degree. As a practicing physician in Portland, Lane won the respect of his profession and was elected to the presidency of both the State Medical Association and the Portland City and County Medical Association. Governor Pennoyer later appointed him Superintendent of the State Insane Asylum. Lane subsequently recalled of those early years: "I used to sit across the table from [Governor Pennoyer] in the olden days and attempt to force the grafters out of the affairs of the people of Oregon."[48] In 1903, Governor Chamberlain appointed Lane to the State Board of Health, and two years later, importuned by civic reformers, he ran for mayor of Portland.

Schism among Portland Republicans in 1905 gave Lane the election. As mayor, he zealously campaigned for better municipal government and acquired a reputation not unlike that of Tom Johnson of Cleveland and "Golden Rule" Jones of Toledo. When job-hungry Democrats besieged the mayor for positions in his administration he refused to reward party members with patronage. As mayor, he remarked later, he attempted to "play it fair down the line"[49] with the citizens of Portland without regard to partisanship. At the end of his administration a California newspaper said of his performance: "Bully for Dr. Lane! It will be a great day when Los Angeles has a Mayor like him."[50] Lane's reelection in 1907 made party history; until then no Democrat had been selected by Portlanders to serve two consecutive terms as mayor.

Lane faced a difficult senatorial race in 1912. With Bourne and Clark in the field, the Democratic candidate could not hope to galvanize all the votes of progressive Republicans behind his candidacy, as did Chamberlain and West when running against standpat Republicans. In a four-way race, however, Progressive and conservative Republicans might neutralize their votes and allow Lane, with some Republican backing, to win the election. Despite the blurred political picture, Lane did not alter the basic Democratic strategy of nonpartisanship.

From the time he campaigned for and won the Democratic primary until the general election, Lane reiterated one theme. "I am unalterably opposed to special privileges . . . being granted to any

---

[48] Harry Lane to Seneca Smith, July 17, 1913, Nina Lane Faubion Papers (University of Oregon, Eugene).

[49] Harry Lane to Seneca Smith, Dec. 4, 1913, Faubion Papers.

[50] Clipping from Los Angeles *Record*, Apr. 7, 1907, Harry Lane Scrapbook, Faubion Papers.

man or set of men at the expense of the mass of the people,"[51] he told Democrats in the primary. Lane directed the same message, without reference to Democratic Party doctrine, to the voters in the general election: "Special interests large and small and both corporate and private do not want me in the United States Senate, and my only hope of election rests in the hands of the plain people of this State, of whom I am one. I will stand by the common people," Lane promised, "through 'thick and thin' and for better or for worse, if I am entrusted with the honorable service which I seek."[52]

In the campaign, Lane lacked adequate funds and the full support of Democrats.[53] But the nature of the Republican campaign partially overcame these disadvantages. More often than not the Republican candidates expended their energies campaigning against one another. The presidential election was injected into the senatorial race when Selling came out for William H. Taft while Clark and Bourne supported Theodore Roosevelt. All announced as proponents of reform and tried to outperform the others in claiming the mantle of reform. This fact caused some consternation among regular Republicans. Describing himself as a "strict partisan," Republican William Colvig explained to a Democrat after the election: "Both Bourne and Selling were each trying to outdo the other in claiming all the honor for imposing upon the people of this state the rotten system known as the 'Oregon System.' Mr. Lane did not make quite so loud claims in that direction, and so I supported him, —not that I loved him more, but that I loved the others less."[54]

After one of the most tumultuous senatorial contests in Oregon history, the voters gave Lane a plurality of approximately 2,000 votes over his nearest competitor, Ben Selling. Bourne ran third, and Clark finished last. Lane's election actually turned on Multnomah County, which he carried undoubtedly because of his progressive administrations as mayor.[55]

In a postelection evaluation of his victory, Lane acknowledged that he probably was "sort of a second choice of the people."

[51] Lane Campaign Letter, Apr. 2, 1912, Neuberger Papers.

[52] *Ibid.*, Aug. 9, 1912.

[53] After the election Lane remarked: "It was a hard campaign for me, for I was shy on cash . . . I wore out my shoes going around the state and almost finished barefooted. I did not have the undivided support of my party. There were some of the party leaders who were too willing to admit my defeat to suit me." Portland *Evening Telegram*, Nov. 9, 1912, p. 2. C. E. S. Wood reported to Lane that the Chamberlain organization did not give full or loyal support to Lane during the election. See C. E. S. Wood to Harry Lane, Mar. 31, 1914, Neuberger Papers.

[54] William M. Colvig to Robert A. Miller, Oct. 18, 1913, Miller Papers.

[55] Blankenship, "Progressives and the Progressive Party in Oregon, 1906-1916," pp. 86-95.

"Strangely enough," he continued, "the Selling people are glad I am elected rather than have Ben beaten by Jack, and the Bourne people are tickled that I won, because they don't want to see Ben beat Jack."[56]

Just as 1912 marked the high tide of Progressivism on the national level, so too did it represent a turning point for Oregon Democrats. Lane was elected to the Senate, and Woodrow Wilson won over Taft in Oregon because of Republican division in the state. Over the next four years, however, the Republican Party gradually united, and by 1916 the state returned to its basic Republicanism.

The elections of 1914 served as a harbinger of the reestablishment of Republican control of state politics. Ralph E. Williams, a candidate for Republican National Committeeman in Oregon, set the tone of that election year when he announced that Republicans would no longer be victimized by "the non-partisan bunk . . . which [had] placed Democrats in nearly every important office in this State and Nation. It is no time to listen again to the duplex voice of the non-partisan who asks his party opponents to vote for the man and who swears his Democratic friends to vote the ticket straight."[57] Driving home his point, Williams later added: "The present campaign is a straight contest along party lines."[58]

In the elections of 1914, Republicans captured nearly every state and federal office. After winning the governorship in three consecutive elections, the Democrats failed to continue their control over that office. When Oswald West, who compiled an outstanding record as a progressive governor, declined to run, the party nominated Charles J. Smith. Though Smith assumed the usual nonpartisan stand, calling on all voters to support his candidacy regardless of party, he was a lackluster candidate compared with West.[59] Smith's defeat by Republican James Withycombe, in addition to the unusually poor showing of Democratic candidates for Congress in the First and Second Congressional Districts, clearly indicated the waning influence of pleas for nonpartisanship.[60]

---

[56] Portland *Evening Telegram*, Nov. 9, 1912, p. 2.

[57] *Voter's Pamphlet—Primary Nominating Election, May 15, 1914* (Salem: Secretary of State, 1914) no. 12, p. 3.

[58] *Voter's Pamphlet—Statements and Arguments of Political Parties and Independent Candidates at the Regular Biennial General Election, Nov. 3, 1914* (Salem: Secretary of State, 1914) p. 9.

[59] Smith, like Lane, had a degree in medicine. He first came to Oregon in 1885 as an assistant surgeon for the Northern Pacific Railroad. Between 1903 and 1909 he served as State Senator from Umatilla County and later was elected mayor of Pendleton. In 1933, Smith attributed his unsuccessful gubernatorial bid of 1914 to the fact that he lacked a state-wide reputation as a reformer. See *Oregon Democrat* 1 (July 6, 1933), p. 4.

[60] Smith lost to Withycombe, 94,594 to 121,037. Willis C. Hawley repre-

Still, party regularity was not entirely restored. Oregon voters returned Democrat George Chamberlain to the Senate in a three-way contest with Progressive Party nominee William Hanley and Republican Robert A. Booth. Significantly, Chamberlain was actively opposed by several Democrats. Chamberlain's neglect of the party in matters of patronage and his failure to support the Wilson administration in voting to repeal the Panama Canal Tolls Act drove C. E. S. Wood and other Democrats into Hanley's camp. "It is sufficient for me to say," wrote Wood to Harry Lane, "that I and many of the leading democrats, including John Gearin, consider Chamberlain too weak a man, are indignant at his attitude on the toll-repeal and infinitely prefer Hanley for what we believe to be loyal and patriotic reasons."[61] Nonetheless, Chamberlain's popularity among Oregonians remained so great that he polled more than the combined vote of Hanley and Booth.

Chamberlain's victory in 1914 coincided with a decline in progressive sentiment in Oregon, as well as a decline in Democratic Party fortunes. Not until 1954 would a Democrat again be elected to the Senate. By 1916, according to a student of the Progressive movement in Oregon, those who bolted the Republican Party in 1912 had returned to the Republican fold.[62] Voting against the national trend, Oregonians cast a majority of their ballots for Charles E. Hughes in the presidential election of 1916. In the same year, for the first time since the turn of the century, Democrats had no candidate for Congress in the Second Congressional District. Two years later the party abandoned the field in the First Congressional District, and not until 1924 did a Democrat again stand for election in that district. In 1918, Oswald West attempted to resurrect the spirit of nonpartisan politics in the senatorial election of that year. Newspapers quickly noted that the strategy had become a "political landmark" of Democratic Party politics and labeled the effort

---

sented the First Congressional District from 1907 to 1933. N. J. Sinnott, elected for the first time in 1912, represented the Second Congressional District from 1913 to 1927. The Third Congressional District, established after the 1910 Census, encompassed Portland and Multnomah County. Races for the House of Representatives were usually much closer here than in the other two districts. The most spirited congressional contest of the entire progressive period occurred here in 1914 with a three-way race between Democrat Austin F. Flegel, Republican C. N. McArthur, and Independent-Progressive A. W. Lafferty. Flegel lost to McArthur by less than 3,000 votes, the closest any Democrat came to defeating Republicans in congressional elections between 1900 and the First World War. See Blankenship, "Progressives and the Progressive Party in Oregon, 1906-1916," pp. 304-309.

61 Wood to Lane, Mar. 31, 1914, Neuberger Papers.

62 Blankenship, "Progressives and the Progressive Party in Oregon, 1906-1916," p. 365.

"nonpartizan propaganda."[63] Republican Charles L. McNary easily defeated West and in the process breathed new life into the expiring appeal of nonpartisan politics, which for the next three decades McNary effectively used in his senatorial career.[64]

In the decade and a half before the First World War, Oregon Democrats had skillfully capitalized on Republican schism. As the decade of the twenties approached, however, it was evident that Republicans had not only found a new unity but also had successfully negated Democratic appeals of nonpartisanship. At the same time, an important segment of the Democratic Party was growing restless under the domination of Senator Chamberlain and others who, it seemed, used nonpartisanship to further their own political fortunes at the expense of a strong, viable party. The years ahead, therefore, scarcely seemed promising, either for party unity or Democratic influence in state politics. Indeed, Oregon Democrats had reached an impasse: the era of the twenties would be a time of factionalism and political debacle.

---

[63] *Oregon Journal*, May 21, 1918, p. 8; Medford *Mail Tribune*, May 2, 1918, p. 4.

[64] For a discussion of the West-McNary campaign and election see Howard A. Dewitt, "Charles L. McNary and the 1918 Congressional Election," *Oregon Historical Quarterly* 68 (June 1967), pp. 125-140.

III   DIVISION AND DEBACLE:
A Party in Shambles

In the decade following the First World War, the nation turned to the Republican Party for political leadership. In Oregon, Republican ascendancy stemmed not from a fundamental conversion of the electorate but from a reaffirmation of basic allegiance to the G.O.P., a political loyalty abandoned only temporarily and on certain occasions under the stress of political change during the progressive era. Anticipating the swing to Republican control of the presidency in the 1920s, Oregon was the only state on the Pacific Slope, and one of two west of the Missouri River, to reject the presidential bid of Woodrow Wilson in 1916.

As the progressive pulse weakened in Oregon, insurgency in the Republican Party ended. Democrats were only occasionally favored by a divided opposition. On the contrary, Oregon Democrats were themselves torn by factionalism, a condition which helped render the party powerless in state politics between 1920 and 1930. Near the end of the decade one friendly commentator lamented: "There exists no party, only the name, and the various factions are far enough apart to even spurn the label rather than unite."[1]

Republican control of Oregon politics during the twenties remained virtually unbroken. With the single exception of 1922, when the Ku Klux Klan became a political force in the state and helped elect a Democratic governor and congressman, Republicans easily carried all elections. Democratic presidential candidates in the elections of 1920, 1924, and 1928 failed to win a single Oregon county. In these contests, no Democrat received more than 34 per cent of the total vote cast for president; in 1924 John W. Davis won only 24.2 per cent of the vote, running behind Robert M. La Follette, the Progressive candidate. In the twelve elections for representative between 1920 and 1928, Republicans usually won by a two-to-one majority, and in some cases three to one.

---

[1] Salem *Capital Journal*, Sept. 8, 1927, p. 4.

Republican candidates for secretary of state, state treasurer, and attorney general either ran unopposed or defeated Democratic rivals by margins similar to those of Republican candidates for Congress. In contests for the state legislature, Democrats consistently failed to elect representatives in proportion to the total party strength.[2] Reflecting the demoralized state of Democratic Party politics, as well as the political bias of Oregonians, Democratic registration remained at a static 28 per cent over the decade.

Because of advantages in registration and the enfeebled nature of Democratic opposition, Republicans frequently ignored Democratic opponents in elections. One knowledgeable Republican advised a candidate for Congress: "Do not allow yourself to be put on the defensive by the opposition candidate . . . Shun all invitations to debate and refuse to answer any of the dozen or so questions that, no doubt, your opponent will demand that you reply to."[3] Following this counsel, the Republican defeated his Democratic rival by a vote of nearly three to one in a race for representative in the Third Congressional District in 1928.

Though Democrats fared badly during the twenties, the party was not torpid. Controversy and factionalism kept the party alive, even in defeat. In some instances, the divisiveness which plagued Democrats in Oregon stemmed from national issues, while on other occasions disputes peculiar to the political scene in Oregon prompted bitter quarrels.

Much of the division among Oregon Democrats over national issues derived from a change in the leadership of the national Democratic Party. Between 1918 and 1932, the locus of power in the party shifted from rural to urban America. This transformation, not completed until the inauguration of the New Deal, was accompanied by intraparty strife. To Democrats of rural orientation and loyalties, the change in leadership from the country to the city seemed to mark not only a political realignment but also an attack on rural values. Throughout the twenties, therefore, the struggle between the rural and urban wings of the Democratic Party frequently centered on social questions and mores.[4] Insofar as a defense

---

[2] In 1920, Democrats cast one third of the total vote, but elected only 1/33 of the membership of the legislature. See Schumacher, "Oregon Legislators," pp. 675-682.

[3] Thomas B. Neuhausen to Franklin F. Korell, Sept. 3, 1927, Neuhausen Papers.

[4] This is the thesis of David Burner, *The Politics of Provincialism: The Democratic Party in Transition, 1918-1932* (New York, 1968). For an excellent study of how the realignment of the national Democratic Party influenced Democratic politics in Missouri during the 1920s see Franklin D. Mitchell, *Embattled Democracy: Missouri Democratic Politics, 1919-1932* (Columbia, 1968).

of prohibition, nativism, and religious fundamentalism typified the rural faction of the party across the nation, that element often held the upper hand in Oregon. The leadership of this group did not go unchallenged, and the resulting controversy explains some of the deep fissures characteristic of the party in the twenties.

In addition to the differences which stemmed from national party politics, Democrats in Oregon quarreled over parochial issues. Distribution of patronage and the question of nonpartisan politics particularly disrupted local party harmony. Throughout the progressive period, one faction of the party was continually alienated by the allocation of patronage to Republicans by elected Democrats. Initially, this group was led by C. E. S. Wood, who refused to support Chamberlain for reelection in 1914 because of the Senator's independence of party. During and after the First World War, leadership of this faction fell to Will R. King, Harvey Starkweather, and Gilbert E. Hamaker, who attempted to oust from party councils those Democrats who continued to cooperate with Republicans.[5]

Because the battles that destroyed party unity in the twenties sometimes centered about national events and in other instances involved local politics, the degree of factionalism, and its cast of characters, vacillated with each issue. Oswald West, however, was at the center of most controversies and consequently became the most divisive personality in the party. Edward F. Bailey, who won election to the lower house of the state legislature in 1922 and was one of the two Democrats elected to the state senate in 1926, states that West encountered the opposition of several important Democratic Party officials in the 1920s. This was so for several reasons. West personified the older politics of nonpartisan progressivism and became the chief antagonist of those who sought to restore party regularity. Furthermore, because of his opposition to the presidential candidacy of Alfred E. Smith in 1928 and to the repeal of prohibition, he was opposed by many who wished to follow the new urban leadership of the national Democratic Party. Finally, West's activity as a utility lobbyist at the state legislature aroused the vociferous opposition of those Democrats who hoped to break the power of corporations and special interests in Oregon.[6] In 1928,

---

[5] This group opposed the candidacy of Oswald West in the Democratic senatorial primary of 1918. Will R. King, the Democratic-Populist fusion candidate for governor in 1898, lost to West in the primary. King, Starkweather, Hamaker, and others saw West not only as a close ally of Chamberlain but one, who, if elected, would ignore the party much as Chamberlain did. See *Oregon Journal*, May 21, 1918, p. 8; Seward W. Livermore, *Politics Is Adjourned: Woodrow Wilson and the War Congress 1916-1918* (Middletown, Conn., 1966), pp. 146-147, 231, 277.

[6] Interview with Edward F. Bailey, Apr. 1, 1968. Investigations by Charles

John W. Kelly, political essayist for the Portland *Oregonian*, observed: "Sometimes we bystanders fall to thinking that Os is really the party, all in himself."[7] Although Oregon Democrats agreed that West attempted to run the party, it was also evident that many considered him the greatest source of schism.

The discord that marked the Democratic Party over the decade of the twenties was first manifested in the senatorial contest of 1920. George Chamberlain, who sought reelection as the incumbent Democrat, angered many Oregon Democrats by some of his activities during the First World War. As chairman of the Senate Military Affairs Committee, he called for an investigation of the War Department and subsequently condemned and criticized the Wilson administration for its handling of war mobilization. At one point the debate between Chamberlain and the President became so heated that Wilson branded the Senator a liar and disloyal in his attack upon the American war effort. Other differences with Wilson came later when Chamberlain accused the War Department of being unprepared and incompetent to direct a program of demobilization. Further, Chamberlain refused to support ratification of the Treaty of Versailles without reservations, a position Wilson tenaciously defended.[8] C. S. Jackson, editor of the *Oregon Journal*, expressed sentiments held by other Democrats when he complained to William Gibbs McAdoo that Chamberlain was "still thinking of the Republican majority in Oregon and that it [would] be effective in re-electing him." The Senator was, Jackson concluded, "always half-Republican-reactionary and privileged."[9]

Beyond Chamberlain's differences with Wilson, some Democrats in Oregon resented the Senator's alliance with Republicans. To some extent, Chamberlain maintained his bipartisan following by granting patronage either to Republicans or Democrats who shunned party regularity. Indicative of this attitude was Chamber-

---

M. Thomas, Public Utilities Commissioner of Oregon, and Claude R. Lester, chief of engineers for the Oregon Public Utilities Commission, revealed that West was retained as a lobbyist by the Northwest Electric Company, Pacific Power and Light Company, Portland Gas and Coke Company, and Pacific Telephone and Telegraph Company. For an itemized account of the salary paid by these companies to West see "Documents Relating to the Investigation of Certain Public Utility Companies by the Oregon Public Utilities Commission," Claude R. Lester Papers (University of Oregon, Eugene); Charles M. Thomas to Henry M. Hanzen, Oct. 31, 1931; *ibid.*, Dec. 9, 1931, Hanzen Papers.

[7] Portland *Oregonian*, Mar. 18, 1928, p. 10.

[8] Sheldon B. Avery, "A Private Civil War: The Controversy Between George E. Chamberlain and Woodrow Wilson" (unpublished master's thesis, University of Oregon, 1967), pp. 70-75, 77, 87.

[9] Quoted in Marshall Dana, *Newspaper Story: Fifty Years of the Oregon Journal, 1902-1952* (Portland, 1951), p. 132.

lain's action in 1913 when he secured the appointment of a Republican as postmaster of Milwaukie, Oregon. When Democrats complained to Senator Harry Lane about the appointment he replied: "The entire affair has placed me in an unfortunate position; without having had anything to do with it I was forced to either stand for his appointment and take a share of the responsibility without having been consulted concerning it, or on the other hand be compelled to fight the appointment."[10] This incident and others naturally angered the Democratic hierarchy in Oregon. Robert A. Miller, a member of the Democratic State Central Committee, wrote Josephus Daniels, Wilson's Secretary of the Navy, that "for years the prominent men of Oregon and the party [had] been sacrificed to Senator Chamberlain's personal interests." The dissident Democrat argued that Wilson failed to carry Oregon in 1916 because "the real leaders and loyal Democrats were not in charge of the various organizations." Yet all was not lost, argued Miller, for if the party "could at once put real Democrats on guard in the Federal positions in Oregon, we might in due time make Oregon a Democratic state."[11]

There were ample reasons, therefore, why, in the senatorial primary of 1920, Chamberlain faced an open revolt in his party. The anti-Chamberlain contingent, composed of almost every member of the party's hierarchy, included Democratic State Chairman Harvey G. Starkweather, Multnomah County Democratic Chairman Gilbert E. Hamaker, former Portland Postmaster Frank S. Myers, and a majority of the State Central Committee. This group threw its support to Starkweather in the primary and attempted to discredit Chamberlain by calling attention to his quarrel with Wilson and his close association with Republicans.

Hamaker addressed a series of public letters to Chamberlain charging, among other things, that the Senator used his influence in Washington during the war to finagle government contracts for Republican friends in Oregon. Oswald West, who supported Chamberlain in the primary, was said to have collaborated in these deals. According to Hamaker, West used his law firm in alliance

---

10 Harry Lane to Seneca Smith, Nov. 27, 1913; Smith to Lane, Nov. 14, 1913; *ibid.*, Nov. 15, 1913, Faubion Papers.

11 Miller also stated: "For many years Senator George E. Chamberlain has controlled Oregon politics. His attacks, however, upon the President and the administration has alienated the great body of the Oregon Democracy from his support. The Oregon Democracy are now trying to reorganize themselves into an effective organization in the interests of Democracy, believing that the great constructive work of President Wilson...makes it possible to accomplish much in the cause of democracy." See Miller to Josephus Daniels, May 3, 1919, Miller Papers.

with Chamberlain's law partners in Washington to lobby for the contracts. For such activities, it was charged, Chamberlain received not only political support from influential Republicans but also such gratuities as a "fine expensive automobile" which the Democrat's "rich Republican [friends] clubbed together and bought . . ."[12]

President Wilson lent his support to Starkweather in an attempt to defeat Chamberlain. Without mentioning the Senator by name, Wilson wired Hamaker that Oregon Democrats should nominate a candidate who would vote to ratify the Treaty of Versailles without the Lodge Reservations. Wilson's telegram, reproduced on handbills, explained that Starkweather promised to support the president while Chamberlain had already made his opposition clear.[13] In spite of the President's opposition, and Starkweather's vigorous campaign, Chamberlain won the primary. He received twice as many votes as Starkweather and carried his opponent's home county by a vote of over two to one.

Chamberlain's victory did not bode well for Republicans. Thomas B. Neuhausen, campaign manager for the Republican senatorial nominee, Robert N. Stanfield, was well aware of Chamberlain's following among Oregon Republicans. As a key figure in Oregon's Progressive Party, Neuhausen had witnessed at first hand Chamberlain's successful senatorial bid in 1914, and now he repeatedly expressed the fear that Chamberlain's nonpartisan reputation would prove too formidable an obstacle for Stanfield. Shortly after the primary, he predicted that Chamberlain would "make a combination with Republicans, throwing his strength to help them elect Harding in this state, in return for his senatorial candidacy."[14] Chamberlain was all the more dangerous because his support extended to influential Republican circles in Oregon. Neuhausen regarded the Chamberlain-West wing of the Democratic Party with as much distaste as did the King-Starkweather-Hamaker faction. Neuhausen observed that "Oswald West [had] various corporation alignments and [knew] how to get corporation presidents and other corporation officials to go to the front for Chamberlain. In fact, the term 'Our George' is heard more frequently and more appropriately around the directors' table of certain banks and other corporation interests than it is in the homes of the working class.

[12] Portland *Evening Telegram*, Apr. 28, 1920, pp. 1, 2. For other criticisms of Chamberlain by Hamaker, see Portland *Evening Telegram*, Feb. 21, 1920, p. 1, and p. 3; Portland *Oregonian*, Feb. 22, 1920, p. 15.

[13] Starkweather also pledged to rebuild the Democratic Party if nominated and elected. Campaign flyer, "Democrats, Stand By Our Noble President!," Neuhausen Papers.

[14] Neuhausen to Robert N. Stanfield, July 4, 1920, Neuhausen Papers.

I doubt whether there is a single working man in Portland or Oregon who speaks of Chamberlain as 'Our George' . . ."[15]

In the campaign, Chamberlain and Stanfield remained silent on the Treaty of Versailles and the League of Nations. While Stanfield argued that Oregonians should honor party regularity and vote Republican, Chamberlain emphasized his past service in the cause of progressive reform.[16] According to a member of the Republican State Central Committee, Chamberlain was "shrewdly and cunningly playing the same old game of 'Non Partisan Politics.' He is a dangerous opponent and his ability to fool Republican voters must not be underestimated."[17]

Stanfield's campaign staff confirmed Chamberlain's strength among Republicans throughout the state. "Our Republicans here are 'hypotmised' [sic] by Chamberlain," complained one correspondent. "The principal thing is to overcome the influence of Chamberlain's magnetic personality," advised another. In Klamath Falls, a Stanfield supporter fulminated, "They have paraded Chamberlain as virtually non-partisan, and [are] exhibiting him over the country in a broken down old Ford . . ." After Chamberlain visited Coos Bay, one Republican wrote: "Chamberlain is a very smoothe [sic] article. He was to [sic] clever to touch on politics in any of his talks, just made friends."[18]

Republican estimates of Chamberlain's strength proved well founded. Chamberlain lost to Stanfield in November, but the close election illustrated the incumbent's popularity over the state. Chamberlain received approximately 17,000 more votes than the number of registered Democrats in Oregon, running well ahead of the Democratic presidential ticket.[19] After his defeat, Chamberlain

---

[15] *Ibid.*, July 15, 1920. Shortly before the election, Neuhausen complained that several members of the Republican National Committee secretly favored the election of Chamberlain over Stanfield because the Democrat fully cooperated with Republican leadership in the Senate. See Neuhausen to Will H. Hays, Oct. 22, 1920; Henry M. Hanzen to Will H. Hays, Oct. 24, 1920, Neuhausen Papers.

[16] *Voter's Pamphlet, Statements and Arguments of Political Parties and Independent Candidates, General Election, Nov. 2, 1920* (Salem: Secretary of State, 1920), no. 3, pp. 37-38, 40-43. Before Stanfield received the Republican nomination, Neuhausen advised him to avoid the League issue. "If a candidate can preserve silence in regard to his attitude toward the league of nations . . . that would be the ideal condition." Neuhausen to Stanfield, Sept. 30, 1919, Neuhausen Papers.

[17] Walter L. Tooze, Sr., to Neuhausen, Aug. 3, 1920, Neuhausen Papers.

[18] Joseph A. Wright to Stanfield, Sept. 25, 1920; J. F. McNaught to Stanfield, Sept. 1, 1920; W. H. A. Renner to Stanfield, Aug. 30, 1920; E. B. Hall to Stanfield, Aug. 30, 1920, *ibid.*

[19] Chamberlain lost to Stanfield 100,133 to 116,696. The only avowed defender of Wilson's position on the League, independent senatorial candidate Thomas A. Hayes, received 4,456 votes.

informed Oswald West that while his future plans were not yet set, he probably would "accept some good place under the new administration."[20] Later that year, President Harding appointed Chamberlain as the Northwest representative on the United States Shipping Board.

Although Democratic Party politics was a model of confusion and chaos during the twenties, the controversy within the party over Chamberlain's candidacy in 1920 typified the more general issues over which Democrats divided. Chamberlain's dispute with Wilson and his refusal to identify his candidacy with that of James M. Cox, the Democratic presidential candidate in 1920, raised the question of whether Oregon Democrats would continue, as in the progressive era, to subordinate their identification with the national party. On the other hand, Chamberlain's calculated attempt to build a following among Oregon Republicans, both through the distribution of patronage and nonpartisanship, was inimical to the creation of a strong and independent Democratic Party on the state level. Consequently, the issue of party regularity at both the national and state level was repeatedly joined throughout the twenties, providing the only thread of continuity in Democratic Party politics.

Before the question of party loyalty again plunged Oregon Democrats into factional dispute, the party unexpectedly became the beneficiary of Ku Klux Klan activity in Oregon. The Klan proved to be a particularly disruptive element in national Democratic politics during the twenties, but it temporarily, and rather improbably, provided Oregon Democrats with an opportunity to challenge Republican control in the state.

The rise of the Klan in Oregon, a reflection of the nativistic intolerance and patriotic fervor that swept the country following the First World War, coincided with the state elections of 1922. The Klan, in alliance with the Federation of Patriotic Societies and the American Protective Association—two groups that also claimed to be the special guardians of "one hundred percent Americanism" —sought two primary objectives in Oregon: the intimidation of the Roman Catholic Church and, more important, control of state politics.[21]

The anti-Catholic attack matured in the form of a Compulsory

---

[20] Chamberlain to West, Feb. 10, 1921, West Papers.

[21] For the growth and activities of the Klan in Oregon see Eckard V. Toy, "The Ku Klux Klan in Oregon: Its Character and Programs" (unpublished master's thesis, University of Oregon, 1959); David M. Chalmers, *Hooded Americanism: The First Century of the Ku Klux Klan 1865-1965* (Garden City, 1965), pp. 85-91; Kenneth T. Jackson, *The Ku Klux Klan in the City, 1915-1930* (New York, 1967), pp. 196-214.

School Bill, sponsored initially by the Scottish Rite Masons and introduced as an initiative measure in 1922. The measure would have required all children between eight and sixteen years of age to attend public school. This thinly-disguised attempt to eliminate parochial education in Oregon immediately became an inflammatory issue.[22]

In an attempt to seize control of state politics the Klan set out to capture the Republican Party, centering its most spectacular bid for power on the Republican gubernatorial primary of 1922. Beset by this extreme pressure, the Republican Party splintered into quarreling factions. Of the six candidates who entered the primary, Ben Olcott and Charles Hall dominated the contest. Olcott, then governor, declared publicly against the Klan, while Hall, a former president of the Oregon Chamber of Commerce, ran as the Klan candidate. When Olcott won nomination by a margin of 500 votes the Klan declared: "Hall's defeat means a Democratic governor next fall."[23]

The results of the Republican primary suddenly and swiftly rebounded to the favor of Democrats. Although the question of the Klan had not been an issue in the Democratic primary, Walter M. Pierce, the Democratic gubernatorial nominee, announced his support of the Compulsory School Bill a few days after the primary. Moreover, Pierce was known to oppose Oriental immigration, alien ownership of land, and the holding of public office by Roman Catholics. Naturally, Klansmen and other nativists flocked to Pierce's standard.[24]

During the campaign, the Democratic Party took no official position on Klan support, leaving party members free to cope with the Klan as they best saw fit. Harvey Starkweather welcomed Klan endorsement; Austin F. Flegel denounced the Klan and the Compulsory School Bill. Edward F. Bailey, a candidate for the state legislature from Lane County in 1922, recalled that the Klan was active in Eugene. Without Klan backing, Bailey wisely exercised

[22] Much has been written on the Compulsory School Bill. For the most recent discussions of this measure see M. Paul Holsinger, "The Oregon School Bill Controversy, 1922-1925," *Pacific Historical Review* 38 (Aug. 1968), pp. 327-341; Lloyd P. Jorgenson, "The Oregon School Law of 1922: Passage and Sequel," *Catholic Historical Review* 54 (Oct. 1968), pp. 455-466; David B. Tyack, "The Perils of Pluralism: The Background of the Pierce Case," *American Historical Review* 74 (Oct. 1968), pp. 74-98.

[23] Quoted in Jackson, *The Ku Klux Klan in the City, 1915-1930*, p. 204.

[24] Pierce served two terms as a state senator from eastern Oregon (1903-1907, 1917-1921). In 1912, he unsuccessfully sought the Democratic senatorial nomination, and in 1918 won nomination as the gubernatorial candidate, but lost to Republican James Withycombe.

caution in his bid for election: "Most of us either ignored the Klan or made a point of not openly criticizing the organization."[25]

For his part, Pierce avoided an overt appeal to racial or religious prejudices in the campaign. Instead, he stressed the need for increased taxes on utility and lumber interests, a position entirely consistent with his past record in the state legislature. As a state senator, he had championed welfare legislation and cast a lone vote against a criminal syndicalism bill in 1919. A review of his performance in the legislature prompted C. C. Chapman of the *Oregon Voter* to describe Pierce in equivocal terms: "One of the most effective and eloquent debaters in the senate; excelled in sob eloquence; invariably favored so-called 'popular' side of every issue; rejoiced in denunciation of business and industry as selfish and rapacious."[26]

Pierce did not emphasize racial and religious issues in the campaign, but he and other Democrats nonetheless won the endorsement and the support of the Klan and other nativist groups. Elton Watkins, Democratic candidate for Congress in the Third Congressional District, zealously campaigned for restriction of immigration, prohibition of Oriental land ownership, and the Compulsory School Bill. A pro-Klan publication, *Murdoch's Magazine*, endorsed Watkins, noting that his political affiliation was of little consequence: "While a Democrat, he knows he will represent a Republican State and will work with Republican senators, and with other members of Congress. Watch him make good in Washington."[27] Watkin's opponent, incumbent Republican Clifton N. McArthur, was marked for political elimination by the Klan and was opposed by the American Legion because of his vote against the soldiers' bonus bill of 1922, but narrowly won renomination over Franklin F. Korell, the Klan-sponsored candidate.

The initiative proposal that would abolish parochial schools overshadowed all campaign rhetoric in 1922. "No matter how rotten or weak the Democrat may be," observed a Pierce partisan, "he will be elected on account of the greatest religious split which the Republican Party has seen in the history of the state."[28] Thomas Neuhausen, though a Republican, voted for Pierce in 1922 on the basis of the initiative proposal. "The race between Olcott and

---

25 Toy, "The Ku Klux Klan in Oregon: Its Character and Program," p. 92, 102; Ralph E. Bunch, "Pierce v. Society of Sisters: The Oregon School Case" (unpublished master's thesis, University of Oregon, 1961), p. 52; Interview with Edward F. Bailey, Apr. 1, 1968.

26 *Oregon Voter* 29 (May 13, 1922), pp. 8-9.

27 *Murdoch's Magazine* 1 (Nov. 1922), p. 11.

28 Quoted in Dorothy O. Johansen and Charles M. Gates, *Empire of the Columbia: A History of the Pacific Northwest*, 2nd ed. (New York, 1967), p. 496.

Pierce," he later argued, "was not Republicanism at all but something entirely different."[29]

On election day in November, Pierce received the largest vote given a gubernatorial candidate up to that time. Watkins defeated McArthur to become the first Democratic representative elected from Oregon since 1879, and Democrats increased their representation in the lower house of the state legislature from two to nine and in the senate from one to four. The controversial Compulsory School Bill was adopted by a vote of 107,498 to 97,204.[30]

After the election, the Klan boasted that it was responsible for the elevation of Pierce to the governorship. Pierce later denied that he made an official alliance with the Klan and that he rewarded Klansmen with patronage, but it seems obvious that he received the votes of those motivated by racial and religious prejudice.[31] It is equally important to recognize that the Federation of Patriotic Societies probably backed Pierce because of his attack on special interests in Oregon. Founded in 1917, the Federation originally had as its major purpose an assault on corporate interests in the state.[32] As a rancher from eastern Oregon who persistently crusaded against excessive profits of big business and the influence of corporate power, Pierce undoubtedly appealed to small farmers who saw in him a champion of their political ideals. And, even though the movement for public power had not yet gained great momentum in Oregon, Pierce and others who advocated the cre-

---

[29] Neuhausen to Stanfield, Mar. 21, 1923, Neuhausen Papers.

[30] The *Oregon Voter* noted that "More inexperienced men will be members of the next legislature in both houses than has been the case in the history of Oregon. This year the religious issue has dominated the election, with the result that the majority of experienced members who sought reelection were defeated. The new members are in the main beholden to some secret organization for their election." *Oregon Voter* 31 (Nov. 11, 1922), p. 5. Of the nine Democrats elected to the House, six had never before served in the legislature. Two years later, in elections for the state legislature, only one of the nine won reelection.

[31] One student of Pierce's political career maintains that "sometime between the 1922 primaries, and the summer of 1923, Walter M. Pierce was 'naturalized' into the Invisible Empire." The evidence offered for this allegation is based on two letters written to Pierce by Klansmen, neither of which provides conclusive proof that Pierce was actually a member of the Klan. See Gerald Schwartz, "Walter M. Pierce and the Tradition of Progressive Reform: A Study of Eastern Oregon's Great Democrat" (unpublished doctoral thesis, Washington State University, 1969), pp. 68-69.

[32] In 1924, the alliance between the Klan and the Federation dissolved when the Klan advanced individuals for membership on the Public Service Commission who were considered captives of the utility corporations. The Federation, long an opponent of telephone and electric utilities, denounced the Klan. See Jackson, *The Ku Klux Klan in the City, 1915-1930*, pp. 210-211.

ation of a hydroelectric power commission were endorsed by the Federation in 1922.[33]

Whether or not bigotry and prejudice or personal economic interest motivated those who supported Pierce, the Democrat clearly owed his election to Republicans. Understandably, Governor Pierce found it necessary to court the opposition party to obtain support for his administrative programs. The need for Republican votes led Pierce to reject party regularity in the presidential election of 1924, thus reviving the feud between regular and maverick Democrats.

Pierce's rejection of party regularity occurred indirectly. In March 1924, when Republican State Treasurer O. P. Hoff died, Pierce appointed a Democrat, Jefferson Myers, to fill the vacancy for the remaining few months of Hoff's term. Because the state treasurer, together with the governor and secretary of state, constituted the Board of Control which ran the state, Pierce deemed it imperative that a fellow Democrat hold this position.

The election of Myers to a full term was likely to be a formidable task. Since 1887, when voters elected the last Democratic state treasurer, Oregonians had returned Republicans to that office with monotonous regularity. Furthermore, in 1924 registered Republicans heavily outnumbered Democrats. Clearly, Myers must seek support outside of his party. Fortunately, the third-party revolt of Progressives in 1924 offered a way out of the dilemma.

To secure the election of Myers, Pierce and other Democrats agreed covertly to support Robert M. La Follette, Progressive presidential candidate, rather than the Democratic presidential nominee, John W. Davis. In exchange, La Follette's forces promised to support Myers for state treasurer and Elton Watkins for reelection to Congress from the Third Congressional District. Alarmed by these developments, Thomas Neuhausen advised the Republican National Committee of the Democratic-Progressive coalition. "Myers' election as State Treasurer is absolutely essential to Governor Pierce," explained Neuhausen. "Unless Pierce can elect Myers with La Follette Republican votes, he will lose control of the Board."[34] The

---

[33] Among those endorsed for the state legislature by the Federation in 1922 was George W. Joseph. Joseph has been popularly identified as that individual most responsible for heading the public power movement in Oregon until his death in 1930. As a state legislator in 1921, Joseph introduced legislation designed to establish a hydroelectric commission to survey the state's water power resources in preparation for public development and marketing of electricity. See "Federation of Patriotic Societies Ticket" (Portland, 1922), Neuhausen Papers; George M. Joseph, "George W. Joseph and the Oregon Progressive Tradition" (unpublished bachelor's thesis, Reed College, 1952), pp. 56-59.

[34] Neuhausen to David Henshaw, Oct. 3, 1924, Neuhausen Papers; Port-

Democratic-Progressive coalition also included fusion candidates for Justice of the Supreme Court and Public Service Commissioner. It was at first rumored that Democrats and Progressives would support a single senatorial candidate to challenge incumbent Republican Charles L. McNary, but this plan went awry.[35]

The attempt at an exchange of political courtesies failed. La Follette ran nearly 10,000 votes ahead of Davis in the presidential contest, but the Democratic-Progressive alliance failed to produce any victory for Democrats on the state level. Republicans captured all congressional districts, McNary retained his senate seat, and Myers was swamped in his bid for state treasurer. The Democratic-Progressive coalition was defeated for two reasons. First, the old Roosevelt progressive group, headed by Thomas B. Neuhausen, refused to support La Follette or make alliance with Democrats.[36] Second, an important faction of the Democratic Party, led by Will R. King, the National Committeeman, remained loyal to Davis and opposed Pierce's efforts at fusion on the state level. King later denounced Pierce as a "hybrid Democrat" because he supported La Follette.[37]

The desire to elect Myers to the post of state treasurer was probably the determining factor in Pierce's support of La Follette. At the same time, Pierce and other Democrats undoubtedly found John W. Davis far too conservative. Especially important to Pierce was the question of public power, a cause he had consistently championed. Since La Follette's position on this issue, as well as others, closely paralleled that of Pierce, the Democratic governor was not simply surrendering to political expediency when he supported La Follette.

land *Oregonian*, July 13, 1924, p. 10; *ibid.*, Oct. 2, 1924, p. 12; Oct. 16, 1924, pp. 1, 4.

[35] Republican agreement on a senatorial candidate was rendered difficult by the activities of Fred T. Gifford, Grand Dragon of the Klan. Both George Baker, mayor of Portland, and K. K. Kubli, Speaker of the lower house of the legislature, sought Klan endorsement in the Republican primary. Gifford originally favored Baker, while Lem A. Dever, editor of the Klan publication *Western America*, backed Kubli. As a result, the Klan split over a candidate and Gifford, after much political maneuvering, eventually came out for McNary. See Chalmers, *Hooded Americanism*, pp. 90-91; Jackson, *The Ku Klux Klan in the City, 1915-1930*, pp. 210-211.

[36] Neuhausen and other progressive Republicans backed Hiram Johnson in the Oregon presidential primary of 1924. Neuhausen served as the state campaign manager for Johnson, who, running unopposed, won the primary. When La Follette became the Progressive presidential nominee, Neuhausen deserted the third party and organized the former Johnson followers for Coolidge. Portland *Oregonian*, Oct. 26, 1924, p. 11; Neuhausen to Stanfield, July 16, 1924; Stanfield to C. Bascom Slemp, Oct. 9, 1924, Neuhausen Papers.

[37] Will R. King to Charles L. McNary, Dec. 8, 1925, Neuhausen Papers.

Regardless of Pierce's reasons for rejecting party regularity in the presidential contest of 1924, the Governor, like Senator George Chamberlain in the presidential election of 1920, had deserted the leadership of the national Democratic Party. Even before the presidential election of 1928, when Democrats would again face the issue of identification with the national party, the question of party loyalty on the state level was renewed in the senatorial election of 1926.

The Democratic senatorial primary of 1926 was not unlike the Chamberlain-Starkweather contest of 1920. The major issue of the primary centered on whether the party would nominate a candidate who was known to cooperate with Republicans in the nonpartisan fashion of Senator Chamberlain or, on the other hand, a candidate who advocated party regularity. These contrasting views were reflected in the candidacies of Bert E. Haney, a prominent Portland attorney, and Elton Watkins, a former Democratic representative.

Haney's association with the Chamberlain approach to politics was more than a coincidence. When Chamberlain resigned from the United States Shipping Board in 1923, he persuaded President Coolidge to appoint Haney, a close personal friend, as his replacement.[38] Haney, like Chamberlain, immediately proceeded to build a following among Republicans. As a member of the Shipping Board, he won strong Republican backing when he sided with Portland shipping interests in opposition to a proposal by Coolidge to reduce the appropriations and powers of the Shipping Board in Portland. When Haney refused to agree to the President's plan, Coolidge demanded his resignation. Predictably, the Portland Chamber of Commerce and the Portland *Oregonian* condemned the President and defended Haney.[39]

The controversy catapulted Haney into political prominence. He was suddenly a leading candidate for the United States Senate. The *Oregon Voter* pointed out that "President Coolidge may have elected a Democratic United States Senator from Oregon when he sent his curt little wire to Bert E. Haney. We have listened to expressions of a number of Republican business men from different parts of Oregon. With few exceptions all said they would vote for

[38] Haney attended Willamette University and the University of Oregon School of Law. After practicing law in Portland for several years he was elected Chairman of the Democratic State Central Committee and served in that position from 1911 to 1915. During Wilson's second administration, Haney was appointed United States Attorney for Oregon. Haney was the unanimous choice of Portland shipping interests to replace Chamberlain in 1923. The next year, he won their endorsement for appointment to a full term.

[39] Portland *Commerce* 9 (Aug. 1, 1925), p. 1; *ibid.* 9 (Sept. 5, 1925), p. 1; Portland *Oregonian*, Sept. 3, 1925, p. 10; Portland *Evening Telegram*, Sept. 2, 1925, p. 6; Sept. 5, 1925, p. 1.

Haney despite the danger of throwing senate control to the Democrats."[40] In December 1925, Haney resigned from the Shipping Board and declared as a candidate for the Senate.

Haney's decision to run for the Senate revived Democratic factionalism. Even before the senatorial primary, when Haney's credentials as a *bona fide* Democrat would be questioned, party leaders quarreled bitterly over Haney's successor on the Shipping Board. Governor Pierce recommended to Senator McNary that Marshall H. Dana, associate editor of the *Oregon Journal,* be appointed to the Board. Will R. King, Democratic National Committeeman, Charles J. Smith, chairman of the Democratic State Central Committee, Harvey Starkweather and others strenuously objected, believing that the post should go to some active Democrat. King reasoned that the selection of Dana, like that of Chamberlain and Haney, would in no way help Oregon Democrats because none of these men was committed to party regularity. Insulted because Pierce had not consulted party leaders before recommending Dana, King wired McNary: "Don't let Republicans and heretofore inactive Democrats fuse on some one for place whom Democrats don't want."[41]

Haney tried to avoid the controversy over his successor, but because he owed his appointment on the Board to Chamberlain he became the target of criticism by anti-Chamberlain Democrats. The simmering dispute reached the boiling point in the primary. Elton Watkins, who entered the primary in April 1926, charged that Haney was unworthy of the nomination because he was not a loyal Democrat. Watkins argued that Haney, as a member of the Chamberlain-West wing of the party and an ally of Republican shipping interests, was "half-Republican" and would do nothing to further the interests of the Democratic Party. "Haney is no longer a Jeffersonian Democrat, neither is he a Jackson Democrat, nor a Wilson Democrat, nor a Bryan Democrat," said Watkins, ". . . he is an Arlington Club Democrat."[42]

Ironically, Watkins was himself not a consistent exponent of party regularity. As a candidate for Congress in 1924, he had joined with Pierce and other Democrats in an attempt at fusion with La Follette Progressives. Despite the inconsistency in Watkin's position, the primary struggle centered about the issue of party regu-

---

[40] *Oregon Voter* 45 (Sept. 5, 1925), pp. 13-14.

[41] Will R. King to Charles L. McNary, Dec. 8, 1925; King and Charles J. Smith to Calvin Coolidge, Dec. 9, 1925; Neuhausen Papers. See also Portland *Oregonian,* Dec. 1, 1925, p. 4; Dec. 4, 1925, p. 10; Dec. 6, 1925, pp. 1, 4.

[42] *Oregon Journal,* May 18, 1926, p. 13. The Arlington Club was an organization which in large part drew its membership from wealthy Republican businessmen.

larity. The campaign became so rancorous that when Haney emerged the victor with a plurality of 2,500 votes, the party was seriously split.

Although Haney did not enter the senatorial race with the undivided support of his own party, he benefited from a divided Republican opposition. The Republican senatorial primary of 1926, one of the few times during the twenties when the G.O.P. was torn with dissension, revolved around the character and personal behavior of Senator Robert N. Stanfield.

After his election to the Senate in 1920, Stanfield became a constant source of embarrassment to his party. Scarcely six months after he assumed his duties in Washington, Stanfield was described by a reporter as a playboy: "Oregon certainly has sent a live one to the Senate this time. I refer to Bob Stanfield. He spends his nights joyriding in taxi cabs with some of the finest stock we have in Washington."[43] Perhaps Stanfield's fondness for Washington nightlife contributed to his frequent absences from the Senate. Whatever the reason, Oregon newspapers were critical of Stanfield's record of absenteeism. The Portland *Oregonian* compared the Senator with "Charles Ross, the most celebrated lost boy in history."[44]

As early as 1922, Thomas Neuhausen informed Stanfield that some Republicans already considered him a "one-termer." Neuhausen lectured Stanfield on the proper personal and political behavior of a United States Senator, warning that unless Stanfield changed his personal and political image he would not be reelected.[45] In spite of this warning, Stanfield continued to embarrass Republican Party leaders and his constituents in Oregon.[46]

If some Oregon voters remained unconvinced of Stanfield's moral and political peccadillos, all their doubt vanished when, seven months before the primary election of 1926, police at Baker, Oregon, arrested the Senator on charges of being drunk and disorderly. Stanfield allegedly resisted arrest, used profane language, and threatened to kill the arresting officer. The Senator heatedly portrayed the episode as a "frame-up all the way" because "old Gover-

[43] W. W. Caviness to Neuhausen, June 4, 1921; Caviness to Neuhausen, June 6, 1921; Neuhausen to Stanfield, June 8, 1921, Neuhausen Papers.

[44] Portland *Oregonian*, July 8, 1922, p. 1; July 4, 1922, p. 2; July 2, 1922, p. 1.

[45] Neuhausen to Stanfield, July 4, 1922, Neuhausen Papers.

[46] Neuhausen warned Stanfield that he had a reputation for being friendly to the meat packers in Oregon, Washington, and Idaho. "One begins to hear ugly comments here on the alleged conspiracy of the packers to keep up the prices of meat beyond reasonable profit, and not infrequently your name is mentioned and dragged in as a sponsor of the packers' evil doings." The fact that Stanfield was an eastern Oregon livestock operator—his 350,000 head sheep ranch was among the largest in the nation—added credibility to the charge. Neuhausen to Stanfield, Feb. 12, 1922, Neuhausen Papers.

nor Pierce wired in here last night to have me arrested."[47] Despite Stanfield's repeated declarations of innocence, the publicity given the affair, coupled with other criticism, endangered his nomination.

Frederick Steiwer, Stanfield's opponent in the Republican primary, began his campaign by calling attention to Stanfield's poor record of attendance in the Senate, but prohibition quickly emerged as the major issue. Steiwer declared his staunch support of prohibition and won the endorsement of the Anti-Saloon League. The Portland *Oregonian* urged Republicans to vote for Steiwer because he could best defend prohibition against the attacks of the wets.[48] A majority of Republican voters apparently agreed with the *Oregonian* and awarded the nomination to Steiwer.

The senatorial primaries of 1926 had divided both parties. Watkins and other Democrats, unhappy with the victory of Haney, vowed to withhold support from the Democratic nominee. Meanwhile, Stanfield's supporters argued that Steiwer had unfairly won nomination because of the episode at Baker—an incident that Stanfield continued to insist was a "frame-up"—and refused to back Steiwer's candidacy. Therefore, in the early months of the senatorial campaign, the political picture was confused. Suddenly, in August, Haney's political fortunes improved when Stanfield declared as an independent senatorial candidate, further splitting his own party and, in the opinion of some Republicans, ensuring Haney's victory.[49]

Stanfield's renewed candidacy again raised the issue of prohibition. Both Haney and Steiwer professed opposition to any tampering with the Volstead Act, and Stanfield advocated a national referendum on prohibition.[50] The presence of Stanfield in the campaign offered Democrats an opportunity to capture the Senate seat; unfortunately for Haney, the party was not united behind him. The anti-Haney group in the Democratic Party, one observer

---

[47] Portland *Oregonian*, Sept. 15, 1925, pp. 1, 8; Sept. 19, 1925, p. 6; Sept. 27, 1925, pp. 1, 3.

[48] Radio Address by Frederick Steiwer, Apr. 6, 1926, Neuhausen Papers; Portland *Oregonian*, Apr. 7, 1926, p. 4, May 3, 1926, p. 1; May 6, 1926, p. 12; May 17, 1926, p. 10.

[49] *Oregon Voter* 46 (Sept. 4, 1926), pp. 3-5.

[50] Portland *Oregonian*, Aug. 28, 1926, p. 3; Sept. 4, 1926, p. 8. Lem A. Dever, who described himself as the "liberal leader of the Klan in Oregon," reported that Stanfield had lost the votes of the "Best People" because of his position on prohibition. "This State is DRY, the whole nation is DRY," said Dever, and Stanfield could expect little help from the wet minority, "composed principally of the alien and semi-alien elements." See Lem A. Dever to Neuhausen, Aug. 30, 1926, Neuhausen Papers. In the election, the Klan reportedly favored Steiwer. Because most politicians had repudiated the Klan by 1926, and its endorsement was considered a political liability, the Klan allegedly spread word that it favored Stanfield. See Chalmers, *Hooded Americanism*, p. 91.

stated, "are reconciled and will . . . vote for the Republican whom they think will have the better chance of defeating Haney, a Chamberlain man. The sentiment among these Democrats is favorable to Stanfield."[51] The November elections validated this analysis. The three-way race for the Senate resulted in the election of Steiwer, though Haney, who ran second, lost by only 8,000 votes. In other contests, Republicans remained firmly in control. Walter Pierce, who sought reelection as governor, was soundly defeated. Governor Pierce had gained some support among progressive Republicans because of his crusade for prison reform, conservation, development of a state-owned hydroelectric program, and a graduated income tax for Oregon, but this support was not enough to bring his reelection.[52]

Robert Stanfield's candidacy in 1926 injected the issue of prohibition into Republican state politics, but the major battle ground for temperance during the decade was the Democratic Party. Until 1928, Oregon Democrats officially, if not unanimously, committed themselves to prohibition.[53] However, as the presidential election of 1928 approached, the party split over the presidential candidacy of Alfred E. Smith and the repeal of prohibition.

In Oregon, Oswald West became the chief opponent of Smith's nomination as the Democratic presidential candidate. West had been elected National Committeeman in 1926, and had full responsibility for conducting the Oregon presidential campaign on behalf of the party's nominee. At the Democratic National Convention of 1924, West stood solidly behind William Gibbs McAdoo for the presidential nomination. Although McAdoo declined to seek the nomination in 1928, he and West considered Smith's candidacy a disaster for the party. "If the Democratic Party had the courage to stand unequivocally . . . for the maintenance of the Eighteenth Amendment and enforcement of the prohibitive laws," McAdoo assured West, Democrats would stand a good chance of winning the election in 1928. But, "If the party is delivered into the hands of Tammany Hall," McAdoo warned, "I see no hope."[54] West,

---

51 *Oregon Voter* 46 (Sept. 4, 1926), pp. 3-5.

52 For a discussion of the progressive legislation Pierce sponsored as governor and the gubernatorial election of 1926, see Schwartz, "Walter M. Pierce and the Tradition of Progressive Reform," pp. 68-86.

53 In 1904, a local option law for prohibition was adopted and finally, in 1914, statewide prohibition was enacted in Oregon. John E. Caswell, "The Prohibition Movement in Oregon, 1904-1915," *Oregon Historical Quarterly* 40 (Mar. 1939), pp. 64-82; James H. Timberlake, *Prohibition and the Progressive Movement 1900-1920* (Cambridge, 1963), pp. 166, 172.

54 William Gibbs McAdoo to West, Sept. 30, 1927, West Papers. At the Democratic Convention of 1924, the Oregon delegation voted solidly against Smith and refused to support censure of the Ku Klux Klan by name.

who zealously defended prohibition, agreed without reservation.[55]

Insisting that the major issue in the presidential election would be prohibition, West devised a twofold strategy to discredit Smith in Oregon. First, he and McAdoo persuaded Senator James Reed of Missouri and Senator Thomas J. Walsh of Montana to enter the Oregon presidential primary against Smith.[56] Second, West initiated a vigorous campaign to herd Oregon Democrats into the dry camp.

In a series of public letters to Democratic voters before the primary, West sounded the alarm: "The Democratic Ship is about to be captured and turned into a rum boat. It is planned to operate her out of the port of New York." The National Committeeman warned Democrats of eastern Oregon that the primary was a "fight between the night clubs and the homes!" To rank and file party members in Benton County, West addressed the following picturesque warning: "The booze hounds are on your trail. You can hear their voices in the distance. If you run you are lost . . . But if you stand and make a fight, you will protect your homes and save the party of Jefferson, Jackson, Wilson, and Bryan. Kick the booze hounds in the slats and send them back to their night clubs with their tails between their legs."[57]

West's uncompromising defense of prohibition and opposition to Smith brought sharp dissent within the party. Democrats who supported Smith formed an Oregon Tammany Society headed by Gilbert E. Hamaker and demanded that West be replaced as National Committeeman by a "true Democrat." George Putnam, editor of the Salem *Capital Journal,* questioned the wisdom of West's opposition to Smith. Under the leadership of Smith, said Putnam, "The Democrats show signs of returning to sanity . . . [and] may emerge from the dismal swamp of political oblivion." Walter Pierce entered the controversy by expressing doubts about the success of the Volstead Act. "Prohibition by legislation has not

---

[55] West established a reputation as a militant dry during his term as governor. In 1914, he dispatched his private secretary to Copperfield, Oregon, with instructions to force saloon owners, who had secured control of the city government, to resign from office. See Stewart H. Holbrook, *Far Corner: A Personal View of the Pacific Northwest* (New York, 1952), pp. 176-185.

[56] Portland *Oregonian,* Mar. 18, 1928, pp. 1, 10; Salem *Capital Journal,* Mar. 24, 1928, p. 1. Walsh, a Roman Catholic dry, was chairman of the Democratic Convention in 1924. Although the McAdoo faction of the party hoped Walsh would get the nomination, they lined up behind Reed as a last-ditch effort when Walsh withdrew his name as a possible candidate after losing the California primary. See Burner, *The Politics of Provincialism,* pp. 190-191.

[57] Salem *Capital Journal,* Mar. 16, 1928, p. 4; Pendleton *East Oregonian,* Mar. 15, 1928, p. 1; Corvallis *Gazette Times,* Mar. 14, 1928, p. 1.

accomplished the results expected of it," Pierce observed, "We cannot legislate people into being moral and temperate."[58]

In spite of vociferous opposition from fellow Democrats, West did not alter his position. Undeterred, he reiterated the conviction that prohibition must remain. In a public letter to Pierce, West stated: "It is reported in private beer circles that you are for Al Smith. Am I to stand alone. The drys need help! The booze dam is about to break! Mount your horse Walter! Join me in spreading the alarm!"[59] To Multnomah County Democrats, West explained that "Miss Democracy, heretofore a perfectly proper old maid, has been slipped a few cocktails by the wets and as a result is about to step out with the boys."[60] The only hope for the party, according to West, lay in stopping Smith in the primary.

The Democratic primary, fueled by the prohibition debate, became so heated, commented the Portland *Oregonian*, that the "republican primary campaign [had] been relegated to the sidelines . . ."[61] Some Democrats regarded the dispute as futile because Republicans would undoubtedly carry the state in November. With this in mind, one member of the Tammany Society declared: "Isn't it funny how democrats will fight over offices they haven't a chance on earth of filling?"[62] Others in the party interpreted the battle as an indication of whether or not "there [were] enough real Democrats in Oregon . . . to untie the apron strings of the W.C.T.U. fastened upon the party by Mr. West and the Klan night-gown regalia capped on by Mr. Pierce."[63]

On May 18, West was repudiated when Smith emerged the victor over Walsh and Reed. Convinced that Smith would receive the nomination, West refused to attend the Democratic Convention in Houston. He did not actively campaign against Smith in the fall, but the Democratic presidential campaign in Oregon suffered from the inactivity of the National Committeeman.[64] As predicted, the Republican Party made a clean sweep of the state in November.[65]

---

[58] *Oregon Journal*, Jan. 19, 1928, p. 2; Mar. 24, 1928, pp. 1, 9; Salem *Capital Journal*, Mar. 16, 1928, p. 4.

[59] *Oregon Journal*, Mar. 24, 1928, p. 1.

[60] Portland *Evening Telegram*, Apr. 14, 1928, p. 1.

[61] Portland *Oregonian*, Mar. 18, 1928, p. 10.

[62] *Ibid.*

[63] Salem *Capital Journal*, Mar. 30, 1928, p. 4.

[64] Portland *Oregonian*, June 19, 1928, p. 10. At the last minute, West gave Smith a weak endorsement. See *ibid.*, Nov. 1, 1928, p. 10.

[65] The election of 1928 in Oregon cannot be considered a "critical election." According to V. O. Key, Jr., such elections occur when new and durable voting blocs are formed. In Massachusetts, for example, the support for Al Smith in 1928 prompted a realignment of votes which established an

After the election, Democrats across the state expressed pessimism about the future of the party. E. B. Aldrich, editor of the Pendleton *East Oregonian*, concluded: "The Smith-Raskob leadership will kill the party if continued, if it has not already done so. It may be hard to do any organization work until people know where the party is headed." The chairman of the Democratic State Central Committee declared, "the way of the democrat in Oregon is like the way of the transgressor," while the president of the Jackson Club decried "the folly of a minority party trying to carry elections by a fevered effort of only a few weeks."[66]

Oswald West, perhaps shaken by another defeat, suggested that unless the party found new leadership, Oregon Democrats were doomed to political impotence: "I feel that it would be a wonderful thing . . . if a lot of us has-beens would retire."[67] Some persons maintained that West was less interested in rebuilding the party than in frustrating the political ambitions of those who earlier opposed him in party quarrels, especially Walter Pierce, Harvey Starkweather, and Will R. King. "If Mr. West is going to ban defeated Democrats, who will there be left in the party?" asked the Salem *Capital Journal*. "Almost every Democrat of any prominence has been drafted for defeat by the party in the past."[68]

Shortly after the inauguration of Herbert Hoover, Walter Pierce summed up the wide-spread disillusionment among Democrats. Noting that party organization was in a state of utter chaos, Pierce remarked: "The draft has been hard against us for many years. Men of money are practically all in the republican camp." But, said Pierce, "we must devise some method by which we can keep to-

---

enduring pattern of Democratic supremacy over the next four decades. Although Smith lost to Hoover, the new electoral grouping which backed Smith presaged Franklin Roosevelt's victory in 1932. Smith's support in Oregon scarcely reflects a realignment of voters. Omitting the presidential contest of 1924, when the Democratic candidate ran last in a three-way race, Smith did not significantly poll more urban or rural votes than did James M. Cox in 1920. Cox won 35.8 per cent of the vote in Multnomah County, the largest concentration of urban votes in Oregon, while Smith received 36.8 per cent. See V. O. Key, Jr., "A Theory of Critical Elections," *Journal of Politics* 17 (Feb. 1955), pp. 3-18. For an evaluation of Smith's support in Oregon see Ruth C. Silva, *Rum, Religion, and Votes: 1928 Re-Examined* (University Park, Pa., 1962). Key's theory has been tested in California and Illinois with negative results. See John L. Shover, "Was 1928 A Critical Election in California?," *Pacific Northwest Quarterly* 58 (Oct. 1967), pp. 196-204; Duncan MacRae and James Meldrum, "Critical Elections in Illinois: 1888-1958," *American Political Science Review* 54 (Sept. 1960), pp. 669-683.

[66] E. B. Aldrich to Robert A. Miller, Jan. 25, 1929; Miller to Mrs. Rose Schiefflin, Feb. 9, 1929, Miller Papers. Portland *Oregonian*, July 31, 1929, p. 12.

[67] Portland *Oregonian*, Jan. 11, 1929, p. 8.

[68] Salem *Capital Journal*, Sept. 26, 1929, p. 4.

gether the straggling fragments of what was once a great, aggressive political party."[69] Fortunately—for the Democratic Party—the adverse political reaction to Republican leadership after the economic collapse of 1929 united the fragments and gave Democrats an opportunity to break with their defeatist and divisive past.

[69] Pierce to Robert A. Miller, Apr. 6, 1929, Miller Papers.

IV THE GREAT DEPRESSION:
Political Challenge and Lost Opportunities

The Great Depression of the 1930s, an economic disaster unprecedented in the history of the nation, prompted a dramatic shift in
the political preferences of the American voter. As the depression
settled over the land, farmers and industrial workers, as well as
ethnic minorities and Negroes, joined in a powerful political alliance that swelled the ranks of the Democratic Party.[1] The support of this coalition, coupled with the leadership of Franklin D.
Roosevelt, enabled the Democratic Party to assume a position of
undisputed prominence on the national scene.

Even before the tide of national politics had clearly demonstrated a reversal in the fortunes of the Republican Party, Democrats in Oregon recognized the political opportunity provided by
the depression. In the spring of 1930, scarcely six months after the
stock-market crash of 1929, a jubilant party official declared that
the economic debacle had at last given Democrats a concrete issue:
"If there was ever a time when Democrats should get together it
is now. If we unite we will sweep all before us."[2] Carl C. Donaugh,
chairman of the Democratic State Central Committee, echoed this
sentiment. "Everyone conceeds [sic] that opportunity knocks at
the Democratic door,"[3] he affirmed. After a decade of division and
defeat, the political horizon seemed unlimited. With hard work at
the state level and the assistance of a Democratic administration in
Washington, Democrats in Oregon believed they could realign the
political balance of the state to a competitive two-party system, if
not win outright control of Oregon politics.

---

[1] For a discussion of the political coalition that supported the New Deal
see Samuel Lubell, *The Future of American Politics* (New York, 1951); Carl
N. Degler, *Out of Our Past: The Forces That Shaped Modern America* (New
York, 1959), pp. 393-410.

[2] Will M. Peterson to Robert A. Miller, Mar. 20, 1930, Miller Papers.

[3] Carl C. Donaugh to Thomas G. Green, Dec. 2, 1930, Thomas G. Green
Papers(University of Oregon, Eugene).

Confident of success, Democrats set out to organize and reunite the party. The State Central Committee called a series of state-wide party meetings between 1930 and 1932 to plan a precinct-by-precinct reorganization. "Nothing means more to a party organization than interest, activity and enthusiasm on the part of its members. This can only be accomplished through continuous meetings,"[4] Donaugh told fellow Democrats. In April 1931, Jouett Shouse, chairman of the national Democratic Executive Committee, visited Portland to coordinate state organization efforts with campaign strategy for the presidential contest of 1932. Later that year a Young Democratic League, an affiliate of the Young Democratic Clubs of America, was formed and shortly thereafter boasted an active membership of 2,500 with chapters in every county of Oregon.[5]

As the work of organization went forward, other forces equally significant were at work for the development of party harmony. Democrats disagreed on some issues, notably the question of public power, but the divisive issues of the twenties subsided as sources of factionalism. Throughout the decade of the 1920s, for example, Oregon Democrats frequently opposed the new urban leadership of the national Democratic Party. As the Democratic convention of 1932 approached, however, a consensus emerged concerning the selection of a presidential candidate. When William G. McAdoo urged Oswald West to work for the nomination of John Nance Garner, West refused and instead threw his support to Franklin Roosevelt, the overwhelming choice of Democratic Party officials in Oregon.[6] Roosevelt, running against Governor William "Alfalfa Bill" Murray of Oklahoma, won 80 per cent of the vote in the Oregon presidential primary of 1932.

The question of prohibition, which had split the Democrats so badly in 1928, also became less controversial. In 1930, Democrat Charles H. Martin, who waged a successful campaign for election to Congress in the Third Congressional District, declared for a national referendum on prohibition and received the backing of West, the most conspicuous champion of prohibition during the twenties.[7] An Oregon chapter of the Association Against the Pro-

4 Donaugh to Green, Dec. 29, 1931, *ibid.*

5 Joseph K. Carson, Jr., to Green, May 2, 1931; Donaugh to Green, May 14, 1931; "Report on the Young Democratic League of Oregon," Apr. 16, 1932, Green Papers; *Oregon Democrat* 1 (Jan. 20, 1933), p. 8; *ibid.*, 1 (Jan. 6, 1934), p. 10.

6 William G. McAdoo to West, Feb. 26, 1932; West to McAdoo, Mar. 1, 1932; Franklin Roosevelt to West, Mar. 11, 1932; Roosevelt to West, Mar. 29, 1932, West Papers.

7 *Voter's Pamphlet—Statements and Arguments of Political Parties and Independent Candidates, General Election, November 4, 1930* (Salem: Secre-

hibition Amendment was established in 1931 and received the enthusiastic support of party leaders, as well as the rank and file.[8] In 1932, the people of Oregon repealed the state's general prohibition law by a decisive margin.[9]

The earlier Democratic practice of avoiding party identification and emphasizing nonpartisanship in elections, a strategy that had proved eminently successful during the progressive era but one that aroused much controversy during the twenties, no longer appeared attractive or desirable. As the party in power at the time of the crash, the G.O.P. was identified with responsibility for the nation's economic problems. Conversely, the Democratic Party presented itself as the exponent of new ideas. Democrats in Oregon, anxious to capitalize on the rising popularity of the national party, now saw the party label as a distinct advantage. For those Democrats who failed to appreciate the wisdom of party loyalty, there were threats. "We intend to dynamite all fence straddlers and all pusillanimous equivocators out of our party,"[10] asserted one advocate of party regularity. Such warnings were scarcely necessary. Without exception, those Democrats elected to office in 1932 identified their candidacies with Franklin D. Roosevelt and campaigned on the basis of the yet unfulfilled promise of a "new deal."

With the schismatic twenties behind them, Democrats greeted Roosevelt's victory in the presidential election of 1932 with uniform and unrestrained glee. "The tide has turned," exclaimed the *Oregon Democrat*, an official party publication that made its debut in January 1933. "Democrats learned the formula for success," the magazine noted, "organization, leadership, and a clearly defined progressive program."[11] Equally important, Roosevelt's popularity helped several Democrats in local contests. The party increased its representation in the lower house of the State Legislative Assembly from seven to seventeen and in the state senate from one to eight. At the same time, Charles H. Martin won re-election in the Third Congressional District; in eastern Oregon, Walter Pierce captured the Second Congressional District for the party for the first time in Oregon history.

tary of State, 1930) no. 5, p. 13. Martin privately confided: "I am against the 18th Amendment to the Constitution, and favor its repeal." Charles H. Martin to Henry H. Curran, July 15, 1930, Charles Henry Martin Papers (Oregon Historical Society, Portland). On West's support of Martin see *Oregon Voter* 61 (May 17, 1930), p. 55.

[8] Jouett Shouse to Nan Wood Honeyman, Oct. 14, 1932; Honeyman to Shouse, Oct. 20, 1932, Nan Wood Honeyman Papers (University of Oregon, Eugene); *Oregon Democrat* 1 (Feb. 6, 1933), pp. 3-6.

[9] Waldo Schumacher, "Ballot's Burden: An Analysis of the 1932 Election in Oregon," *Commonwealth Review* 15 (Nov., 1933), p. 98.

[10] *Oregon Democrat* 1 (June 6, 1933), p. 2.

[11] *Ibid.*, (Jan. 20, 1933), p. 4.

Amid the rejoicing and self-congratulation of 1932, thoughtful Democrats recognized that Roosevelt's success in Oregon and the gains of the state party stemmed primarily from the disaffection of Republicans who backed Democrats in the elections of 1932. Roosevelt won 53 per cent of the popular vote in Oregon at a time when Democratic registration stood at 32 per cent. Neither Martin nor Pierce won on the basis of a straight party vote; Democrats constituted less than 40 per cent of the registered voters in their congressional districts. Republican votes also determined a majority of the victories scored by Democrats in elections to the state legislature. Commenting on Republican support for Democratic candidates, the *Oregon Democrat* observed: "The large number of progressive Republicans who voted the Democratic ticket, either in part or whole, are Democratic at heart and by a little process of education in Democracy may be converted to our course."[12]

The challenge for Democrats in Oregon was obvious. The future success or failure of the party hinged on forging a coalition with liberal forces in the state. "The West believes in liberal and progressive ideas regardless of party," stated one Democrat, "and it is this element which forms the reserve strength of the Democratic Party."[13] Unlike the power base of the national Democratic Party, which included many disparate elements, a New Deal coalition in Oregon, as envisioned by party leaders, would consist of two groups: farmers and industrial workers, represented by the Grange and State Federation of Labor, in league with the state Democratic Party. This political alliance would, of course, be based on common support of the Roosevelt administration and the programs of the New Deal. Peter Zimmerman, a recognized leader of progressive Republicans in Oregon, pointedly underscored the importance of this fact when he explained that so long as the Democratic Party of Oregon endorsed the New Deal and sought to develop its programs in the state, liberal Republicans would back the party. If not, Zimmerman warned, "the Democratic party is going to be in bad in this state in the future."[14]

Zimmerman's admonition proved prophetic. Although the task ahead was clear and all signs promised Democratic ascendancy, the party failed in its bid to reshape Oregon politics. As the decade progressed, ominous clouds appeared on the once bright political horizon, continued to gather, and finally brought a storm of controversy that split the party into warring factions and dispelled all hope of a New Deal coalition on the state level. In fact, a few years

---

[12] *Ibid.*, (March 21, 1933), p. 10.

[13] *Ibid.*, p. 11.

[14] Peter Zimmerman to Walter Pierce, Jan. 15, 1935, Walter Pierce Papers (University of Oregon, Eugene).

after Roosevelt's election in 1932, the party was in turmoil, its discipline virtually gone. This ruinous state of party affairs continued throughout the later thirties until one party spokesman resignedly concluded that Oregon Democrats might as well "fold the party up and call it a day," while another argued it was futile for the party to run candidates against Republicans because they would meet certain defeat. "What the hell's the use?," he exclaimed.[15]

Paradoxically, while Democrats blundered toward ignominious defeat, more Oregonians than ever before joined the party. Between 1900 and 1930, Democrats never constituted more than 30 per cent of the state's registered voters. But in the thirties, Democratic registration climbed to a high of 48 per cent. In Multnomah County, with the state's largest city, Portland, Democratic registration jumped from 25 per cent in 1930 to 53 per cent in 1938. The increase in registration reflected not only the sagging appeal of the Republican Party but, more important, support for the New Deal. After first carrying Oregon in 1932, Roosevelt went on to capture the state easily in the presidential elections of 1936 (68.5%), 1940 (54.1%), and 1944 (52.5%).

Oregonians voted for Roosevelt, but they refused to support other Democratic candidates with equal enthusiasm. During the Roosevelt years, Democrats in Oregon were unable to win a single senatorial election. The party attained some success in congressional elections, but even here made a poor showing. After winning three of the nine congressional contests between 1930 and 1932, the party failed to gain significantly. Walter Pierce, elected to Congress in 1932 from the Second Congressional District, won re-election four times before his defeat in 1942. The election of Nan Wood Honeyman in the Third Congressional District in 1936 marked the only other Democratic congressional victory during the decade.

Contests for state offices revealed a similar pattern. Between 1930 and 1942, Democrats won only one of the four gubernatorial elections. The party captured no other state executive position, but in 1934 and again in 1936, Democrats gained control of the lower house of the State Legislative Assembly. These victories were only temporary; in 1938, Democrats lost twenty-five seats in the house and once again assumed a minority position.

The inability of Oregon Democrats to ride the tide of national politics during the thirties, or measurably benefit from the inauguration of the New Deal, is not without parallel. The political fortunes of the Democratic parties of Minnesota, Wisconsin, and Michigan, as well as those in most of the Western states, did not

---

[15] *Oregon Democrat* 10 (June 1942), p. 11; 10 (Nov. 1942), p. 7.

improve enough during the depression to permanently alter Republican domination of state politics.[16] Indeed, as James T. Patterson recently argued, the political impact of the New Deal on state parties was minimal at best. Many state Democratic organizations, on the other hand, were unable to emulate the political achievements of the national party, and a common set of problems explain their failure.[17]

The most vexing problem that beset Oregon Democrats during the New Deal centered around a contest between liberals and conservatives for domination of the party. At the time of Roosevelt's election in 1932, conservatives were firmly in control, but liberals immediately announced their intention to overthrow the established leadership and assume command. "There is no excuse or necessity for the existence of a Democratic Party in Oregon unless that party advocates and executes radical changes," argued a member of the Multnomah County Central Committee. "We intend," he declared, "to drag out all of the little Mellons, Mitchells, Morgans, Insulls and all of the other little tin icons and display their little clay feet."[18] Conservatives warned that such talk would result in schism and, beyond that, State Chairman Donaugh made it clear that the party would not be run by what he called "radicals." "It is high time to muzzle these die-hards," said Donaugh. Vernon Williams, editor of the *Oregon Democrat*, wrote a blistering editorial in which he urged party members to "Clip that Left Wing."[19]

In spite of a spirited challenge from liberals, conservatives were able to maintain their hold on the party apparatus. But the intraparty struggle produced an incorrigible factionalism that prevented party unity. As the battle raged, conservatives eventually moved to a position of opposition to Roosevelt and the programs of the New Deal. As a result, voters in Oregon who stood behind the national administration came to view the state Democratic Party and its leaders as reactionary. Under the circumstances, Republicans and Democrats alike, in an attempt to secure the benefits of the New Deal, frequently exercised an independence of party and a nonpartisanship reminiscent of the progressive era. Republican

---

[16] For a general description of the political impact of the New Deal on the Democratic parties in these states see Epstein, *Politics in Wisconsin;* John H. Fenton, *Midwest Politics* (New York, 1966); Robert E. Burke, *Olson's New Deal for California* (Berkeley, 1953); and the essays on state politics in Frank H. Jonas, ed., *Politics in the American West* (Salt Lake City, 1969).

[17] James T. Patterson, "The New Deal and the States," *American Historical Review* 73 (Oct. 1967), pp. 70-84; Patterson, *The New Deal and the States: Federalism In Transition* (Princeton, 1969).

[18] *Oregon Democrat* 1 (June 6, 1933), p. 2.

[19] *Ibid.,* 1 (May 22, 1933), p. 9; 1 (June 21, 1933), p. 8.

Senator Charles Linza McNary established a reputation for cooperation with the Roosevelt administration, and thereby gained bipartisan support in senatorial campaigns during the New Deal. In some circles McNary was known as the "Republican New Dealer,"[20] and even though the *Oregon Democrat* never endorsed him for reelection the magazine was obliged to admit that he displayed "the ear marks of a good democrat."[21] Active Democratic support for McNary was demonstrated in the senatorial contest of 1942 when Willis Mahoney, a liberal Democrat who came within 6,000 votes of unseating the Republican Senator in 1936, endorsed McNary rather than support Walter W. Whitbeck, a conservative Democrat.[22]

A second problem, one that bedeviled both conservative and liberal Democrats, concerned the distribution of patronage by the Roosevelt administration. Democrats in Oregon counted on patronage from Washington in their efforts to perfect party organization, but the anticipated assistance did not materialize, at least in the quantity desired. Moreover, when patronage was available, Democrats complained that the state party had little control over its distribution. Bitter criticism of the administration's patronage policy was first voiced in 1933 when Rosemary Schenck, Vice-Chairman of the Democratic State Central Committee, angrily charged: "We have not been permitted to even name our own postmasters [because] outside influences dominate our appointments."[23] Equally distressing was the fact that the Civil Works Administration produced more jobs for Republicans than Democrats in the state. This situation came about because New Deal relief directors, anxious to speed assistance to the unemployed, utilized the existing state relief agency in Oregon, which was staffed and administered by Republicans. In 1934, the *Oregon Democrat* reported that of 19 CWA positions in Multnomah County, 15 were held by Republicans. The remaining four were divided between three Democrats, two of whom had changed their party registration to Democratic in 1932, and one independent who had campaigned for Hoover

20 John D. Phillips, "Charles L. McNary: Progressive Ideology and Minority Politics During the New Deal" (unpublished master's thesis, University of Oregon, 1963), p. 57. Another of the Senator's biographers has stated that McNary "established a better relationship with Franklin D. Roosevelt than he had ever had with any other President he had known." See Roger T. Johnson, "Charles L. McNary and the Republican Party During Prosperity and Depression" (unpublished doctoral thesis, University of Wisconsin, 1967).

21 *Oregon Democrat* 1 (July, 1929), p. 12; 1 (Sept. 6, 1933), p. 8; 1 (July 6, 1933), p. 9.

22 *Ibid.*, 10 (Mar. 1942), p. 8.

23 Rosemary Schenck to Milton A. Miller, Nov. 27, 1933; *ibid.*, Nov. 8, 1933, Milton A. Miller Papers (Oregon State Library, Salem).

against Roosevelt. Describing the appropriation of jobs under CWA the magazine lamented, "The big warm nest built by Democracy was filled with a weird assortment of Republican cuckoo eggs."[24]

Unfortunately for the party, the dispute over patronage was not settled in the thirties. The Roosevelt administration, caught between the liberal and conservative factions, first tried to placate each group but succeeded only in alienating both. Typical of the disappointment expressed by Oregon Democrats during the New Deal was the complaint of one conservative who described himself as a "loyal party man." Why, he asked, should the party faithful "be required to continually spend time, effort and money in behalf of our party without hope of reward."[25] In 1938 a liberal observed: "Frankly, our whole group here is getting pretty weary of everlastingly battling for the New Deal, and yet seeing virtually every key Federal post in the hands of the opposition."[26] In 1942, the *Oregon Democrat* agreed that the lack of patronage had severely hampered effective party organization. "The absolute failure of the big shots in Washington to play ball with the state organization in passing out the jobs . . . caused the organization efforts, and everything that goes with it, to be shot to hell."[27]

Conflict between the AFL and the CIO on the national labor scene was another stumbling block to Democratic gains in Oregon during the 1930s. Although many Democrats hoped at first to form an alliance with organized labor similar to the national New Deal coalition, these plans went awry when conservative Democrats proved unsympathetic to the aspirations of labor. Nevertheless, individual liberals within the party frequently won the endorsement of the State Federation of Labor. But when the battle between the AFL and the CIO erupted, and then spread to Oregon, the State Federation of Labor and the AFL withdrew support from liberal Democrats, who tended to side with the CIO.

The plight of liberal Democrats, caught in the sulphurous labor dispute, is illustrated by the case of Nan Wood Honeyman. In

---

24 *Oregon Democrat* 1 (Jan. 6, 1934), p. 9; 2 (Jan. 21, 1934), p. 9.

25 Dellmore Lessard to Walter Pierce, May 12, 1937, Pierce Papers.

26 Monroe Sweetland to E. L. Oliver, Dec. 5, 1938, Oregon Commonwealth Federation Papers (University of Oregon, Eugene).

27 *Oregon Democrat* 10 (Nov. 1942), p. 7. For recurring criticisms of the Roosevelt administration's patronage policies see *Oregon Democrat* 1 (June 21, 1933), p. 3; 1 (Jan. 6, 1934), p. 5; 2 (Mar. 21, 1934), p. 8; 2 (Oct. 6, 1934), p. 5; 2 (July 6, 1935), p. 8. After a trip around Oregon in 1938, one Democratic Party official reported that a "substantial block" of the Democratic Party was "generally disgruntled at the state and national administrations because of patronage matters." Thomas W. Delzell to Edgar W. Smith, Mar. 30, 1938, Martin Papers.

1936, Mrs. Honeyman was endorsed by the State Federation of Labor in a successful campaign for Congress in the Third Congressional District. After the election, however, labor violence flared in Oregon when the Lumber and Sawmill Worker's Union broke with the AFL, reconstituted itself as the International Woodworkers of America, and affiliated with the CIO.[28] Mrs. Honeyman, outspokenly sympathetic to the organizational efforts of the CIO, was actively opposed by the AFL and the State Federation of Labor when she ran for reelection in 1938.[29] In spite of the support of the CIO and Harry Bridges's International Longshoremen and Warehousemen's Union, she lost to Republican Homer D. Angell, though by less than 3,000 votes out of over 135,000 cast.[30]

Another difficulty facing Oregon Democrats was the caliber of candidates who ran on the Democratic ticket during the depression. With but few exceptions, the aspirants to high offices did not generate much enthusiasm. Some were merely politically inept or self-seeking, while others were older Democrats who had repeatedly been defeated for political office in the past. Harvey G. Starkweather, an unsuccessful Democratic candidate for state and federal office since the progressive era, failed in his bid for election to Congress in the First Congressional District in 1932. Thomas R. Mahoney, who failed to win election to the state legislature as a Republican in 1930, 1932, and 1936, switched his registration to Democratic in 1938. Mahoney won a seat in the state senate in 1938 from Multnomah County, but seemed uninterested in rebuilding the party.[31] Willis Mahoney, a new face on the Oregon political scene, ran against Senator McNary in 1936, but received only qualified support from either conservative or liberal Democrats. According to one conservative spokesman, Mahoney was a "baloney peddler."[32] Liberals, on the other hand, castigated him as an opportunist.[33]

Undoubtedly the most controversial Democrat who held office during the thirties—one who contributed to the party's poor image in recruiting—was Charles Henry Martin. In 1927, after serving

[28] Walter Galenson, *The CIO Challenge to the AFL: A History of the American Labor Movement* (Cambridge, 1960), pp. 387-389, 391-392.

[29] E. B. O'Grady to Honeyman, May 23, 1938; J. W. Estabrook to Honeyman, Oct. 14, 1938, Honeyman Papers; Jill H. Herzig, "The Oregon Commonwealth Federation: The Rise and Decline of a Reform Organization" (unpublished master's thesis, University of Oregon, 1963), pp. 51-54.

[30] Although the State Federation of Labor did not formally endorse Angell, members of that organization unofficially aided his campaign. Angell also had the support and assistance of several AFL unions.

[31] *Oregon Voter* 94 (Dec. 31, 1938), p. 28.

[32] *Oregon Democrat* 2 (Oct. 6, 1934), p. 11.

[33] Sam H. Brown to J. L. Steinbach, Nov. 4, 1934, Brown Papers. Interview with Monroe Sweetland, Dec. 21, 1967.

forty years in the United States Army, Martin retired with the rank
of major general and moved to Portland. As a registered Republican, he became active in civic affairs and eventually worked his
way into politics. In 1930, though still a Republican, he won a write-
in campaign as the Democratic nominee for Congress in Portland's
Third Congressional District. After winning election to Congress
in the fall of 1930, and reelection in 1932, he announced for governor in 1934, and won a narrow victory in a three-way race. Until
1934, Martin's political career was not marked by controversy; but
as chief executive of the state, and titular head of the Democratic
Party, he dramatically altered his public image.

Aside from the fact that as a Democratic governor he repudiated
the Roosevelt administration and many programs of the New Deal,
Martin possessed the unhappy faculty of repeatedly attracting to
himself allegations of ruthlessness which, true or not, served to discredit him and the party. Perhaps this was in part due to his philosophy of human relationships, summarized by his statement: "Man
is a fighting animal."[34] If this statement did not necessarily suggest
a lack of compassion or humanity, some of Martin's other words
and acts demonstrated otherwise. When a suggestion was made
that the aged and feeble-minded wards of the state be chloroformed,
Martin commended the idea. If 900 of the 969 inmates at the Fair-
view Home in Salem were "put out of their misery," the Governor
stated, it would save the state $300,000 on the next biennial budget.[35]
On another occasion Martin asserted that the able-bodied unemployed should not be given federal or state assistance: "The need
for the necessities of life will force these people to get some kind of
work and to care for themselves." For those unable to work because
of physical or mental impairments, the Governor remarked, "I
believe $10.00 a month ample to care for them."[36] When a group
of farmers, fearing that the state legislature was about to adopt a
sales tax, petitioned the Governor to veto any such legislation,
Martin advised the group that what the legislature did was "none
of their business." He added: "Go home and listen to the birdies
sing."[37]

While Martin ignored the economic and social plight of Oregonians during the thirties, he zealously emphasized law and order.
At the height of the depression, he declared that the most pressing
problems of the day was sterilization of persons convicted of sex

34 Turnbull, Governors of Oregon, p. 83.

35 Salem Capital Journal, Mar. 12, 1936, pp. 1, 13; Portland Oregonian,
Mar. 18, 1936, pp. 1, 5; Richard L. Neuberger, Our Promised Land (New York,
1938), p. 314.

36 Salem Capital Journal, July 14, 1936, p. 7.

37 Salem Capital Press, Apr. 29, 1938, pp. 1, 8.

crimes. "Governor Martin," reported the *Oregon Democrat*, "is preparing . . . a far-reaching program of sterilization."[38] That Martin's attention should be occupied by such a peripheral problem must have seemed curious to those who were concerned with employment and survival in an era of economic collapse.

Party factionalism, the lack of sufficient patronage to build and maintain party organization, the turbulent labor scene, and candidates of little political ability or appeal all played a part in preventing the Democratic Party from building a strong party or altering the political complexion of the state during the depression. But the major obstacle to Democratic success during the New Deal was the failure of Democratic Party leaders to support the administration's public power program and, most specifically, the power program as interpreted by the Oregon Grange and the State Federation of Labor. This issue, above all others, became the chief source of schism in the Democratic Party.

Public power as a political issue had long been important in Oregon politics. Richard Lewis Neuberger, a liberal Democrat and an active participant in Oregon politics during the thirties, observed in 1938 that the "fate of governors, senators, and presidential electors" often turned on "how forthrightly a candidate approaches, or how expertly he straddles, the question of hydroelectric development."[39] The public power movement in Oregon, initiated by the state Grange during the late nineteenth century, had steadily gathered strength. During the decade of the depression, it dominated most elections and was a source of division in both the Republican and Democratic parties.[40]

The public power dispute of the depression years first took shape in the gubernatorial election of 1930. George W. Joseph, a longtime advocate of hydroelectric development and vociferous critic of private electric utilities, won the Republican gubernatorial primary on a platform that promised state and municipal development of water power resources without expense to the taxpayer.[41] One

---

[38] *Oregon Democrat* 3 (Aug. 21, 1935), pp. 8-9.

[39] Neuberger, *Our Promised Land*, p. 88.

[40] For a general discussion of the origins and growth of the public power movement in Oregon see Daniel M. Ogden, "The Development of Federal Power Policy in the Pacific Northwest" (unpublished doctoral thesis, University of Chicago, 1949), pp. 87-102, 215-227. New Deal power policies in the Pacific Northwest are treated in Charles McKinley, *Uncle Sam in the Pacific Northwest* (Berkeley, 1952); Herman C. Voeltz, "Genesis and Development of a Regional Power Agency in the Pacific Northwest, 1933-43," *Pacific Northwest Quarterly* 53 (Apr. 1962), pp. 65-76. See also Voeltz, "Proposals for a Columbia Valley Authority: A History of Political Controversy" (unpublished doctoral thesis, University of Oregon, 1960).

[41] Joseph's decision to seek the Republican gubernatorial nomination was based as much on his advocacy of public power as on a desire to vindicate

month after the primary Joseph suddenly died, and the Republican State Central Committee selected as his successor Phil Metschan, a member of the old guard who opposed Joseph's platform. Liberal Republicans, outraged by the choice of Metschan, nominated Julius Meier as an independent candidate for governor. Meier, a Portland merchant and close friend of Joseph, adopted Joseph's primary platform, literally word for word, and promptly received the endorsement of the State Federation of Labor and the Oregon Grange.

If Republican Party politics seemed chaotic in 1930, the Democratic Party was far from united on the power issue. Democrats were divided into two groups: one faction, led by Democratic National Committeeman Oswald West, opposed Joseph's stand on public power while a second, headed by Walter Pierce, ardently endorsed state and municipal development of water resources. After much political sparring—at one point both Pierce and West threatened to enter the race for governor—the two wings of the party each fielded a candidate for the gubernatorial nomination.[42] West, whose activities as a utility lobbyist put him at odds with the Grange and other public power advocates,[43] persuaded State Senator Edward F. Bailey to enter the primary. Bailey remained silent on the power issue, but George R. Wilbur, the candidate of the Pierce faction, campaigned on a platform nearly identical to that of Joseph.[44]

Interest in the Democratic primary increased when Pierce entered the race for National Committeeman against Oswald West. Like Joseph and Wilbur, Pierce inserted a long statement in the *Voter's Pamphlet* declaring that the state should assume responsibility for hydroelectric development and distribute it at cost. West, like Bailey, sidestepped the power issue. "I cherish no political

himself in the face of disbarment proceedings. For a discussion of the events that prompted Joseph's candidacy see Joseph, "George W. Joseph and the Oregon Progressive Tradition," pp. 115-130; Henry M. Hanzen, "The Joseph-Meier Political Revolution" unpublished manuscript, Hanzen Papers; Stephen A. Stone, *Oregon Memorabilia: Stories from the Files of an Oregon Newsman* (Eugene, 1967), pp. 137-149.

[42] Portland *Oregonian*, Mar. 21, 1930, p. 1; Joseph, "George W. Joseph and the Oregon Progressive Tradition," pp. 132-133.

[43] In 1928 the Portland Electric Power Company proposed a merger with the Northwest Electric Company. The merger required approval by the electorate, and in the election West took the side of the utility company while Joseph fought the merger. The Grange denounced West as a puppet of the utilities. Joseph, "George W. Joseph and the Oregon Progressive Tradition," pp. 76-83.

[44] Bailey opposed Joseph's position but decided not to declare himself on the power issue until after the primary. Interview with Edward F. Bailey, June 4, 1968.

ambitions. I have only a sincere desire to serve the party," said West.[45]

The result of the Democratic primary proved inconclusive for both factions. Bailey won a razor-thin victory over Wilbur for the gubernatorial nomination, but Pierce, by a vote of nearly two to one, defeated West for the post of National Committeeman.

Once the gubernatorial campaign commenced, public power remained the preeminent issue; Joseph's death had only increased its significance. Both Bailey and Metschan rather belatedly announced their support for hydroelectric development but emphasized that the federal government, and not the state, should underwrite the expense of such a program.[46] Neither, however, endorsed a constitutional amendment sponsored by the state Grange to establish public-utility districts. Meier, on the other hand, declared that he stood "four square on the platform of the late Republican party nominee" and also urged the adoption of the Grange measure.[47]

The power question dominated the campaign for governor, and also became the main issue in other contests. Practically all candidates for major political office made statements in support of public power, if not specifically in terms of the Joseph-Meier proposal. Senator Charles L. McNary, running for reelection, followed the advice of Meier's campaign manager and carefully avoided association with the position of Metschan and the Republican State Central Committee on public power.[48] McNary endorsed the Grange proposal for public-utility districts and stated further that he was "a staunch advocate of the principle that the people come first when the ownership, development, and control of water power of the country are concerned."[49] Elton Watkins, the Democratic senatorial candidate, made a similar statement and tried, unsuccessfully, to picture McNary as a captive of the power trust. "If you like [the] Joseph platform, vote for me," said Watkins.[50] In the election

[45] *Voter's Pamphlet—Statements of Democratic Candidates for Nomination or Election at the Primary Election, May 16, 1930* (Salem: Secretary of State, 1930) pp. 3-4.

[46] *Voter's Pamphlet—Statements and Arguments of Political Parties and Independent Candidates, General Election, November 4, 1930* (Salem: Secretary of State, 1930) no. 5, pp. 14 and 17-20. Metschan stated: "There may be times and conditions under which public ownership is advisable, but seldom should it be adopted to the exclusion of private ownership."

[47] *Ibid.,* pp. 15-16.

[48] Henry M. Hanzen to Charles McNary, Sept. 17, 1930, Hanzen Papers.

[49] *Voter's Pamphlet—Statements and Arguments of Political Parties and Independent Candidates, General Election, November 4, 1930* (Salem: Secretary of State, 1930) no. 5, p. 4.

[50] *Ibid.,* p. 7: Manuscript copy of radio address by Elton Watkins, Sept. 16, 1930, Neuhausen Papers. Thomas B. Neuhausen warned McNary that Watkins posed a serious threat because he had "flopped completely over into the Meier

for representative in the Third Congressional District, Democrat Charles H. Martin and Republican Franklin F. Korell both endorsed the concept of public power, but did not make specific reference to the Joseph platform, nor did they urge enactment of the constitutional amendment for public-utility districts.

Before the campaign was over, Bailey concluded that Meier would probably win the governorship. Bailey later recalled that although Joseph had died shortly after the primary, he, and then Meier, had captured the support of most voters. "My campaign efforts seemed useless. I was running against a dead man."[51] Compounding Bailey's dilemma was the demand of several Democrats that he dissociate himself from Oswald West and adopt Joseph's platform. When Bailey refused, many Democrats defected to Meier. The Pierce wing of the party moved, almost *en masse*, into Meier's camp. Pierce did not publicly endorse Meier, but it was clear that he sided with the independent candidate. Mrs. Walter Pierce, Bert E. Haney, Dr. Charles J. Smith, and William C. Culbertson openly backed Meier.[52]

In November, Meier won an overwhelming victory, receiving more votes than his two opponents combined. In addition, the constitutional amendment for public-utility districts was adopted. The only major Democratic victory was that of Charles H. Martin in the Third Congressional District.[53]

Meier's victory in the gubernatorial election of 1930 did not end the public power controversy. Before long, the depression made it apparent that Oregon did not have sufficient funds to proceed with a state program of hydroelectric development. At the same time, the power issue temporarily ceased to be a source of division within the Democratic Party. The concept of federal responsibility for construction of power sites in Oregon had been advanced by Democrats who opposed the Joseph plan in 1930. Accordingly, the party united behind Roosevelt during the presidential election of 1932 and endorsed his proposal for federal development of water

---

camp, declares himself in entire accord with the Joseph platform, and is endeavoring to win over as many [Republican] votes as possible." Neuhausen to McNary, Oct. 29, 1930, Neuhausen Papers.

[51] Interview with Edward F. Bailey, June 4, 1968.

[52] *Ibid.*; *Oregon Voter* 62 (Aug. 16, 1930), p. 20; 61 (Sept. 13, 1930), pp. 6-7; Portland *Oregonian*, Aug. 10, 1930, p. 1; Hanzen, "The Joseph-Meier Political Revolution," chaps. 30-34; Joseph, "George W. Joseph and the Oregon Progressive Tradition," pp. 132-133.

[53] The vote in the gubernatorial election was Meier 135,608; Bailey 62,434; Metschan 46,840. The constitutional amendment for public-utility districts was approved 117,776 to 84,778. The *Oregon Democrat* later said of Bailey's defeat: "It will always be the general feeling of his friends and supporters that had he received the whole-hearted backing of his party . . . Bailey would have won." *Oregon Democrat* 1 (July 6, 1933), p. 3.

resources in Oregon. Furthermore, party leaders did not react unfavorably when Roosevelt, speaking at Portland during the campaign, suggested that the cost of electricity produced by federally financed power projects should be used as a national yardstick for power rates.[54]

Once elected, Roosevelt acted on his campaign suggestion. In 1933, the Public Works Administration began construction of Bonneville and Grand Coulee Dams on the Columbia River. As work on these projects went forward, two important questions arose: what type of agency would distribute the power produced at Bonneville and Grand Coulee Dams, and would private or public interests be the chief beneficiary of the new power?

The Oregon Grange and the State Federation of Labor generally favored the creation of a Columbia Valley Authority, a federal agency patterned after the Tennessee Valley Authority. Such an agency would provide for the integrated development and administration of the Columbia River Valley projects and also ensure federal distribution of power from the dams. Whether Congress created a federal agency similar to TVA was not nearly so important as the demand of farmers and workers that electricity produced at Bonneville be allocated principally for farms and homes in Oregon. Integral to the idea of a CVA was the expectation that the state or federal government would build transmission lines from Bonneville, thus providing electricity at cost to domestic consumers.[55] A representative of the Grange later summarized this position: "The use of electricity has come to the point where it is a social necessity . . . We are interested in having this power given to the people of the state at the cheapest possible rate."[56]

A contrary view was held by utility companies, the Portland Chamber of Commerce, and industrial interests. While favoring the federal development of the Columbia River Valley, these groups maintained that Bonneville and Grand Coulee Dams should not be jointly administered by one federal agency but separately administered by the U.S. Corps of Army Engineers and the Bureau of Reclamation. Portland businessmen believed that power generated at Bonneville could be distributed at a lower rate if the dams were not combined under an authority-type organization. Although they argued that the power produced at the dams should serve both private and public use, it became clear that inexpensive

[54] William E. Leuchtenburg, *Franklin D. Roosevelt and the New Deal* (New York, 1963), p. 11.

[55] Voeltz, "Proposals for a Columbia Valley Authority: A History of Political Controversy," pp. 195-212.

[56] G. W. Thiessen, "The Grange Program for Bonneville Power Distribution," *Conference on Distribution of Bonneville Power* (University of Oregon Commonwealth Series) 2 (July 1937), pp. 39-40.

power for industrial purposes was their prime concern.[57] Walter W. R. May, speaking for the Portland Chamber of Commerce, argued: "It is vital that we remember that Bonneville was not built as a subsidy for public-ownership agitation. It will produce more power than we can now use in the state," May continued, "and the quickest way to put it to use is to attract industries to use it in large blocks."[58]

As the debate between private and public-power forces grew in intensity, it once more entered the political arena. In fact, the power issue became another, perhaps the major, reason that the Democratic Party of Oregon was unable to arrange the type of coalition that would have allowed it to assume political control of Oregon during the New Deal. If Oregon Democrats had made common cause with the Grange and the State Federation of Labor on this issue, they undoubtedly could have reconstituted the party and assumed a dominant position in state politics. Instead, the party split over the issue, much as it had in 1930, and remained permanently divided during the thirties. The gubernatorial election of 1934 demonstrated the continuing significance of the power issue and the debilitating influence it had on Democratic unity. Democrats captured the governorship, but it was only because the proponents of public power dissipated their strength by quarreling among themselves.

The gubernatorial primaries of 1934 revealed deep divisions in both parties over the power issue. When Governor Meier announced that he would not seek reelection, five candidates entered the Republican primary for governor. Only three of them were considered serious contenders: State Senators Sam H. Brown and Joe E. Dunne and State Treasurer Rufus Holman. Brown and Holman, both prominent in the Joseph-Meier campaign of 1930, sought nomination on the basis of a public-power platform. In addition, both announced support of an initiative sponsored by the Grange which would empower the state to build transmission lines from Bonneville to distribute power at cost to domestic consumers. By contrast, Dunne was cautious on the power issue. He declared his support for "cheap power," but he was careful not to explain for whom.[59] This ambiguous position, coupled with his

[57] Voeltz, "Genesis and Development of a Regional Power Agency in the Pacific Northwest, 1933-43," pp. 65-67.

[58] Walter W. R. May, "Industrial Uses of Bonneville Power," *Conference on Distribution of Bonneville Power* (University of Oregon Commonwealth Series) 2 (July 1937), p. 35.

[59] Brown asserted that the power produced at Bonneville should go "to the common people," while Holman advocated "cheap hydroelectric power for the benefit of the people, rather than permit its exploitation by power trusts." *Official Republican Voter's Pamphlet—Primary Election May 18, 1934* (Salem: Secretary of State, 1934) no. 1, pp. 29-34.

refusal to endorse the initiative for state construction of transmission lines and his opposition to the Grange power bill in 1930, seemed to class Dunne as a representative of the Portland Chamber of Commerce and utility companies.[60]

With Brown and Holman in the race, the public-power wing of the Republican Party faced an unhappy situation. Three months before the primary Morton Tompkins, a leader of the Oregon Grange, warned that either Brown or Holman must withdraw from the primary or run the risk of dividing the public-power vote, thus giving the nomination to Dunne. "Some one must yield," said Tompkins, "or we are going to be defeated."[61] When Brown and Holman persisted in their candidacies, Tompkin's prediction came true. Dunne received the nomination with but 30 per cent of the primary vote; Brown and Holman each received approximately 20 per cent.[62]

In the Democratic gubernatorial primary, Representative Charles H. Martin, who was induced by Oswald West to enter the race, ran on a platform that promised equal distribution of Bonneville power to both industry and domestic consumers.[63] It was immediately obvious that Martin sided with the Portland Chamber of Commerce and industrial interests on the primary use of Bonneville power. In the fall of 1933, Martin had told the Portland Realty Board that the "power which the government will develop at Bonneville dam is not intended to force down the rates of existing power companies. This power is intended for the great chemical and metallurgical reduction plants whose first consideration is cheap power and an inexhaustible supply."[64] After announcing his candidacy, Martin reiterated this view. The suspicion that Martin was no friend of public power was confirmed by West's role as an instigator of Martin's candidacy. The *Oregon Statesman* reasoned that Martin was a puppet of West, who in turn was "the political representative of utility interests."[65] Another newspaper maintained that the utility companies commissioned West to draft Mar-

---

[60] Sam H. Brown to A. M. Esson, Feb. 8, 1934; Morton Tompkins to W. E. Burke, Feb. 26, 1934, Brown Papers.

[61] Morton Tompkins to Sam H. Brown, Feb. 26, 1934, Brown Papers.

[62] The vote was Dunne 42,563; Brown 29,913; Holman 27,804. Two other candidates, both of whom advocated public power, received a total of 35,678 votes.

[63] "I was the one," wrote Oswald West, "who induced General Martin to enter the race for Governor." West Scrapbook, West Papers. On West's role as an instigator of Martin's candidacy see Portland *Oregonian*, Jan. 14, 1934, pp. 1, 6; Salem *Oregon Statesman*, Feb. 9, 1934, p. 4; Salem *Capital Press*, Feb. 9, 1934, p. 1.

[64] *Oregon Journal*, Oct. 15, 1933, p. 8.

[65] Salem *Oregon Statesman*, Feb. 9, 1934, p. 4.

tin for the governorship because Martin was short on progressive principles and had said that "Bonneville should not be allowed to infringe upon the marauding privileges of privately owned utilities."[66]

Martin's position on the distribution of Bonneville power was unacceptable to the public power bloc within the Democratic Party, but no one of consequence in this group was willing to enter the primary. Walter Pierce, leader of the public power faction, was seeking reelection to Congress in the Second Congressional District and declined to challenge Martin. Finally, Willis Mahoney, mayor of Klamath Falls, entered the primary contest. There was no question about Mahoney's stand on power. Shortly after the election of Roosevelt in 1932, Mahoney said: "The [Democratic] party and the party candidates cannot be put down as doormats for the power trusts. The Democratic Party in Oregon and its leaders must be right on the power issue . . . or else they will be in for some unpleasant surprises."[67] When he entered the race for governor, Mahoney stated his opposition to the "Portland Chamber of Commerce ideas" on power and in a reference to West asked Democrats to "repudiate the self-appointed leaders who've run things for the last quarter of a century."[68] Mahoney's platform was identical with the positions of Brown and Holman on public power, but in addition advocated several social and economic reforms: federal old age pensions, a 50 per cent tax on incomes and inheritances in excess of $50,000, increased benefits under the Workman's Compensation Law, and "redistribution of wealth."[69]

Mahoney's bid for the nomination was seriously hampered by his reputation within the Democratic Party. Though his position on power corresponded with the views of Walter Pierce, Bert E. Haney, George R. Wilbur, and other Democrats active in the public-power movement, many in this group considered Mahoney an opportunist and dangerous demagogue. In part, this view prevailed because of Mahoney's attempt to win the support of the Townsendites and those who were enamored of Senator Huey P. Long's "Share-Our-Wealth" program. Sam Brown reported that Walter Pierce and other prominent Democrats in eastern Oregon helped him in his primary campaign rather than support

[66] Salem *Capital Press*, Feb. 9, 1934, p. 1.

[67] *Oregon Democrat* 1 (June 6, 1933), p. 5.

[68] Portland *Oregonian*, Mar. 9, 1934, p. 1. "I am unalterably opposed to letting Bonneville power be turned over to the utility gangsters," said Mahoney, "who have had their hands in the pocket-books of our people for a generation." *Oregon Democrat* 2 (Mar. 21, 1934), p. 4.

[69] *Official Democratic Voter's Pamphlet—Primary Election May 18, 1934* (Salem: Secretary of State, 1934) no. 25, p. 29.

Martin or Mahoney.[70] On the other hand, Bert E. Haney and George R. Wilbur reluctantly joined Martin's campaign because they saw Mahoney as a "crafty, plausable [sic] demagogue."[71]

Division within the public-power faction of the Democratic Party materially aided Martin. Subsequently, he won the nomination for governor with 58 per cent of the vote. Martin's nomination was one thing; to win the election in November was another. Already there were rumors of a third-party movement like that of 1930 and, in addition, some strategy had to be devised to keep those Democrats who voted for Mahoney within the party.

On the day following the primary, Bert Haney advised Martin that he must win "the more progressive and radical vote" in order to defeat Dunne and neutralize any third-party candidate. To accomplish this feat Haney recommended that Martin alter his position on the power question. "Your campaign in the primary election was injured by support from those notoriously known by reason of their utility connections, and their past record as lobbyists," explained Haney. The same advice was offered by Donald J. Sterling, managing editor of the *Oregon Journal.*[72]

Whatever Martin might do to change his image, it seemed unlikely that those who voted for Mahoney would back his candidacy. Similarly, those who voted for Brown or Holman in the Republican primary were adamantly opposed to Dunne. As the contest for governor got under way, it became evident that neither Martin's nor Dunne's campaign promises could satisfy the advocates of public power. To attract the votes of all these dissidents, Republican State Senator Peter Zimmerman announced as an independent candidate for governor on a public-power platform.

In his social, economic, and political outlook, Zimmerman was as much a Socialist as anything else. He first entered politics in 1922 after winning election to the state senate from Yamhill County. At that time, C. C. Chapman, editor of the *Oregon Voter*, described him as the personification of the "dirt farmer of Oregon." Comparing Zimmerman to "Pitchfork" Ben Tillman, Chapman stated that Zimmerman was "thoroughly and sincerely steeped in the prejudices and arguments used most frequently by those who claim to see a tendency on the part of the government and big business to . . . enslave the mass of producers."[73] As an active member of the Nonpartisan League, a partisan of La Follette in the presiden-

---

[70] Brown to A. M. Esson, Mar. 19, 1934; Brown to Mrs. Sam Brown, May 11, 1934, Brown Papers.

[71] Bert E. Haney to Charles H. Martin, May 19, 1934, Martin Papers.

[72] Haney to Martin, May 19, 1934; Donald J. Sterling to Martin, June 5, 1934, Martin Papers.

[73] *Oregon Voter* 31 (Dec. 30, 1922), pp. 57-58; 45 (Apr. 17, 1926), pp. 28-30.

tial election of 1924, and enthusiastic follower of George Joseph in
1930, he clearly deserved the adjective progressive.[74]

In his campaign, Zimmerman not only advocated Bonneville
power for the people and enactment of the initiative for state construction and ownership of power lines, but broadened his appeal
by calling for such reforms as old-age pensions and increased income and inheritance taxes. A statement in the *Voter's Pamphlet*
proclaimed that Zimmerman believed "humanity is above money
. . . labor is above capital."[75]

Zimmerman's obvious popularity among farmers sent shock
waves through the Democratic and Republican parties. In an attempt to stem defections to Zimmerman, as well as secure the votes
of liberals, Martin urged old-age pensions, unemployment insurance, and tax reductions. Moreover, Martin explained that the
federal government would build transmission lines from Bonneville
to supply domestic consumers with inexpensive power and therefore the Grange initiative for state construction of transmission
lines was not only unnecessary but an unwarranted expenditure of
state funds when other problems demanded a heavy economic
outlay. Dunne, probably realizing that the liberal vote was lost,
made no concessions to the public power bloc. His platform, as
published in the *Voter's Pamphlet*, stressed his loyalty to the
Constitution, his opposition to Communism, and the fact that he
was "Father of the $5 Auto License."[76]

By the last month of the campaign, Zimmerman had won the
active support of Sam Brown. In two radio addresses, Brown delivered scathing denunciations of Dunne. Among other things,
Brown charged that Dunne was an enemy of the "common people"
on the power question and a disreputable politician who had
"gained his political education as a democrat in the alleys of Chicago."[77] Zimmerman also had the support of the Grange and the
official endorsement of the State Federation of Labor.[78] But the
support of Willis Mahoney did not materialize.

---

[74] *Ibid.;* Hanzen, "The Joseph-Meier Political Revolution," chap. 30. After
Zimmerman entered the gubernatorial race, Chapman described him as "the
Socialist who registers as a Republican and runs as an Independent." *Oregon
Voter* 79 (Oct. 27, 1934), p. 6. Richard Neuberger, a liberal Democrat who
joined Zimmerman's campaign staff, remarked: "Zimmerman is the most
extreme left-winger ever to be within hearkening of a Pacific Northwest
gubernatorial chair." Richard L. Neuberger, "The Northwest Goes Leftish,"
New Republic 80 (Nov. 7, 1934), p. 357.

[75] *Official Voter's Pamphlet for the Regular General Election, November
6, 1934* (Salem: Secretary of State, 1934) no. 8, pp. 34-35.

[76] *Ibid.,* pp. 30-33.

[77] "Stand By Your State," Oct. 11, 1934; "State or Party?", Nov. 1, 1934,
manuscript copies of radio address by Sam H. Brown, Brown Papers.

[78] Peter Zimmerman to Sam Brown, July 24, 1934, Brown Papers. Also see

In September, Mahoney's partisans created the Oregon Democratic League, an organization dedicated to reorienting the Democratic Party along liberal lines. Mahoney announced that he would withhold the support of his followers from all gubernatorial candidates unless one candidate agreed to endorse certain social and economic reforms. Chief among Mahoney's demands, in addition to the Grange power program, was the adoption of Upton Sinclair's E.P.I.C. program (End Poverty in California).[79] When none of the candidates acceded to Mahoney's wishes, he refused to declare for any.[80]

Although Martin did not have the support of Mahoney, or the full backing of the Democratic Party, the nature of the campaign overcame these disadvantages. The Dunne and Zimmerman forces expended their energies combating one another. Brown's denunciation of Dunne probably convinced some conservatives that Martin was the more respectable candidate.[81] Also, unlike 1930 when prominent Democrats defected to Meier, no major Democratic leader endorsed Zimmerman. Elton Watkins, for instance, acted as Mahoney's campaign manager in the primary but later joined Martin's campaign.[82]

Furthermore, Martin experienced a sudden conversion to the New Deal in the closing weeks of the campaign, and sought the public power vote by appealing to anti-utility prejudices. The *Oregon Democrat* said that President Roosevelt, not Oswald West, persuaded Martin to run for governor. "General, I don't like to spare you from Congress," Roosevelt allegedly told Martin, "but I wish you'd go back to Oregon and be governor. When the Columbia River is harnessed I must have the cooperation

---

Zimmerman campaign paper *Human Rights* 1 (Nov. 1934), Neuberger Papers. Zimmerman's campaign staff included the entire executive committee of the Grange.

[79] Portland *Oregonian*, Sept. 25, 1934, pp. 1, 4; Sept. 26, 1934, pp. 1, 2; *Oregon Journal*, Sept. 25, 1934, pp. 1, 5. *Oregon Democrat* 2 (Sept. 21, 1934), p. 5.

[80] After the election Mahoney wrote: "It is true I did not support Governor Martin in the General Election, and I also realize that when I refused to endorse Senator Zimmerman it was a great disappointment to many loyal friends . . . My reason for not supporting Senator Zimmerman was because I would not be a party to turning the affairs of this State over to Ray Gill, Morton Tompkins, and their clique." Willis Mahoney to Mrs. Grace M. Charlton, June 7, 1935, Martin Papers.

[81] Democrats on Martin's campaign staff were delighted with Brown's attack on Dunne. Referring to the radio addresses, Carl Donaugh wrote Brown: "not only do I consider them a contribution to good government, but also the two most effective political addresses made during the present campaign." Carl C. Donaugh to Brown, Nov. 2, 1934, Brown Papers.

[82] Portland *Oregonian*, Sept. 25, 1934, p. 1.

of that state to save the resulting benefits from the light and power companies that are lying in wait for them."[83]

By this combination of circumstances and events, and after one of the most chaotic gubernatorial contests in Oregon history, Martin emerged the victor with a plurality of 21,000 votes, 39 per cent of the total vote cast for governor. Zimmerman ran a close second with 32 per cent of the vote, and Dunne finished last with 29 per cent. The Grange initiative for state construction of power lines was defeated.[84]

Martin's election as governor proved to be a disaster for Democratic Party unity. Despite the fact that he had campaigned as a champion of the New Deal, and continued to insist that he supported the national Democratic administration, his actions belied his words. Those Democrats who voted for Martin on the supposition that he would cooperate with President Roosevelt and perhaps inaugurate a "little New Deal" in Oregon soon became the Governor's strongest critics and most vocal opponents. "Whenever I recall that I voted for him," said one disillusioned Democrat, "I am so humiliated that I feel like migrating to South America to live among the Indians of the upper Amazon for the balance of my natural life."[85]

The problems that Martin faced as Governor would have taxed the most skillful politician. Under pressure, however, he exhibited an unfortunate lack of political acumen and a basic conservatism that alienated liberal Democrats and put him at odds with the Roosevelt administration. The Governor eventually opposed several New Deal programs,[86] but it was his conservative stance on public power that remained the single most contentious issue in the Democratic Party. Construction of Bonneville Dam was not completed until 1937, and in the interim Martin demonstrated his militant opposition to the proposal for a CVA and the position of the

[83] *Oregon Democrat* 2 (Oct. 6, 1934), p. 13.

[84] The vote was Martin 116,677; Zimmerman 95,519; Dunne 86,923. Martin later said of his victory: "Enough good Republicans came to my support to secure my election over a weak Republican candidate." Martin to Charles G. Dawes, June 21, 1935, Martin Papers.

[85] Wilbur F. Brock to Walter Pierce, June 3, 1937, Pierce Papers.

[86] Among other things, Martin remarked, "the New Deal's social security program is driving this country into national socialism." Concerning federal relief, which he opposed, Martin declared himself a "Hoover Democrat" and asserted: "democratic nations have lost their moral force through pampering their people." Salem *Capital Journal*, Oct. 14, 1938, p. 1. One of Martin's political advisers commented: "There is no doubt in my mind that one of the weak spots in [Democratic Party unity] is that a substantial number of what may be called regular Democrats question the fealty of Governor Martin to the Democratic cause, and more particularly to the aims of President Roosevelt." Thomas W. Delzell to Edgar W. Smith, Mar. 30, 1938, Martin Papers.

Grange and the State Federation of Labor on the primary use of power produced at Bonneville. Martin's Democratic critics pointed out that the Governor was diametrically opposed to Roosevelt, who expressed support for CVA and the distribution of inexpensive power from Bonneville to domestic consumers.[87] "Politics are certainly funny," wrote a member of the Oregon Public Utility Commission. "Here I am supporting Roosevelt's power program and am opposed by a man [Martin] who was elected on a program to support the President and then [I was] ordered . . . to fight the President on Bonneville."[88]

Within the Democratic Party, Congressman Walter Pierce, an apostle of CVA and paladin of the public power movement, became the leading antagonist of Martin in the power feud. W. E. Burke, Byron F. Carney, Dr. J. F. Hosch, William Strayer, Henry Hess, G. W. Thiessen, Mark V. Weatherford, Nan Wood Honeyman, and Willis Mahoney, among others, sided with Pierce. These Democrats did not hold formal positions of power within the party's hierarchy, but many of them won election to the state legislature in 1934 and re-election in 1936. Their unrelenting opposition to Martin, specifically on the power issue, gave rise to internecine warfare between the Democratic majority in the lower house of the legislature and the Democratic Governor. "My most virile enemies in the legislature are Democrats and most ardent supporters are Republicans," complained Martin. "I have been bedeviled from morning to night by a lot of small, mean, contemptible people."[89]

While liberal Democrats continued in their denunciations of Martin, conservatives who sided with the Governor held the reins of power in the party. Martin's contingent included Mayor Joseph K. Carson, Jr., of Portland, Howard Latourette (elected National Committeeman in 1936), Frank Tierney (elected chairman of the State Central Committee in 1936), Oswald West, Carl C. Donaugh, and Vernon Williams (editor of the *Oregon Democrat*).

By 1937, the bitter quarrel between conservative and liberal

---

[87] In a letter to Walter Pierce one Democrat said: "I do hope that if you ever have the opportunity to tell President Roosevelt that our present Governor rode into office on Roosevelt's policies and then has been untrue to that trust you will do so." Another wrote: "All know now, what many did not appreciate before, that Walter is for the people, while Charles is for the utilities." See Dr. J. F. Hosch to Pierce, Apr. 12, 1935; Andrew C. Smith to Cornelia M. Pierce, May 10, 1937, Pierce Papers. Also see W. E. Burke to Pierce, Apr. 1935; Steve Kahn to Pierce, June 8, 1936; Harvey G. Starkweather to Pierce, Apr. 12, 1937; Richard Neuberger to Pierce, May 14, 1937; Mark V. Weatherford to Pierce, May 23, 1938, *ibid.*

[88] Charles M. Thomas to Pierce, June 11, 1935, *ibid.*

[89] Charles H. Martin to Paul R. Kelty, Nov. 21, 1935, Martin Papers.

Democrats had resulted in a deadlock. Because neither the Democratic nor the Republican party officially acted as a spokesman for public power or other New Deal programs, liberals in Oregon joined to create the Oregon Commonwealth Federation. The Federation, which declared itself a "nonpartisan league of progressives," included Democrats, Republicans, and Socialists. Among the founders and sponsors of the OCF were Peter Zimmerman, Ben T. Osborne, executive secretary of the State Federation of Labor, Daniel D. Whedon, a representative of AFL unions in Portland, Monroe Sweetland, a young Socialist, and several prominent leaders of the Grange. While the OCF advocated many liberal programs, its major emphasis was on public power. This issue not only served as the catalyst to draw liberals together but also remained a *cause celebre* of the OCF until its end in 1942.[90] When the Federation, at its first convention in April 1937, devised a program of political action, the first item in its platform read: "Public ownership of all natural resources, utilities, banks, and monopolies. Bonneville power made available to the people of Oregon by publicly constructed transmission lines, and by a blanket rate to public distributing agencies; endorsement and support of the creation of people's utility districts."[91]

While public power was the major long-range concern of the OCF, its immediate principal adversary was Governor Martin.[92] Almost immediately, the OCF joined with liberal Democrats, many of whom joined the Federation, in preparing plans to defeat Martin in the Democratic gubernatorial primary of 1938. At its first convention, the OCF passed a resolution denouncing the "tyranny of the Martin regime" and further put its charges to music. To the tune of "Fare Thee Well," the convention sang:

> There is a general in the town, in the town
> Oh how he's let the people down, let us down
> And we'll vote, vote, vote until we've won the day
> And brought the New Deal here to stay![93]

---

[90] Herzig, "The Oregon Commonwealth Federation," pp. 8-12; Interview with Monroe Sweetland, Dec. 21, 1967.

[91] "Program of the Oregon Commonwealth Federation," Apr., 1937, Oregon Commonwealth Federation Papers. An organizer and leader of the OCF put public power as the major objective of the organization. "We don't want the big boys to grease their snouts in the trough until the common people have had first chance at the cheapest power in the world." Stephenson Smith to Lillian Herstein, June 1, 1937, *ibid.*

[92] Martin believe the OCF to be a "subsidiary to the Communist Party of the Soviet Union." He ordered Charles Pray, chief of the state police, to compile weekly reports on OCF activities. They were labeled "Weekly Reports of Communist Activities." See Martin to Charles Pray, Aug. 10, 1937; "Weekly Reports of Communist Activities," Martin Papers.

[93] "Oregon Commonwealth Federation Song Sheet, 1937," Oregon Commonwealth Federation Papers.

As the primary of 1938 approached, Governor Martin clearly faced an uphill battle. In addition to opposition from the OCF and the Grange, the Governor encountered the enmity of labor. During the first years of his governorship, Martin excoriated labor leaders who, seeking to win union recognition under Section 7A of the National Recovery Act (1933), plunged Oregon into labor-management disputes by encouraging strikes against employers who refused to comply with the provisions of that legislation. The Governor referred to union organizers as "pestiferous peewees" and allegedly advised law enforcement officers in the state to "beat hell out of 'em."[94]

Formidable opposition to Martin was also found in the ranks of the Democratic Party, not only among liberal Democrats who had been feuding with the Governor since his election, but from former supporters. On the liberal side, Oregon's two Democratic congressional representatives, Walter Pierce and Nan Wood Honeyman, made it clear that they would not support Martin if he sought reelection. "I think the old fello [sic] should be reprimanded by the people of Oregon," declared Pierce. "We must show up the old Governor."[95] Joining with liberals in denouncing Martin was Vernon Williams, influential editor of the *Oregon Democrat*. Williams had earlier defended Martin in his battle with liberals but in January 1938, he reversed his position and read the Governor out of the party in a searing editorial entitled: "CHARLES H. MARTIN HAS PROVED TRAITOR TO THOSE BY WHOSE VOTES HE WAS ELECTED." Asserted Williams: "By word and deed Charles H. Martin has demonstrated that at heart he is not a Democrat, that he never was a Democrat, and that his endorsement of Democratic principles was pretense and sham." The editor went on to castigate Martin for "egotistic intolerance," "stubborn conceit," "inordinate vanity," and "excessive use of profanity."[96]

Undeterred by his critics and encouraged by promises of support from many conservative Republicans,[97] Martin announced for a second term as governor. In contrast with his earlier campaigns for Congress, or for the governorship in 1934, Martin ran on a decidedly conservative platform in 1938. The Governor stressed

---

[94] Martin to Walter E. Pearson, May 16, 1935, Martin Papers; Neuberger, *Our Promised Land*, p. 315.

[95] Pierce to Tom Quigley, May 26, 1937, Pierce Papers.

[96] *Oregon Democrat* 5 (Jan. 6, 1938), p. 3.

[97] For typical letters of support received by Martin from conservative Republicans see W. H. Buoy to Martin, June 13, 1935; R. M. Tuttle to Martin, June 21, 1935; C. C. Crow to Martin, Aug. 16, 1936; F. S. Senn to Martin, Feb. 1, 1938; Will B. Levy to Martin, Feb. 5, 1938; Paul E. Spangler to Martin, Jan. 28, 1938; Lawrence T. Harris to Martin, Jan. 31, 1938; K. R. Crookham to Martin, Mar. 26, 1938; M. L. Johnson to Martin, Apr. 1, 1938, Martin Papers.

law and order, "preservation of the American form of government," and "sound economic development." No mention was made of Bonneville or the power question.[98] Oswald West and Edgar W. Smith, Martin's campaign strategists, devised a plan to ensure the Governor's nomination with the help of conservative Republican votes. Through "Martin-for-Governor" clubs, West attempted to persuade Republicans who favored the Governor to register as Democrats and vote for Martin in the primary.[99]

Martin's opponent in the primary, State Senator Henry Hess, had the support of liberal Democrats, the OCF, the Grange, and labor. Unlike the Governor, Hess expressed his admiration of the New Deal, depicting himself as a "Progressive, Roosevelt Democrat." Hess's platform endorsed public power, regulation of private light and power companies, the appropriation of federal and state funds for the unemployed, and recognition of the rights of labor.[100]

From the beginning of the campaign, Martin seemed determined to further antagonize his already aroused opponents. In February 1938, when Republican Senator Frederick Steiwer resigned from office, Martin appointed Democrat Alfred E. Reames to fill the vacancy. The selection of Reames, an attorney and lobbyist for various Oregon utility companies, was vigorously contested by the proponents of public power, and considered conclusive proof that Martin was a lackey of the utilities.[101] The Governor also exercised his talent for brusque political epithets by referring to the OCF, which met in convention during the primary, as "a convention of 250 nuts."[102]

Perhaps inevitably, the contest between Martin and Hess became more than a local struggle between Democrats. Martin had been at sword's point with the Roosevelt administration since 1935, first in disputing the authority of Secretary of Labor Frances Perkins to dispatch arbitrators to the state to settle labor difficulties and later by opposing the views of Secretary of the Interior Harold Ickes on the disposition of Bonneville power.[103] In 1937, the Salem

98 *Official Voter's Pamphlet—Democratic Party Primary Election, May 20, 1938* (Salem: Secretary of State, 1938) no. 29, p. 9.

99 West to Martin, Jan. 10, 1938; Martin to West, Jan. 11, 1938; Martin to West, Feb. 4, 1938; W. L. Gosslin to West, Feb. 4, 1938; West to Gosslin, Feb. 11, 1938; West to Gosslin, Feb. 17, 1938, Martin Papers.

100 *Official Voter's Pamphlet—Democratic Party Primary Election, May 20, 1938* (Salem: Secretary of State, 1938) no. 29, p. 8.

101 Sam Brown to Martin, Jan. 7, 1938; Walter Pierce to Martin, Jan. 8, 1938; Elton Watkins to Martin, Jan. 28, 1938, Martin Papers.

102 Portland *Oregonian*, May 13, 1938, p. 3.

103 Martin and Joseph K. Carson, Jr., to Frances Perkins, Nov. 2, 1936; Martin and Carson to Perkins, Nov. 13, 1936, Martin Papers. Bernard F. Donahoe, *Private Plans and Public Dangers: The Story of FDR's Third Nomination* (Notre Dame, 1965), pp. 69-70; Neuberger, *Our Promised Land*, p. 318.

Capital Press reported that Martin was "openly denouncing the president." "As a pseudo democrat at war with the democrat president . . . his position is quite ridiculous," concluded the newspaper.[104] Therefore, it was not altogether unexpected when, two weeks before the election, Senator George Norris and Secretary Ickes sent letters of endorsement to Hess. "Martin is at heart no New Dealer," wrote Ickes.[105] The letters were given wide publicity and interpreted as a repudiation of Martin by the Roosevelt administration.

The combined strength of the Governor's opponents in Oregon, coupled with the endorsement of Norris and Ickes, proved decisive in the election. Hess emerged the victor with a plurality of 7,000 votes but in the process so divided the party that his prospect for success in the general election was diminished.[106] In a letter to James Farley after the primary, one of Martin's political lieutenants wrote: "The party is badly split. It is doubtful if Hess can be elected, and the adverse tide on that election may sweep other Democratic candidates out of the picture."[107]

This evaluation was later confirmed. Hess lost the gubernatorial election to Republican Charles Sprague, editor of the Salem *Oregon Statesman*. Sprague, generally regarded as a progressive, endorsed the administration's public power program and proved far more friendly to Roosevelt than had Martin. At the same time, Democrats lost control of the lower house of the state legislature, and Nan Wood Honeyman was defeated in her bid for reelection in the Third Congressional District. Martin and several of his followers campaigned for the Republican candidates against Hess and Honeyman.[108]

---

[104] Salem *Capital Press*, Dec. 31, 1937, p. 4.

[105] Harold Ickes to Henry Hess, May 14, 1938, Oregon Commonwealth Federation Papers. Upon hearing rumors that the Roosevelt administration was about to endorse Hess, Oswald West wrote James Farley: "Is it true a high administration official is about to give Martin a resounding oratorical spanking. Please, is there any truth in this?" Telegram, West to Farley, May 10, 1938, Martin Papers.

[106] Martin received 3,780 write-in votes in the Republican gubernatorial primary. During the primary campaign, the chairman of the Democratic State Central Committee reported that there was more open support for Martin among Republicans than Democrats and that Republicans were openly wearing Martin campaign pins. Frank Tierney to Thomas W. Delzell, Mar. 22, 1938, Martin Papers.

[107] Thomas W. Delzell to James A. Farley, May 25, 1938, Martin Papers.

[108] After the election, the chairman of the Multnomah County Republican Central Committee wrote Martin, thanking him for his help in the campaign. "I want to express to you my very great appreciation for your support given to the Republican cause in the recent campaign in which we were engaged with the Oregon New Deal contingent of the Democratic Party." Fred W. Brown to Martin, Nov. 14, 1938, Martin Papers.

Following the reversals of 1938, the Democratic Party declined rapidly as a political force in Oregon politics. Members of the OCF, especially Monroe Sweetland who was the driving force behind the organization from its initial formation to its decline, sought to revitalize the Democratic Party along New Deal lines but met the determined opposition of conservative Democrats. Oswald West commenced a campaign of invective against the Federation, alternately referring to members of that organization as "punks," "bums," "drunken libertines," and "communists." West warned that the Federation had plans to "Russianize" the Democratic Party and advocated that OCF members be "given a bath sweetened with sheep dip." Declared West: "If I have hurt anybody's feelings, I am glad."[109]

Despite attacks of this nature, Sweetland and others continued in their efforts to rehabilitate the party. They endorsed liberal Democrats for state and federal office, contributed to their campaigns, and attempted to seize control of positions in the party hierarchy. The Roosevelt administration, recognizing these endeavors, awarded OCF members with patronage over the objections of Howard Latourette, Democratic National Committeeman, and Frank Tierney, chairman of the Democratic State Central Committee. Liberal Democrat Byron G. Carney, first vice-president of the OCF, was named as the state director for the census of 1940, and Sweetland was regularly consulted by the administration on patronage appointments.[110]

The battle between conservative Democrats and the OCF assured the restoration of Republican rule in Oregon. Although Roosevelt carried the state in the presidential elections of 1940 and 1944,[111] Republicans substantially increased their strength during these years. In the gubernatorial election of 1942, the Democratic candidate received only 22 per cent of the vote. Meanwhile, the defeat of Walter Pierce in 1942 removed the last Democrat from federal office.

109 Portland *Oregonian*, June 16, 1939, p. 16; Salem *Capital Journal*, June 16, 1939, p. 9; June 17, 1939, p. 4; Feb. 26, 1940, p. 4; Eugene *Register-Guard*, Feb. 27, 1940, p. 4.

110 Interview with Monroe Sweetland, Dec. 21, 1967.

111 In 1940, Martin and other conservative Democrats campaigned for Wendell Willkie. Martin also assisted Republican Homer Angell in his campaign against Nan Wood Honeyman. "I cast another vote with the Republicans in November," Martin confided to a friend. "We took care of Nan Wood Honeyman, the coattail hanger, who helped slaughter me in the Democratic primary two years ago. Her treachery and that of the Administration . . . will not soon be forgotten." Martin to Richard B. Wigglesworth, Dec. 30, 1940; Martin to Homer Angell, Nov. 7, 1940; Martin to Angell, Nov. 10, 1940, Martin Papers.

During the 1930s, Oregon Democrats had lost their greatest opportunity to win political control of the state. Nevertheless, the decade brought some important and encouraging changes in Oregon. Democratic registration, which had never exceeded 30 per cent before the depression, rose to a high of 48 per cent. Even though those who registered as Democrats did not consistently vote the Democratic ticket, their numerical strength was not diminished by Republican victories during the 1940s. In addition, the depression spawned a new generation of liberal Democrats who were ready and willing—and perhaps able—to lead the party in new directions. Potentially, therefore, two important ingredients for rebuilding the Democratic Party were at hand: numbers and leadership. But rejuvenation of the party with vigorous, effective leadership and mobilization of the Democratic electorate was delayed until after the Second World War.

V   THE DEMOCRATIC PARTY IN TRANSITION

Several months before the end of the Second World War, a series of meetings took place in the Southwest Pacific that would prove significant for Oregon politics. At Kwajalein, and later in Honolulu, Monroe Sweetland, a Red Cross field secretary, and Howard Morgan, a young naval lieutenant, discussed plans for rebuilding the Democratic Party in Oregon after the war. Sweetland later recalled that his talks with Morgan centered on strategy, especially the need for forceful, liberal leadership of the Democratic Party. Although both agreed that much work lay ahead, Sweetland and Morgan looked forward eagerly to the challenge, hopeful that they and others would infuse the Democratic Party with new life.[1]

While Sweetland and Morgan laid plans for reordering Oregon politics, certain events were working in their favor. The Great Depression had already brought a new political balance to Oregon. Though the Democratic Party had not made permanent gains on the state level, many Oregonians had revised their political preferences while passing through the depression. By 1938, Democrats claimed 48 per cent of the registered voters in the state.

In addition to the impact of the depression, developments of another nature altered the political picture in Oregon during the 1940s. In his analysis of the complicated and diverse factors that produce realignments of partisan forces in state politics, V. O. Key, Jr., has suggested that minority parties frequently gain ascendancy "not by the excellence of their candidates or the intensity of their campaign exertions, but by the slow culmination of the effects of economic and demographic changes."[2] Key's observation is espe-

---

[1] Interview with Monroe Sweetland, Dec. 21, 1967. Morgan, a student at Reed College in Portland during the late thirties and early forties, was not an active participant in Democratic politics during the depression, but did support President Roosevelt and the programs of the New Deal. Interview with Howard Morgan, Apr. 13, 1968.

[2] Key, *Politics, Parties, and Pressure Groups*, p. 287. See also Donald E. Stokes and Gudmund R. Iversen, "On the Existence of Forces Restoring Party

cially appropriate as an explanation for one of the factors that produced political change in Oregon.

From the time Oregon was admitted to the Union in 1859 until the Second World War, farm produce led the state's economy. Beginning in the late 1930s, however, the economic structure of the state began to change. Farm products yielded first place to lumber and wood products, and by 1940 Oregon surpassed all other states in timber production. But the Second World War brought the greatest diversification to the economy. In fact, one historian of the Pacific Northwest has argued that the war years marked the turning point in the region's economic growth, while another has asserted that the war "brought probably the most drastic changes in the Far West since 1849."[3]

Government contracts for shipbuilding at Portland, the establishment of aluminum reduction plants and electroprocess industries, food processing, and other industries, all designed to meet the production demands of the war, collectively broadened the economy. After 1945, several of the new federally controlled industries that had emerged during the war were sold to private industry. The total number of workers employed in manufacturing industries in Oregon increased 85 per cent between 1939 and 1949, and manufacturing output tripled between 1939 and 1954.[4]

The economic growth in Oregon during and after the war, though important, did not remake the state into a replica of industrial areas in other parts of the nation. Oregon remained heavily dependent upon products from its farms and forests; in spite of increased industrialization the state was basically "a place of small shops and branch plants."[5] The lumber industry, which experienced a boom following the war because of the nationwide demand for building materials, employed 63 per cent of those classified as industrial workers in the mid-fifties.[6] Still, economic diversification stemming from the war provided new sources of employment and encouraged migration to the state.

During the decade of the depression, the population of the state increased 14 per cent, from 953,786 in 1930 to 1,089,648 in 1940.

Competition," *Elections and the Political Order,* ed. Angus Campbell, *et al* (New York, 1966), pp. 180-193.

[3] Johansen and Gates, *Empire of the Columbia,* p. 539; Pomeroy, *The Pacific Slope,* p. 297.

[4] Johansen and Gates, *Empire of the Columbia,* pp. 529-533, 539-541; Swarthout and Gervais, "Oregon: Political Experiment Station," *Politics in the American West,* pp. 307-308; Seligman, "Political Change: Legislative Elites and Parties in Oregon," pp. 177-178.

[5] Johansen and Gates, *Empire of the Columbia,* p. 531.

[6] Swarthout and Gervais, "Oregon: Political Experiment Station," *Politics in the American West,* pp. 312-313.

But between 1940 and 1950, Oregon grew by nearly half a million, so that at mid-century the population totaled 1,521,347, an increase of 40 per cent over 1940. Oregon's population continued to multiply after 1950, but the rate of growth appreciably declined. In 1960 the population totaled 1,757,691, an increase of 16 per cent over 1950.

Census figures indicate that before 1950 well over half of the state's population growth derived from migration. During the forties, when Oregon was almost inundated by newcomers, over 80 per cent of them came from the Western states, principally California. Undoubtedly, many of these persons reached Oregon after first moving from other parts of the nation to the West and then, in a second stage of migration, to Oregon.[7]

Those areas of the state with the largest increase in population during the 1940s were located adjacent to new or expanding industries. Opportunities for employment in the shipyards of Portland and other wartime industries located in and around the Portland metropolitan area contributed to a population growth of 33 per cent in Multnomah County. Washington and Clackamas counties, which border Multnomah on the west and the south, had increases of 56 and 52 per cent respectively. South of Portland, up the Willamette Valley, population growth was even more striking. Here smaller manufacturing firms in the middle Willamette Valley, coupled with timber and lumber-based industries in southwest Oregon, provided employment for immigrants and accounted for a large portion of the increase in population. Linn and Lane counties grew by 78.2 and 82 per cent respectively; further to the south, Douglas County jumped 112 per cent, Josephine 63 per cent, and Jackson 62 per cent.

The popularity of the national Democratic Party during the depression, added to the economic and demographic changes of the 1940s, produced important political change in Oregon. Even though the state Democratic Party failed to become the majority party during the 1930s and was moribund during the war years, the political setting in the state had been altered. That the Democratic Party benefited from these developments may be dramatized by comparing party registration, the geographical distribution of Democratic Party strength, and Democratic voting trends before and after the depression.

For the first three decades of the twentieth century, Democrats in Oregon never constituted more than 30 per cent of all registered voters. But beginning in the 1930s, and continuing throughout the

---

[7] *Historical Statistics of the United States: Colonial Times to 1957* (Washington, D.C., 1960), p. 45; *1950 U.S. Census of Population: Population Mobility —States and State Economic Areas* (Washington, D.C., 1956), pp. 32, 34.

TABLE 3

Summary Of Voting Figures For President In Oregon, 1900-1948

		1900	1904	1908	19
Votes in thousands:	Democratic	33	17	38	
	Republican	47	60	63	
	Others	4	11	10	
	Total	84	88	111	1
Democratic per cent for state:		39	19	34	
Democratic per cent by counties:	Mean	40	20	33	
	Lowest	29	7	23	
	Highest	51	28	44	
Total number Democratic counties:		5	0	0	

SOURCE: Compiled from Svend Petersen, *A Statistical History of American Presidential Elections* (New York: Frederick Ungar Publishing Company, 1963) and

TABLE 4

Summary Of Voting Figures For Governor In Oregon, 1902-1948

		1902	1906	1910	19
Votes in thousands:	Democratic	41	46	55	
	Republican	41	43	49	1
	Others	7	7	14	
	Total	89	96	118	2
Democratic per cent for state:		46	47	46	
Democratic per cent by counties:	Mean	44	46	45	
	Lowest	32	38	31	
	Highest	59	54	57	
Total number Democratic counties:		12	19	20	

SOURCE: Compiled from *Trends in Oregon Voting, 1858-1960* (Salem: Secretary of State, 1962).

916	1920	1924	1928	1932	1936	1940	1944	1948
120	80	67	109	213	266	258	248	243
127	144	142	205	136	122	219	225	261
14	14	69	5	18	24	3	6	20
251	238	278	319	367	412	480	479	524
46	34	24	34	58	65	54	52	47
45	32	25	33	59	62	53	52	46
37	30	13	23	42	47	36	34	30
57	38	35	40	68	72	65	64	58
18	0	0	0	35	36	27	19	16

hard M. Scammon, *America at the Polls: a Handbook of American Presiden-Statistics, 1920-1964* (Pittsburgh: University of Pittsburgh Press, 1965).

918	1922	1926	1930	1934	1938	1942	1946	1948
65	133	93	62	116	158	62	106	227
81	99	120	46	86	214	220	237	271
6	0	12	139	98	0	0	0	11
152	232	225	247	300	372	282	343	509
42	57	41	25	39	43	22	31	45
40	55	45	31	38	40	19	24	42
29	33	29	13	23	25	12	18	30
51	71	67	57	51	55	29	39	55
6	28	16	5	21	4	0	0	5

1940s, an important shift in party allegiance occurred. By 1936, Democrats totaled 46 per cent of all registered voters in Oregon; in 1938, 48 per cent; and in 1940, 49 per cent. During the forties, Democratic registration remained at a static 48 per cent until finally, in 1950, Democrats outnumbered Republicans for the first time in the twentieth century with 51 per cent of the state's voters. Those who declared as Democrats did not regularly vote the Democratic ticket—indeed, during the war years the party fared very poorly— but the time had passed when Republicans could count on a three-to-one margin in registration.

A shift in the geographical distribution of Democrats over the state paralleled the rise in party registration. Between 1900 and 1932, the distribution of Democrats in Oregon remained nearly constant, with over 70 per cent of the party membership clustered in four geographical areas. Multnomah County, with the largest city of the state, Portland, accounted for an average of 27 per cent of the party, the greatest single concentration in Oregon. The second largest number of Democrats, 18 per cent of the party, was centered in four counties of the lower and middle Willamette Valley: Clackamas, Marion, Linn, and Lane. In the southwest corner of the state, Coos, Douglas, Jackson, and Josephine counties contributed 14 per cent of total Democratic strength before the depression. Finally, in the northeast section of the state, Umatilla, Wallowa, Union, and Baker counties contained 13 per cent of the party's members.[8]

As a result of the depression and the heavy migration to Oregon during the war years, the earlier Democratic pattern was altered. Democratic gains were registered over most of the state. Multnomah County remained the single most important source of party strength, but increased its proportion of Democrats from 27 per cent to an average of 36 per cent between 1932 and 1950. Washington and Clackamas counties, adjacent to Multnomah County, contained a combined total of 10 per cent of the party between 1932 and 1950, an increase of 5 per cent. Contrary to this trend, the counties of northeast Oregon, with the exception of Umatilla, lost population during the 1940s. Consequently, Umatilla, Wallowa, Union, and Baker counties dropped from their previous average of 13 per cent to 6 per cent of the party between 1932 and 1950.

In the Willamette Valley, Lane County, second only to Multnomah in the number of Democrats, embraced 7 per cent of the

[8] Baker was the most consistent Democratic county in the state before the depression. In 1914 and 1924, when Democrats constituted less than one-third of all registered voters in the state, Baker County had Democratic majorities of 51 per cent. No other Oregon county had a majority of Democrats before the New Deal.

party. Marion and Linn counties, in the middle Willamette Valley, accounted for a combined total of another 7 per cent; four counties in southern Oregon, Coos, Douglas, Jackson, and Klamath, each contained 3 per cent of Democratic Party members. Democrats constituted no more than 2 per cent of the total party strength in all other counties.

The geographical configuration of the Democratic Party during and after the depression reveals a decided shift to urban areas. Thus, almost half of the party, 46 per cent, was located in Portland and its suburbs in Washington and Clackamas counties. At the same time, it is important to note that the party usually made its greatest gains in those areas where populations grew and where the economy was more diversified. The Portland metropolitan area grew over 60 per cent between 1930 and 1950, and the party substantially increased its representation in this area.[9]

While the Democratic Party dramatically improved its numerical strength during the 1930s and 1940s, voting trends do not consistently reflect this fact. The party enlarged its share of the vote in presidential elections, but the same was not always true in elections for state and federal offices.

An analysis of Oregon's role in presidential elections is presented in Table 3. The data illustrate that the state's Republican bias was dissolved by the depression. With the exception of the three-way presidential election of 1912, when Woodrow Wilson carried Oregon with 34 per cent of the vote, Republican presidential candidates easily carried the state with as much as 67 per cent of the two-party vote. The presidential contest of 1932, however, marked a reversal of this pattern. Oregonians supported Roosevelt with 95,000 more votes than Democrats had attracted in the election of 1928, an increase in the Democratic presidential vote from 34 to 58 per cent. Between 1928 and 1936, the nation increased its absolute Democratic percentage in presidential elections from 41 to 60 per cent. Oregon, in the same period, jumped from 34 to 65 per cent.[10] Though the Democratic vote in the presidential elections of 1940 and 1944 declined, Roosevelt captured the state with comfortable margins, and although Harry S. Truman lost Oregon in 1948, he won a greater percentage of the vote than any Democratic presidential candidate who lost the state in the preceeding half century.

The larger state-wide vote for the Democratic Party in presidential elections during the 1930s and 1940s was in part the result of a sudden shift in the urban vote. The vote for president in Port-

---

[9] Donald J. Bogue, *Population Growth in Standard Metropolitan Areas 1900-1950* (Washington, D.C., 1953), p. 34.

[10] Louis H. Bean, *How America Votes in Presidential Elections* (Metuchen, N.J., 1968), pp. 13, 103, 139.

land during the twenties, unlike the vote for president in major urban areas across the nation, did not reflect a trend counter to the interests of the Republican Party.[11] In 1920, Warren G. Harding won 61 per cent of the two-party vote for president in Multnomah County; in 1924, Calvin Coolidge 69 per cent; and in 1928, Herbert Hoover 63 per cent. The presidential election of 1932, however, brought an end to the huge Republican majorities in Multnomah County. Franklin D. Roosevelt carried the county with 63 per cent of the two-party vote in 1932, 72 per cent in 1936, and 57 per cent in 1940 and 1944. Even Harry S. Truman carried Multnomah County with 52 per cent of the two-party vote.[12]

The Democratic vote for governor and senator before and after the depression, when compared with the vote for president, reflects a different pattern. Democrats actually maintained a higher average of the total vote for governor and senator before the depression

[11] Samuel J. Eldersveld, "The Influence of Metropolitan Pluralities in Presidential Elections Since 1920: A Study of Twelve Key Cities," *American Political Science Review* 43 (Dec. 1949), pp. 1189-1206.

[12] Woodrow Wilson won a narrow plurality of 1,400 votes in Multnomah County in 1912. Although Dwight D. Eisenhower carried Multnomah County in 1952 and 1956, along with the rest of the state, his per cent of the two-party vote in Multnomah was lower than that of previous Republican presidential candidates who carried the county.

TABLE 5

Summary Of Voting Figures For Senator In Oregon, 1906-1948

		1906	1908	1912	1914	19
Votes in thousands:	Democratic	39	52	40	112	
	Republican	43	51	38	88	
	Others	10	9	55	46	
	Total	92	112	133	246	1
Democratic per cent for state:		43	47	30	46	
Democratic per cent by counties:	Mean	42	45	30	44	
	Lowest	30	38	21	32	
	Highest	51	52	37	56	
Total number Democratic counties:		12	13	13	24	

SOURCE: Compiled from *Trends in Oregon Voting, 1858-1960* (Salem: Secretary of State, 1962).

than during the thirties and forties. Table 4 indicates that in the seven elections for governor between 1902 and 1926, Democrats won an average of 45 per cent of the vote. Conversely, the party captured an average of only 34 per cent of the vote in the six gubernatorial elections between 1930 and 1948. The figures in senatorial elections illustrate a smaller discrepancy. Table 5 shows that in the eight senatorial elections from 1906 to 1926 Democratic candidates won an average of 39 per cent of the vote; in the seven senatorial elections between 1930 and 1948 the average was 37 per cent.

Several factors explain the difference between Democratic voting trends before and after the depression. Nonpartisanship during the progressive era, frequent three-way races for governor and senator, and short-term partisan forces such as the peculiar circumstances surrounding the so-called "Klan election" of 1922 allowed Democratic candidates, who normally subordinated the party label, to win a substantial per cent of the vote for governor and senator before the New Deal period. On the other hand, the eight presidential elections between 1900 and 1928 occurred at a time when the Democratic Party, in both Oregon and the nation, was the minority party. Like the rest of the country, Oregon voted its Republican bias in most presidential elections before the depression.

1920	1924	1926	1930	1932	1936	1938	1942	1944	1948
100	65	81	66	137	193	167	63	174	199
116	175	89	137	186	199	203	214	269	299
13	25	53	33	29	7	0	0	0	0
229	265	223	236	352	399	370	277	443	498
44	25	36	28	39	48	45	22	39	40
43	26	37	23	36	47	43	21	37	36
32	16	23	10	24	31	27	12	25	24
56	38	48	37	45	59	56	29	48	60
6	0	11	0	1	12	6	0	0	1

The Great Depression of the 1930s and the ascendancy of the Democratic Party on the national scene created serious problems for the Democratic Party in Oregon. While more and more Oregonians came to identify with the Democratic Party and its national programs during the thirties, the conservative leadership of the state Democratic Party rejected the New Deal. Consequently, while Oregonians demonstrated their support of the New Deal by voting for Franklin Roosevelt, they frequently supported independent or liberal Republican candidates in gubernatorial and senatorial elections, candidates more favorably inclined toward New Deal programs than their Democratic opponents.

During the war years, conservative Democrats presided over a torpid party. Party leaders, far to the right of the New Deal, made no effort to capitalize on the changing political scene in Oregon.[13] Union membership doubled during the 1940s, but labor found Republicans more responsive to its interests than Democrats. In Multnomah County, a center of union strength and Democratic by registration since 1938, Republican Homer D. Angell repeatedly defeated Democratic opponents for representative during the 1940s. Angell, who never failed to win the endorsement of the State Federation of Labor during the forties, was known as an active friend of labor, unlike several of his Democratic opponents.[14] During the senatorial contest of 1944, Republican Wayne L. Morse received the endorsement of the State Federation of Labor, the AFL, and the CIO in his campaign against Edgar W. Smith, a conservative Democrat who attacked organized labor and excoriated the New Deal. Labor's support of Morse proved so offensive to conservative Republicans that they pictured him as a "New Dealer

[13] Democratic National Committeemen Howard Latourette (1936-1944) and Lew Wallace (1944-1948) were among the most conservative Democrats during the 1930s. In 1934, the staunchly conservative *Oregon Voter* endorsed Latourette and Wallace for the state legislature because of their "reputation for conservatism." *Oregon Voter* 79 (Nov. 3, 1934), p. 19.

[14] Angell, who represented the Third Congressional District from 1939 to 1955, prided himself on nonpartisanship. "I realize that Multnomah County is heavily Democratic," he wrote a fellow Republican, "but many of my best supporters belong to the Democratic party which I believe is due to the fact that . . . I represent all the people, Democrats and Republicans alike." One Portlander, describing himself as a "life-long" Democrat who never failed to vote for Roosevelt, told Angell he voted for him "on the basis of the indorsement of your record by the union press." See Homer Angell to Douglas McKay, Mar. 6, 1950; Angell to Ralph J. Anderson, May 12, 1954; Edward A. Zenner to Angell, Mar. 2, 1954, Homer D. Angell Papers (University of Oregon, Eugene). Angell ascribed his long tenure in a Democratic district to the fact that he backed various New Deal programs, worked for labor, and consistently supported the Townsend Plan. See Portland *Oregonian*, Jan. 26, 1964, p. 33.

masquerading as a republican" and crossed party lines to support Smith.[15]

The weak showing of the Democratic Party in state politics during the period of the war was not solely based on its failure to attract the vote of labor. The party continued to suffer from a deplorable lack of organization and an inability to recruit attractive candidates. In 1942, over a third of the Democratic county chairmen failed to attend a state-wide meeting to plan strategy for the elections that year. The apathy of Democratic voters was demonstrated when only 30 per cent of the party voted in the primaries of 1942 and, worse yet, the Democratic gubernatorial and senatorial candidates received but 22 per cent of the vote in the general election.[16] Fred Fisk, chairman of the Democratic State Central Committee, attributed the overwhelming defeat of Democrats in 1942 to the "unpopularity of the war."[17] A more realistic evaluation might have mentioned other factors, especially the lack of appeal of Democratic candidates. Lew Wallace, the party's candidate for governor, was more conservative than his Republican opponent, Earl Snell. Democrat Walter Whitbeck, who opposed Charles McNary in the senatorial election, was actively opposed by liberal Democrats because of his failure to support the New Deal.

The results of other elections during and immediately after the war reflected the continuing impotence of the Democratic Party. In spite of this, the possibility of reviving the party was not hopeless. The economic and demographic changes of the 1940s provided solid ground upon which to rebuild. But before the passive Democratic electorate could be galvanized, the hold of the old guard on the party would have to be broken. It was this task that absorbed the attention and energy of liberal Democrats after the war.

15 Portland *Oregonian*, Oct. 16, 1944, p. 4. For conservative Republican opposition to Morse see Rufus C. Holman to Henry M. Hanzen, Feb. 1, 1944; Harry A. Jung to Rufus C. Holman, Mar. 29, 1944; "Do the Republicans of Oregon Want to Put a New Dealer in the Senate?" manuscript copy of radio address by C. C. Crow, Apr. 29, 1944; Ralph E. Moody to Rufus C. Holman, May 1, 1944; Charles C. Hall to Henry M. Hanzen, July 5, 1944; "Yours for the elimination of all New Dealers, including Professor Morse," campaign circular, 1944, Hanzen Papers.

16 *Oregon Democrat* 10 (Aug. 1942), p. 8.

17 *Ibid.*, 10 (Nov. 1942), p. 3.

VI THE LIBERAL CHALLENGE:
Building a New Party

Oswald West, concerned about the leadership of the Oregon Democratic Party, addressed a plaintive question to old-guard Democrats: "Must we 'Old Time' Democrats sit idly by while Communist squatters, on Oregon political soil, execute quit-claim deeds
favoring their gods residing behind the Iron Curtain?"[1] West's
emotional philippic, like others delivered in the postwar period by
worried conservatives, was prompted by the activities of liberal
Democrats who sought to remove conservatives from positions of
influence and power in the party. The battle for control of Oregon's Democratic Party, a contest that raged unabated from 1946
to 1952, destroyed unity and temporarily rendered the party powerless in state politics. Still, despite the intraparty struggle, the
eventual victory of liberals not only was a necessary first step in
rebuilding the party, but also foretold the establishment of a competitive two-party system in Oregon.

The program of liberal Democrats in Oregon after the war was
similar to that of political movements in other parts of the nation.
In fact, political developments in Oregon were much like those in
Minnesota, Wisconsin, and Michigan. Those who sought to revitalize the Democratic Party in these states were guided by a desire to
create what political scientists term programmatic or issue-oriented
parties as opposed to traditional or job-oriented parties. According
to one student of state politics, the distinction between these desig-
nations centers on the motivation of party leaders. People in the
traditional parties "are active in politics because they want a job,
and issues are perceived as tools by which to secure the jobs." On
the other hand, those "in programmatic parties are in politics not
for the jobs as such, but because the job is seen as the means of
securing the policy goals they regard as desirable."[2] That program-

---

[1] Oswald West, "A Guide to Sweetland," undated manuscript copy in
West Papers.
[2] Fenton, *Midwest Politics*, p. 4.

matic politics motivated liberal Democrats in Oregon after the war
was illustrated by the nature of the criticism they directed at old-
guard Democrats, by the policies they articulated, and the nature
of the liberal coalition they hoped to build.

Most of those dedicated to rebuilding the Democratic Party
were scornful of what they sometimes referred to as "Republocrats," individuals who had ruled the party since the New Deal.[3]
Several of the so-called "Republocrats" welcomed conservative
Republican support in the thirties when liberal Democrats and the
Oregon Commonwealth Federation challenged their right to lead
the party. During the forties, when the party was at a low ebb,
these same Democrats accepted patronage from Republicans.
"They were quite comfortable as big frogs in a little puddle," one
liberal Democrat explained, a status they maintained by "picking
up crumbs off the Republican table."[4] Democratic National Committeeman Lew Wallace (1944-1948) and Democratic State Senator Walter J. Pearson, for example, were both insurance agents
who, some liberals charged, appeared more interested in using their
political positions to sell insurance to Republicans than in vitalizing
the Democratic Party.[5] Democratic State Senator Thomas R. Mahoney, who had campaigned for the state legislature as late as 1936
as a Republican, switched his registration to Democratic in 1938.
A member of the legislature from Multnomah County from 1938,
Mahoney was reportedly connected with gambling interests in
Portland and used his position in the legislature to do their bidding.[6]

The issue orientation of liberal Democrats was also reflected in
statements of party principles and the advocacy of certain programs. Believing that the Democratic Party should be a vehicle
for improving society and promoting public service, liberals sought
to remake the party's image along these lines. They urged the enactment of legislation designed to improve the social and economic
well-being of Oregonians, and adopted President Harry S. Truman's Fair Deal as a model for political action. Among the programs
sponsored by liberals in Oregon were federal aid to education,
public housing, increased social security benefits, national health
insurance, a permanent Fair Employment Practices Commission,
the Brannan Farm Plan, repeal of the Taft-Hartley Act, and a
Columbia Valley Authority.[7]

---

[3] Interview with Monroe Sweetland, Dec. 21, 1967; interview with Howard
Morgan, Apr. 13, 1968. See also Portland *Oregonian*, Aug. 10, 1947, p. 1.

[4] Interview with Howard Morgan, Apr. 13, 1968.

[5] *Oregon Democrat* 10 (June, 1942), pp. 8-9; interview with Monroe
Sweetland, Dec. 21, 1967.

[6] *Oregon Voter* 94 (Dec. 31, 1938), p. 28; interview with Howard Morgan,
Apr. 13, 1968.

[7] Interview with Monroe Sweetland, Dec. 21, 1967; interview with James

The programs endorsed by liberals were primarily aimed at farmers and industrial workers in Oregon, the two major groups they hoped to entice into a liberal Democratic coalition. It was no accident, therefore, that CVA became a *cause celebre* of liberals. The Grange and State Federation of Labor had supported the concept of a CVA since the 1930s. In addition, repeal of the Taft-Hartley Act would benefit labor, while the Brannan Farm Plan would, liberals believed, assist the farmer.[8]

Before liberal Democrats could make programmatic politics the focus of the state Democratic Party, they faced a bewildering array of problems. The most obvious task was to overthrow the conservative leadership of the party. At the same time, the problems of apathy and defeatism among the party's rank and file, the party's poor reputation, the lack of organization, inadequate finances, and the need to recruit attractive candidates for state and federal office had to be resolved. While all these difficulties demanded attention, the primary objectives immediately after the war were rebuilding the party at the grass roots and seizing control of positions of leadership in the party.

The most troublesome problem was that of party organization. At both the state and local levels, the party was without effective organization. "The state headquarters was an unmanned office with a few pathetic filing cabinets,"[9] recalled James Goodsell, who became executive secretary of the party in 1949. Equally appalling was the lack of organization at the precinct and county level. Monroe Sweetland summarized the situation this way: "When I returned to Oregon after the war the party was hard to find. In a majority of counties of the state you could not find a Democratic Party committee functioning, if indeed a committee existed."[10] To correct this situation, an ambitious program of party reorganization was initiated.

The job of rebuilding the party at the grass roots was not accomplished easily. In some counties success was immediate, while in others progress was slow. No single strategy was employed in all counties, and those who undertook the arduous work of local organization were drawn equally from the ranks of young men and women new to politics and older liberals active in Oregon politics since the 1930s.

The approach of young liberal Democrats new to politics was

Goodsell, Apr. 6, 1968; interview with Howard Morgan, Apr. 13, 1968. See also Richard Neuberger to Monroe Sweetland, Dec. 27, 1948, Neuberger Papers; *Oregon Journal*, Sept. 14, 1949, p. 32.

[8] Interview with Monroe Sweetland, Dec. 21, 1967.

[9] Interview with James Goodsell, Apr. 6, 1968.

[10] Interview with Monroe Sweetland, Dec. 27, 1967.

demonstrated in Clatsop, Lane, and Baker counties. In 1947 James Goodsell, a newspaper reporter on the *Astorian Budget*, and Robert Holmes, an executive with radio station KAST, went to work with others to revive Democratic organization in Clatsop County. After founding a chapter of Americans For Democratic Action, which provided a temporary base from which to work, Goodsell, Holmes and others campaigned for and won election to the Clatsop County Democratic Central Committee in 1948. Meanwhile, other liberal Democrats in Clatsop County won appointment as precinct committeemen and committeewomen. After consolidating their power, Clatsop liberals inaugurated a campaign to recruit strong candidates to run for the State Legislative Assembly. As a result of these efforts, for the first time in the twentieth century a Democrat was elected to the state senate from Clatsop County in 1948.[11]

The strategy employed by Goodsell and Holmes was repeated in Lane County somewhat later. Charles O. Porter and Keith D. Skelton, two Eugene attorneys, joined with William F. Maddron, Keith Bacon, and A. L. Ellingson to establish a local chapter of ADA. Using this organization as a base of power, Porter and Skelton then sought to gain control of the Lane County Democratic Central Committee. In 1952, Skelton was elected secretary and Porter finance chairman of the Central Committee; one year later, liberals won the chairmanship.[12]

In eastern Oregon, Al Ullman spearheaded a drive to revitalize the Democratic Central Committee in Baker County. Ullman encouraged the creation of amateur political clubs which used the issue of CVA as a catalyst to draw liberals together. By 1950, public-power advocates were in control of the Central Committee.[13]

Those new to politics usually relied on local chapters of the ADA or amateur political clubs as a means to rebuild the party on the local level; older liberals whose roots reached back to the Oregon Commonwealth Federation used a different approach. At the height of its power, the OCF drew support from the Grange and labor. Now, after the war, former OCF members sought to renew the old alliance in an attempt to rebuild local Democratic organization. Nathalie E. Panek, Dave Epps, and Wendell Barnett, one-time OCF activists, joined with members of the Grange in an attempt to resurrect the Marion County Democratic Central Committee. Dr.

---

[11] Interview with James Goodsell, Apr. 6, 1968.

[12] Robert E. Burton, "Charles O. Porter: Embattled Liberal" (unpublished master's thesis, University of Oregon, 1964), pp. 16-19; *Oregon Democrat* 21 (Nov. 1953), p. 17.

[13] Stephen A. Mitchell, *Elm Street Politics* (New York, 1959), pp. 45-46; interview with Monroe Sweetland, Dec. 21, 1967; *Oregon Democrat* 22 (Nov. 1954), pp. 6-7.

Albert Slaughter and Morton Tompkins, prominent members of the Grange, and A. C. Hyman, president of the Farmer's Union, worked with old OCF members in Clackamas, Washington, and Linn counties to revitalize the party. Among former OCF members who assisted in rebuilding the Democratic Party in Multnomah County were John Broast, Ernest Baker, and Al Hartung of the Longshoreman's Union; George Baker, executive secretary of the AFL-CIO in Oregon; Nan Wood Honeyman, a representative during the late 1930s; and Edgar Williams, Kelly Foster, and Ruth Flowers, members of Portland's Negro community.[14]

Although one-time OCF members were not always conspicuous as party leaders, their activity on behalf of a revived Democratic Party was fundamental to the eventual success of liberals. "In county after county, we would know who the pre-war people were," Sweetland recalled. "When we wanted a county chairman we would tap someone we trusted and knew, usually a Federation member." In Sweetland's judgment, OCF members proved to be the most effective and dedicated party workers. This was so because "they knew the tricks of the trade in practical politics," talents derived from "intensive training in politics under very adverse conditions in the late thirties and early forties."[15]

Simultaneously with work at the local level, liberals tried to take over positions of leadership in the hierarchy of the state Democratic Party. The first confrontation between liberal and old-guard Democrats came in the spring of 1947 over the election of a chairman for the State Central Committee. Conservatives, led by Democratic National Committeeman Lew Wallace, backed Lester W. Humphreys for the post, while liberals threw their support to Byron G. Carney, former first vice-president of the OCF. When the Central Committee met, conservatives seemed assured of victory because Wallace held enough proxies to elect Humphreys. Liberals, however, gained control of the committee on credentials and threw out the proxies held by Wallace, charging that they represented nonexistent county committees. Carney won the election by a vote of over two to one. At the same meeting, Sweetland was chosen publicity chairman of the Central Committee.[16]

The election of Carney touched off a bitter feud between Wallace and liberal Democrats. Wallace insisted that the election of Carney was a fraud and further charged that liberals were out to wreck the party.[17] Because Wallace remained unreconciled to the election of Carney and refused to work with the State Central

14 Interview with Monroe Sweetland, Dec. 21, 1967.
15 *Ibid.*
16 Portland *Oregonian*, May 18, 1947, pp. 1, 25.
17 *Ibid.*, Aug. 10, 1947, p. 1.

Committee, liberals recognized that they could do little in reconstructing the party at the state level until they controlled the
office of National Committeeman. With this in mind, Sweetland
declared as a candidate for that office in the primary elections of
1948.

The contest for National Committeeman in 1948 involved four
candidates: Henry C. Aiken, W. E. Wilkins, Mike M. DeCicco,
and Monroe Sweetland. Of the four, Sweetland was the only declared liberal. As the contest got underway, DeCicco emerged as
the major threat to liberals. When Lew Wallace declined to seek
reelection, he and other conservatives threw their support to De-
Cicco. From the liberal point of view, DeCicco personified all that
was objectionable in the old style of Democratic politics. Operator of a Portland tire firm and automotive repair shop, he first entered Democratic politics during the New Deal as a defender of
Governor Martin. During the forties, he was counted among the
anti-New Deal clique that ruled the party; his election, liberals
thought, would be a calamity.[18]

Fortunately for Sweetland, Aiken of Morrow County and Wilkins of Union County were both older Democrats of a conservative orientation. He hoped, therefore, that they would siphon off
support from DeCicco. This analysis was eventually confirmed
when Sweetland emerged the victor with a narrow margin of
2,600 votes.[19]

Sweetland's election as National Committeeman was the most
important party victory for liberals in the late 1940s. As National
Committeeman, he could now coordinate strategy with the State
Central Committee to reconstruct the party. Moreover, Sweetland
could begin the task of realigning the state Democratic Party with
the national Democratic Party. "Once elected," Sweetland said
later, "this gave me a position from which to go to work in the
state and also allowed me to make a liaison with the Truman administration. After 1948 we had strong support from the Democratic
National Committee."[20] Support from the Truman administration
and the National Committee materialized in the form of financial
assistance, patronage, and the dispatch of prominent Democratic
figures to Oregon to rejoice over the rebirth of the party. Among
the many who visited the state were Truman's Secretary of the
Navy, Francis P. Matthews, and Senators Hubert H. Humphrey
and J. Howard McGrath. "Oregon has been called the Vermont

---

[18] Interview with Howard Morgan, Apr. 13, 1968; interview with Monroe
Sweetland, Dec. 21, 1967.

[19] The vote was Sweetland 43,004; DeCicco 40,425; Wilkins 33,182; Aiken
31,223.

[20] Interview with Monroe Sweetland, Dec. 21, 1967.

of the west," Matthews noted, but assured Oregonians that was no longer the case. Humphrey, who was national chairman of the ADA, declared in his most ebullient style that Democratic leaders in Oregon were, like himself, "new deal, fair deal, rip-snortin' Democrats." In the year following the election of Sweetland, said McGrath, the Democratic Party of Oregon had "shown 200 per cent improvement."[21] Sweetland also aided the drive to publicize the rebirth of the party by purchasing the *Oregon Democrat* in 1949. Under his editorship, the party's magazine became a forceful voice for liberalism in the postwar period.

Sweetland's election as National Committeeman marked a turning point in liberal efforts to restructure the party, but much hard work lay ahead. This fact was confirmed by the party's poor showing in the election of 1948. Liberals had only begun to consolidate their power, and as yet had been unsuccessful in recruiting strong candidates for major office. As a consequence, conservatives, without opposition in the Democratic primary election, dominated the field of candidates for high state and federal office in 1948. Lew Wallace ran as the Democratic gubernatorial candidate, and Walter J. Pearson sought the office of state treasurer. Manley J. Wilson, a former OCF member who won the Democratic senatorial nomination, was the only liberal candidate for major office. The Portland *Oregonian* surveyed the field of Democratic candidates, observing that the party seemed to have an over-abundance of "shopworn" candidates. "One may not expect much this year," said the *Oregonian*, "or maybe never."[22]

In an attempt to make the best of a bad situation, Sweetland directed liberals to conduct a vigorous campaign for President Truman. A group of conservative Democrats, however, staged an equally vigorous campaign for Thomas E. Dewey. Dellmore Lessard, who sided with the anti-New Deal Democrats during the 1930s, denounced Truman and liberals in Oregon for being "tainted with New Dealism." As chairman of the "Jeffersonian Democrats For Dewey," Lessard advised Oregon Democrats to vote for Dewey because they could "deliver the punch below the belt that Republicans can't give."[23]

Not unexpectedly, the election that November produced few Democratic victories in Oregon. Dewey carried the state in the presidential contest, and Republicans remained in control of nearly every major state office.[24] Even though liberals found the defeat

---

[21] Portland *Oregonian*, Aug. 15, 1949, p. 1; *Oregon Journal*, Aug. 16, 1949, p. 1; Nov. 7, 1949, p. 2.

[22] Portland *Oregonian*, Mar. 15, 1948, p. 10.

[23] *Ibid.*, Oct. 14, 1948, p. 25; Oct. 15, 1948, p. 9.

[24] Walter Pearson surprised liberals by winning the election for state

of Wilson and Truman disappointing, they could take comfort from the fact that some among their ranks scored victories in elections to the state legislature. Howard Morgan was elected to the lower house of the legislature; Richard L. Neuberger, Robert D. Holmes, and Vernon D. Bull won election to the state senate.

The lesson of the election of 1948 was not lost on liberals. Unless they could diminish the influence of conservatives, recruit appealing candidates, and strengthen their hold on the party, future success seemed unlikely. Consequently, liberals redoubled their efforts to refurbish the party in time for the election of 1950. Old-guard Democrats immediately served notice that they would tenaciously resist such efforts. Throughout 1949, the two wings of the party battled. The intraparty quarrel ranged over several issues but grew to its greatest intensity over elections to party office, liberal efforts to purge disreputable Democrats from the ranks of the party, and the allocation of patronage.

Liberals made their first move early in 1949 when party officials met to select a chairman for the State Central Committee. Mike M. DeCicco, who ran against Sweetland for National Committeeman in 1948, declared as a candidate for chairman with the backing of conservatives.[25] Byron G. Carney, elected chairman in 1947, had not proved to be a forceful or decisive leader. While dedicated to liberalism, the seventy-four-year-old chairman lacked the physical and intellectual vigor necessary to rebuild the party. Hoping to elect a more forceful chairman, liberals realized when the State Central Committee met that they did not have a clear majority of votes. Determined to defeat DeCicco at any cost, they decided to back William L. Josslin, a candidate who claimed some support among conservatives but professed sympathy with liberal goals.[26] The result of the election proved inconclusive for both factions of the party. Josslin was elected chairman, but DeCicco was chosen treasurer.[27]

---

treasurer. Sweetland made no effort to assist Pearson in his campaign. See Waldo Schumacher, "The 1948 Elections In Oregon, "*Western Political Quarterly* 2 (Mar. 1949), pp. 121-123.

[25] Portland *Oregonian*, Mar. 17, 1949, p. 23.

[26] Josslin first became active in Democratic politics during the 1930s. He organized the Young Democrats of Oregon in 1931 and subsequently became the first president of that organization. After the election of Governor Charles H. Martin in 1934, Josslin became the governor's secretary. During Martin's hectic tenure as governor, Josslin frequently sided with conservatives, a fact that caused him some embarrassment in the postwar period. As chairman of the State Central Committee, Josslin often found himself leaning toward the conservative side in disputes between liberals and the old guard. See *Oregon Democrat* 17 (Mar. 1949), p. 7; *ibid.* 20 (Feb. 1952), p. 3; Salem *Capital Journal*, Mar. 2, 1950, p. 4.

[27] *Oregon Democrat* 17 (Apr. 1949), p. 4.

Sweetland, Morgan, and Goodsell were clearly unhappy with the selection of DeCicco as treasurer. Therefore, they devised a plan to lessen his influence in the party. On the pretext of making organization more effective, Sweetland proposed that the Central Committee hire a full-time executive secretary. Among other duties, the secretary would be empowered to handle party funds and disburse money, power which DeCicco held as treasurer. DeCicco, Thomas R. Mahoney, and Lew Wallace immediately declared their opposition to the proposal, correctly guessing that Sweetland's intent was to deny DeCicco influence in the State Central Committee.[28] What promised to be a tumultuous party battle was averted when DeCicco played into the hands of liberals.

DeCicco's undoing followed an incident at Gearhart, Oregon, on the morning of May 3, 1949. According to newspaper reports, DeCicco was attacked and beaten by four sailors who broke into his summer home. But two days later, Mrs. Ramona Laurion told a different story. Mrs. Laurion explained that she and DeCicco had been living together for two years when DeCicco decided to find another girl friend. When Mrs. Laurion found DeCicco with another woman at Gearhart on the morning of May 3, she flew into a rage and administered the beating herself, a beating which ended when she pushed DeCicco through a window. DeCicco denied Mrs. Laurion's version of the episode, but the whole incident clouded his reputation. The Portland *Oregonian* declared the affair "a scandal in a high place," and added: "There have been other symptoms of ill omen in the Democratic Party."[29]

After the incident at Gearhart, Sweetland and others called on DeCicco to resign as treasurer. Although DeCicco refused to resign, and conservatives continued to oppose the appointment of an executive secretary, liberals won the struggle. Before the end of May, James Goodsell was appointed executive secretary of the State Central Committee.[30]

The attempt to deprive DeCicco of power in the hierarchy of the Democratic Party stemmed initially from his conservative orientation. The episode at Gearhart, however, raised another question that troubled liberals. "The party was not taken seriously," one liberal asserted, "because we had too many drunks, crooks, stumble bums, has-beens, and never-wuzes."[31] Besides DeCicco, there were other Democrats who contributed to the party's poor image, most notably Marion L. "Mike" Elliott.

[28] Interview with Monroe Sweetland, Dec. 21, 1967.

[29] Portland *Oregonian*, May 4, 1949, p. 11; May 6, 1949, p. 11; May 7, 1949, p. 6.

[30] *Oregon Journal*, May 24, 1949, p. 1. Goodsell's salary was paid by the Democratic National Committee. Interview with James Goodsell, Apr. 6, 1968.

[31] Interview with Howard Morgan, Apr. 13, 1968.

Elliott, who switched his registration from Republican to Democrat early in 1948, was elected sheriff of Multnomah County in November 1948, defeating veteran Sheriff Martin Pratt by only 800 votes. Elliott had boasted of a distinguished war record, a college degree from the University of Michigan, and an outstanding record as a college athlete. Shortly after the election, it was learned that Elliott had grossly misrepresented himself. He had actually received a bad conduct discharge from the Marine Corps before the Second World War, had gone no further than the second year of high school, and had not engaged in college athletics. Added to these disclosures was the allegation that Elliott maintained a liaison with gambling interests in Portland and Las Vegas. The controversy that swirled around the sheriff reached a climax when Elliott dismissed the county's chief criminologist, allegedly because he refused to hire an Elliott campaign worker who had a past criminal record.[32]

Liberal Democrats recognized that Elliott had to be recalled if they were to improve the reputation of the party. But Mike DeCicco, Thomas R. Mahoney, and other old-guard Democrats opposed recall and moved to the defense of Elliott. DeCicco asserted that Elliot was the target of a conspiracy perpetrated by liberals, a conspiracy that earlier had resulted in his own demotion in party councils.[33] Despite the opposition of conservative Democrats, liberals joined with Republicans in Multnomah County and eventually succeeded in recalling Elliott.[34]

Party schism over the demotion of DeCicco and the recall of Elliott was further widened when Sweetland attempted to engineer the appointment of a liberal Democrat to a new federal judgeship created by Congress in 1949. With the agreement of the Truman administration, Sweetland nominated Gus J. Solomon, former treasurer of the OCF. To contest the nomination of Solomon, Walter Pearson, Thomas Mahoney, Mike DeCicco, and Lew Wallace nominated their own candidate, Earl C. Latourette. Seeking to embarrass Sweetland and discredit Solomon, Mahoney declared that the National Committeeman and Solomon had once been ringleaders of a "left wing organization," a reference to the OCF.[35] Pearson angrily warned Sweetland that if he persisted in

[32] Salem *Capital Journal*, July 8, 1949, p. 2; Portland *Oregonian*, July 12, 1949, p. 14; Oregon *Journal*, July 20, 1949, p. 1.

[33] Salem *Oregon Statesman*, July 30, 1949, p. 2.

[34] Salem *Capital Journal*, Oct. 22, 1949, pp. 3, 4. Elliott later ran afoul of the law. In 1955, he was convicted of forging checks in Los Angeles. In 1968, he was convicted for possession of counterfeit travelers checks, and sentenced to a one-to-fourteen-year prison term in California. Eugene *Register-Guard*, Mar. 29, 1968, p. 5A.

[35] Salem *Oregon Statesman*, July 7, 1949, p. 2.

his support of Solomon it would "split the Democratic Party in Oregon right down the middle."[36] Ignoring the protest of conservatives, Sweetland continued in his support of Solomon. The result was another victory for the liberal faction: President Truman officially nominated Solomon, who was subsequently confirmed by the Senate.[37]

Even though liberals had won several important skirmishes with the old guard during 1949, they had not silenced conservatives or truly relegated them to a position of impotence in party affairs. Worse yet, the feuds of 1949 tended to discredit both factions of the party. One newspaper cautioned: "Democrats—stop fighting among yourselves and go to work or you'll have fewer elected candidates in 1950 than you did in 1948."[38] A different evaluation, one which emphasized the positive accomplishments of liberals in 1949, appeared in an *Oregon Journal* editorial under the title 'Rejuvenated Donkey?" The *Journal* noted that while the national Democratic Party had been ascendant since 1932 "the Democratic donkey in Oregon [had] been a bewildered, frustrated split-personality critter without purpose, confidence, leadership or motive." Nonetheless, the newspaper observed, "There are signs that the Oregon donkey is taking a new lease on life and showing some purpose about things that affect all people of the state."[39] As the election of 1950 approached, liberals hoped their efforts to revive the party would pay dividends.

While the power base of liberals within the party was somewhat tenuous, and party organization still not perfected in many parts of the state, liberals viewed the election of 1950 as their first real opportunity to carry on a "fighting campaign."[40] Because of his attention to organization, Sweetland was especially encouraged when in 1950 Democratic registration surpassed Republican for the first time in the twentieth century.

As early as the spring of 1949, liberals had served notice that the major issue of the coming campaign would be CVA.[41] To dramatize this fact, they launched a publicity campaign designed to create public support for CVA. After meeting with President Truman at the White House, Sweetland declared: "The people of Oregon are for the CVA on a non-political and bi-partisan basis. If the Republicans persist in making a political issue out of it, the Demo-

---

[36] Salem *Capital Journal*, Aug. 5, 1949, p. 1.

[37] Cornelius P. Cotter and Bernard C. Hennessy, *Politics Without Power: The National Party Committees* (New York, 1964), pp. 26-27.

[38] Portland *East Side Post*, June 23, 1949, p. 2.

[39] *Oregon Journal*, Sept. 14, 1949, p. 32.

[40] Interview with Monroe Sweetland, Dec. 21, 1967.

[41] *Oregon Democrat* 17 (Mar. 1949), p. 8.

crats will carry Oregon in 1950."[42] Echoing these sentiments, Richard Neuberger urged Republican Governor Douglas McKay to call the legislature into special session to consider adoption of a referendum on CVA to be presented to the voters. In September 1949, liberal Democrats attended a Democratic Party conference at San Francisco where they and other Democrats adopted a platform calling for the creation of CVA, as well as other Fair Deal programs. The Truman administration dispatched C. Girard Davidson, assistant secretary of the Interior, to Portland to assist liberals in drumming up enthusiasm for CVA. Finally, in January 1950, the Democratic State Central Committee adopted a platform endorsing CVA, repeal of the Taft-Hartley Act, and the Brannan Farm Plan.[43]

Farm and labor groups joined with liberal Democrats on the CVA issue before the election of 1950. Morton Tompkins, master of the Oregon Grange, James T. Marr, executive secretary of the State Federation of Labor, and Stanley W. Earl, secretary of the Oregon CIO, all endorsed CVA at a meeting of the League for CVA in Portland in 1949. The Grange, the State Federation of Labor, and the CIO later endorsed CVA in separate conventions during 1950.[44]

Liberals found the adoption of a political platform an easy matter; the nomination of candidates who would support their program proved to be a more difficult problem. In addition to several lesser political positions, Oregon was to elect a United States senator, a governor, and four representatives in 1950. Liberals not only faced the threat of conservative opposition in the primary but, more important, they had trouble in recruiting attractive candidates, especially for offices at the top of the ticket. Most of the younger Democrats were reluctant to risk their political careers at a time when the party was only partially reconstructed. Furthermore, the incumbent Republican governor, Douglas McKay, and senator, Wayne L. Morse, would be formidable candidates to defeat. Because of these considerations, liberals recruited veteran Democrats.

State Senator Austin F. Flegel became the liberal candidate for the gubernatorial nomination. Flegel had been active in Democratic Party politics for several decades, but had never held high elective office. As president of the Willamette Iron and Steel Company, a director of the Hyster Company, and a member of a prominent

<hr>

[42] Salem *Oregon Statesman*, Aug. 4, 1949, p. 2.

[43] *Ibid.*, Aug. 30, 1949, p. 1; *Oregon Journal*, Sept. 20, 1949, p. 1; Portland *Oregonian*, Sept. 25, 1949, p. 1; Salem *Oregon Statesman*, Jan. 8, 1950, p. 6.

[44] Voeltz, "Proposals For A Columbia Valley Authority: A History of Political Controversy," pp. 195-202, 209-211.

Portland law firm, Flegel scarcely personified the new look liberals had in mind for the party. "Austin Flegel," said Monroe Sweetland, "was a wealthy, distinguished, prominent, successful, traditional Democrat—but one who was strongly for us on the public power issue."[45] Flegel's long standing in the Portland business community, and then his sudden conversion to liberalism, prompted political doggerel:

> Austin's a man with much to say
> He makes all his speeches for CVA
> He's caused a hub-bub
> At the Arlington Club
> And even confused Doug McKay[46]

In their search for congressional candidates, liberals were only partially successful in recruiting new personalities. Dr. Louis A. Wood, a member of the faculty at the University of Oregon who unsuccessfully sought election to Congress from the Fourth Congressional District in 1946, agreed to run for the senatorial nomination. Liberals managed to recruit candidates for all four congressional districts, but most were Democrats who had unsuccessfully sought office in the past.[47] David C. Shaw, who ran for the Democratic nomination in the Fourth Congressional District, was one of the few liberal candidates without a record of defeats.

As liberals had expected, old-guard Democrats made the primary of 1950 a struggle for control of the party. Determined to regain political ground lost in 1949, conservatives declared for almost every major office. Howard Latourette, National Committeeman between 1936 and 1944, ran for the senatorial nomination; L. T. Ward, editor of the Benton County *Review* and vociferous opponent of CVA, sought the nomination in the First Congressional District; Walter A. Swanson, who was described by one newspaper as an opponent of the "New Deal, Fair Deal and all they stand for,"[48] announced for representative in the Fourth Congressional District. Unfortunately for conservatives, the political ambitions of Lew Wallace and Walter Pearson prevented a united front in the gubernatorial contest. Both declared as candidates, a development that naturally aided Flegel in his bid for nomination.[49]

---

[45] Interview with Monroe Sweetland, Dec. 21, 1967.

[46] Portland *Oregonian*, Nov. 21, 1949, p. 13.

[47] Liberals supported Roy R. Hewitt for representative in the First Congressional District and Vernon D. Bull in the Second Congressional District. In the Third Congressional District, liberals were divided between Carl C. Donaugh and Phil Dreyer. Donaugh, like Josslin, had been in Democratic Party politics since the New Deal.

[48] Eugene *Register-Guard*, Oct. 31, 1952, p. 10B.

[49] Salem *Oregon Statesman*, Feb. 20, 1950, p. 1; *Dalles Chronicle*, Feb. 22, 1950, p. 1.

While acrimonious debate punctuated all the contests between liberal and conservative Democrats in the primary, the greatest amount of political bloodletting occurred in the race for the gubernatorial nomination. Flegel, campaigning as a champion of the Fair Deal, asserted that neither Wallace nor Pearson was "fit to occupy the governor's chair" because of their reactionary records. Wallace, in turn, attacked Flegel's credentials as a liberal, while Pearson called on Flegel to withdraw from the race.[50] The campaign became so bitter that Josslin, chairman of the State Central Committee, sent letters to Flegel, Wallace, and Pearson in which he asked them to "bury your barbarous hatchets."[51] The hatchets were not buried; nor did liberal Democrats feel constrained to remain silent. State Senator Richard Neuberger accused Wallace and Pearson of being captives of the "power trust" because of their opposition to CVA. According to Neuberger, both Wallace and Pearson were "more conservative than [Republican Governor] McKay." "The Democratic Party is not going to win in Oregon as a conservative party," said Neuberger. "That has been tried for the past 20 years and what has been the result? Our state does not need two conservative political parties."[52] Howard Morgan, who was running unopposed in the primary for Commissioner of Labor, joined in the attack on Wallace and Pearson. While touring the state with the three gubernatorial candidates, Morgan took every opportunity to advance the candidacy of Flegel, a circumstance that greatly annoyed the two conservatives.[53]

After several months of intensive political warfare, the primary struggle came to an end. With but one exception, liberals captured the nominations. Howard Latourette, who won the senatorial nomination over Dr. Louis A. Wood, was the only winning member of the old guard. Latourette's nomination turned on Multnomah County, which he carried by nearly 16,000 votes.[54] Liberals could be proud of their victory in the primary, but they faced an uphill battle in the general election. Oregon Republicans, solidly united behind an anti-CVA platform, enjoyed the benefit of unity, while the Democratic Party had emerged from the primary seriously divided.

[50] Salem *Oregon Statesman*, Mar. 22, 1950, p. 4; Salem *Capital Journal*, Mar. 25, 1950, pp. 1, 5.

[51] Salem *Oregon Statesman*, Mar. 22, 1950, p. 4.

[52] Manuscript copy of radio address by Richard L. Neuberger, Mar. 23, 1950, Sawyer Papers. Salem *Capital Journal*, Mar. 25, 1950, p. 5.

[53] Interview with Howard Morgan, Apr. 13, 1968.

[54] Latourette defeated Wood 81,168 to 71,098. The race for the gubernatorial nomination was very close: Flegel 59,417, Wallace 57,730, and Pearson 46,549.

The shape and course of the general election in 1950 seemed in doubt for several months following the primaries. There had been earlier signs that conservative Republicans and Democrats might brandish the cudgel of McCarthyism, a phenomenon that was only beginning to take hold in the nation. Charles V. Stanton, editor of the Roseburg *News Review*, had charged earlier in the year that the Democratic Party was "absorbed in the advance of Fabian Socialism," and was now controlled by "Socialists and Fellow Travelers."[55] Tom McCall, Portland newsman and secretary to Governor McKay, described CVA as "creeping socialism" and "fascism."[56] Conservative Democrats had frequently characterized Sweetland, Morgan, and Neuberger as the ringleaders in a plot to convert the Democratic Party to socialism and "left-wingism."[57] These allegations proved to be harbingers of the campaign.

Howard Latourette, the Democratic senatorial candidate was the first to use communism as a campaign issue. His sensational charges drew attention away from other races and made the senatorial campaign the major contest in 1950. Latourette's ire was aroused when, belatedly, he received a check for $2,000 from the Democratic National Committee, an amount some $4,400 under his original request. Latourette returned the check for $2,000, accusing Sweetland and the National Committee of sabotaging his campaign because they preferred to see Senator Wayne Morse reelected. "It is apparent certain administration advisers prefer to retain a political straddler who will work both sides of the street rather than elect a senator who believes in . . . Democratic principles free from socialistic influences."[58] Warming to his subject, Latourette asserted: "We have a hot war at home. It is again the Russians who have spread the false doctrine that we must tolerate so-called liberals among our ranks. Step by step—first socialism, then enslavement through communism."[59] Oswald West joined Latourette in the assault on liberal Democrats. West charged that Sweetland was in league with "other red revolutionaries" to take the Democratic

---

[55] Roseburg *News Review*, Jan. 16, 1950, p. 4.

[56] Ashland *Tidings*, Nov. 11, 1949, p. 1.

[57] Portland *Oregonian*, Sept. 17, 1949, p. 6; Oct. 26, 1949, p. 6; *Oregon Journal*, Dec. 21, 1949, p. 14; Salem *Capital Journal*, Mar. 29, 1950, p. 4.

[58] *Oregon Journal*, Oct. 5, 1950, p. 1; Salem *Capital Journal*, Oct. 6, 1950, p. 2.

[59] *Oregon Journal*, Oct. 10, 1950, p. 10; Portland *Oregonian*, Oct. 8, 1950, p. 14. During the campaign, Latourette had thousands of leaflets dropped over Portland which explained that he had "never played with Pinks or Communists." The leaflets also bore a picture of Harry Bridges, Wayne Morse, and Monroe Sweetland with the caption "strange fellow travelers." A. Robert Smith, *The Tiger in the Senate: A Biography of Wayne Morse* (Garden City, N.Y., 1962), p. 208.

Party on a "left-wing ride." Apparently to make his case stronger, West added that Sweetland was an advocate of "free love."[60]

Latourette's allegation of collusion among Sweetland, the Democratic National Committee, and Senator Morse was, according to Sweetland, not true. Sweetland had sought funds for Latourette, but because there was little hope of defeating Morse, the National Committee hesitated to give Latourette the amount he originally requested.[61] On the other hand, many liberal Democrats had decided to vote for Morse as a matter of personal conviction.[62] This decision came only after much soul-searching. In the fall of 1949, Senator Morse had announced his opposition to CVA, the major campaign issue of liberals in 1950. At that time, Sweetland characterized Morse as a "prisoner of the power trust" and vowed to see him retired from office.[63] But time and circumstance softened that determination. While opposed to CVA, Morse was far more liberal than Latourette and had supported some Fair Deal measures, most notably the repeal of the Taft-Hartley Act. After Latourette's denunciation of Sweetland and the National Committee, and his subsequent repudiations of the Fair Deal and President Truman, liberals moved to open support of Morse. "One anomaly of Oregon law," wrote Sweetland in the *Oregon Democrat*, "is that when a candidate like Latourette disavows his own party, the officials of that party are nevertheless bound to support him. This stricture, however, does not bind the individual voter, as the November returns will in our opinion abundantly prove."[64]

Latourette and West were not the only ones who pictured liberal Democrats as the agents of a communist conspiracy. Republican Harris Ellsworth, who was seeking reelection in the Fourth Congressional District, proclaimed that the major issue of the campaign was "not a contest between Republicans and Democrats but

---

[60] Salem *Capital Journal*, Oct. 9, 1950, p. 3; Oct. 10, 1950, p. 10; Oct. 11, 1950, p. 3; Oct. 12, 1950, p. 14.

[61] Interview with Monroe Sweetland, Dec. 21, 1967.

[62] *Ibid.;* interview with James Goodsell, Apr. 6, 1968; interview with Howard Morgan, Apr. 13, 1968.

[63] Portland *Oregonian*, Sept. 25, 1949, p. 1. Among those who were most upset by Morse's anti-CVA stand was Richard Neuberger. "I certainly was disappointed by your stand on CVA today," Neuberger wrote Morse. "It always had been my hope that you would be a liberal in the Norris tradition. I am afraid you did not help yourself today." In a letter to a close friend, Neuberger wrote of Morse: "He is a man of intellect and brilliance, but I fear he is short on character. Morse carries water on both shoulders. One minute he is posing as a friend of the common man, a Fair Dealer, then the next minute he is denouncing CVA. Neither liberal nor conservative can be certain of Morse's real loyalties. I get the feeling Morse will do anything to be reelected." See Neuberger to Morse, Sept. 23, 1949; Neuberger to Leslie M. Scott, Nov. 21, 1949, Neuberger Papers.

[64] *Oregon Democrat* 18 (Oct. 1950), p. 5.

a contest between Communists and fellow travelers and the rest of us."[65] Ellsworth pictured his Democratic opponent, David Shaw, as a "left-winger" with "pink ideas."[66] "Deadwood" Dave Hoover, who had unsuccessfully challenged Morse in the Republican senatorial primary, echoed the views of Latourette and Ellsworth. After endorsing Latourette, Hoover declared that Latourette was the only Democrat running for high office whose "Americanism" and loyalty "to our form of government [was] unquestioned."[67]

The balloting on November 7 was a disaster for liberal Democrats. The G.O.P. scored an overwhelming victory, winning the races for governor, senator, and representative. Except in the senatorial contest, old-guard Democrats saw the election returns as a victory in their battle with liberals. "The question before the democrats of this state Tuesday," said Oswald West, "was whether old-time party members should be permitted to have a voice in party councils or be pushed aside to make way for pap-sucking socialistic elements who seem to have the ear of the so-called Washington big-shots. A majority of the voting democrats proved their sanity."[68]

West was undoubtedly correct about conservative Democratic support for Republicans in 1950, but this alone does not explain the liberal debacle. The indictment of liberal Democrats as communists, socialists, or fellow-travelers probably influenced some Oregonians to vote Republican, but the decisive victory of Senator Morse, who was described by Latourette as a "strange fellow traveler," seems to diminish the significance of this factor.[69]

Perhaps most important in explaining the Republican victory in 1950 was the lack of appeal of liberal Democratic candidates, party factionalism before and during the election, and the issue of CVA. At the time of the Democratic primary in 1950, one newspaper noted that a majority of liberals who sought nomination had "been

[65] Portland *Oregonian*, Oct. 29, 1950, p. 1. "I have repeatedly stated in this campaign that it is not so much a contest between Democrat and Republican philosophies," said Ellsworth, "as it is a contest between American concepts of government and socialist and left-wing doctrine." See Harris Ellsworth to David Cochran, Nov. 1, 1950, Harris Ellsworth Papers (University of Oregon, Eugene).

[66] Ellsworth compiled a dossier on Shaw during the campaign to support his assertion that Shaw was connected with communism. Ellsworth to Fulton Lewis, Jr., Oct. 22, 1950; Louis E. Miller to Ellsworth, Oct. 31, 1950; Ellsworth to Arthur Priaulx, Nov. 13, 1950; Ellsworth to Louis E. Miller, Nov. 11, 1950; "David Shaw File," Ellsworth Papers.

[67] *Oregon Journal*, Oct. 24, 1950, p. 10.

[68] Salem *Oregon Statesman*, Nov. 10, 1950, p. 4.

[69] Morse, who ran at the top of the Republican ticket, defeated Latourette 376,510 to 116,730.

on the ballot since Hec was a pup."[70] This was true of Flegel and
three of the four candidates for representative. If Oregonians found
most liberal candidates in 1950 without personal appeal, they were
perhaps also persuaded to vote Republican because of factionalism
within the Democratic Party. The battle in the Democratic Party
primary, coupled with Latourette's attack on Sweetland and attacks by Wallace and Pearson on Flegel during the general election,
did not improve the party's image. A final stumbling block to
liberal success may have derived from the choice of CVA as the
primary issue of the campaign. Morgan and Sweetland later suggested that CVA was probably a poor issue in 1950. Not only did
the proposal for a CVA arouse determined and well-organized
opposition, but charges that CVA represented "creeping socialism"
blurred the issue. In addition, while those labor and farm leaders
who were associated with the old OCF supported CVA, many in
the State Federation of Labor and the Grange appeared indifferent
to CVA. This was especially true of rank-and-file union members
who had migrated to Oregon during the Second World War.[71]
Following the election, Charles Sprague, editor of the *Oregon
Statesman*, published an editorial, "CVA—Requiescat In Pace!" The
gist of Sprague's comments was that support for CVA was an illu-
sion, even among labor and farm groups. "The CVA issue," said
Sprague, "may be regarded as buried, at least until some fresh
political Gabriel blows a resurrection horn."[72] After 1950, liberal
Democrats in Oregon, as well as the Truman administration,
dropped the issue.

In spite of the Republican victory in 1950, liberal Democrats
could point to some positive accomplishments in their efforts to
rebuild the party. In 1948, conservative Democrats won virtually
every nomination for major political office. But in the Democratic
primary of 1950, liberals successfully challenged old-guard Democrats, winning all but one nomination for major office. Furthermore, young liberal Democratic candidates, untarnished by past
defeats, ran very well against their Republican opponents in 1950.
Even though Morgan lost his bid for Commissioner of Labor, he
finished at the top of the Democratic ticket, some 42,000 votes
ahead of Austin Flegel. In the Fourth Congressional District, David

---

[70] Salem *Oregon Statesman*, Mar. 13, 1950, p. 4.

[71] Interview with Monroe Sweetland, Dec. 21, 1967; interview with
Howard Morgan, Apr. 13, 1968; Voeltz, "Proposals For A Columbia Valley
Authority: A History of Political Controversy," pp. 220-236. In an analysis of
labor's vote the *Oregon Democrat* noted: "Many voters who are union members made up their minds independently on the Congressional and gubernatorial races—Morse, McKay and Angell were the chief beneficiaries." See
Oregon Democrat 18 (Dec. 1950), p. 5.

[72] Salem *Oregon Statesman*, Nov. 13, 1950, pp. 1, 4.

Shaw won a greater per cent of the two-party vote in his race against Harris Ellsworth than had any previous Democratic candidate. Thus, even in a year of political defeat, liberal Democrats remained stubbornly optimistic about the future. Their optimism was confirmed within two years. In 1952, liberals brought their battle with conservatives to an end when they assumed firm control of the party and permitted old-line Democrats to run for office only after an appropriate act of contrition.

In February 1952, liberal and conservative Democrats clashed for the third and last time over the selection of a chairman for the State Central Committee. Liberals threw their support to Howard Morgan while conservatives backed Walter Pearson. After a two-week campaign, during which the retiring chairman, William Josslin, endorsed Pearson, the State Central Committee met for the balloting. "The high tension meeting," reported the *Oregon Democrat*, "featured considerable oratory . . . and sharp debate."[73] Morgan emerged the victor by a vote of 29 to 28.

Morgan's election as chairman of the State Central Committee proved most significant. The two previous chairmen, Byron G. Carney and William Josslin, had not been effective or decisive party leaders. By contrast, Morgan possessed youth, energy, intellect, and a dedication to the liberal cause which made him the most effective and talented party chairman in the decade after the war. Sweetland observed that Democratic leaders across the state had expressed a desire "to make a clear break with the unhappy past of Oregon Democracy" through the election of Morgan. "Morgan is the first state chairman in 20 years," said Sweetland, "who had no ties with old alliances, allegiances, and intrigues."[74]

Paralleling Morgan's election as chairman of the State Central Committee was the reelection of Sweetland as National Committeeman in 1952. Mike M. DeCicco, who challenged Sweetland for a second time, ran on a platform which promised "$100-a-month old age pensions." Describing himself as a "Jeffersonian Democrat," DeCicco declared the major issue of his race with Sweetland to be "Americanism against Communism."[75] "LET'S DRIVE COMMUNISM OUT OF OREGON," urged DeCicco's statement in the *Voter's Pamphlet*.[76] The results of the election clearly indicated the waning influence of conservatives in the party. Sweetland carried every county in the state, defeating DeCicco by a vote of over two to one.

---

[73] *Oregon Democrat* 20 (Feb. 1952), p. 3.

[74] *Ibid.*

[75] *Ibid.*, p. 17.

[76] *Official Voter's Pamphlet for the Democratic Party Primary Nominating Election, May 16, 1952* (Salem: Secretary of State, 1952) no. 29, p. 3.

After seizing the two highest posts of power in the party, liberals intensified their campaign to further lessen the influence of old-guard Democrats. Between his election in February and the Democratic primary in May, Morgan worked closely with Sweetland to recruit strong liberal candidates for the election of 1952. Aside from four representatives, Oregon was to elect three major state officers: secretary of state, state treasurer, and attorney general. With the exception of candidates for representative in the Second and Fourth Congressional Districts, Sweetland and Morgan succeeded in fielding an attractive slate of liberals. Among this group were Edith Starrett Green, who ran for secretary of state, and Robert Y. Thornton, who sought the office of attorney general. Green and Thornton ran unopposed in the primary; other liberals captured the nominations for state treasurer and representative in the First and Third Congressional Districts.

Not content with simply recruiting strong candidates for major offices, Morgan decided that the party had to advance presentable candidates for lesser office. With this in mind, Morgan and Volney Martin, secretary of the State Central Committee, decided to oppose actively the reelection of State Senator Thomas R. Mahoney in 1952.[77]

Mahoney, who won renomination in the Democratic primary of 1952, was a veteran of seven terms in the state senate from Multnomah County. As an old-guard Democrat he had repeatedly opposed the attempt of liberal Democrats to restructure the party. Moreover, as a member of the state legislature, Mahoney had clashed with Richard Neuberger, Robert Holmes, Phil Brady, and other liberal Democratic legislators on a number of issues.[78] Neuberger prepared and circulated a petition among Democratic members of the state senate repudiating Mahoney as a Democrat.[79] In 1951, Mahoney was selected by Oregon newsmen as one of the five worst state senators, a form of recognition that gave liberal Democrats another reason for purging him from the ranks of the party.[80]

Under Oregon law, the chairman of the State Central Committee was required to sign the statements of Democratic candidates which appeared in the *Voter's Pamphlet*. But when Mahoney submitted his statement, Morgan refused to approve it on the grounds that Mahoney had falsified his record as a state legislator.[81] "His

[77] Interview with Howard Morgan, Apr. 13, 1968.

[78] *Oregon Democrat* 18 (Jan. 1951), pp. 9-10, 26-28; *ibid.* 19 (Sept. 1951), p. 5.

[79] Richard Neuberger to E. B. MacNaughton, Mar. 31, 1951; *ibid.*, Apr. 24, 1951, Neuberger Papers.

[80] *Oregon Democrat* 19 (Sept. 1951), p. 14.

[81] Among other things, Mahoney claimed that he had opposed loyalty oaths

entire statement implies that he is a responsible and respected legislator," said Morgan, "when in truth his espousal of gambling legislation . . . made him a leading source of embarrassment to the party." Angered by Morgan's public denunciation of his record, Mahoney retorted: "Just fine and dandy. I want no votes from commies, fellow travelers and leftists."[82]

The efforts of Morgan and Sweetland to improve the caliber of Democratic candidates brought the party some political rewards in the election of 1952. Although Republicans carried the state in the presidential election, won all four contests for representative, and captured the positions of secretary of state and state treasurer, Robert Y. Thornton won election as attorney general. Even though Democrats captured only one major office, Morgan and Sweetland saw the election as a victory for liberal leadership of the party. Thornton, who carried 26 of the state's 36 counties, was the first Democrat since 1892 elected to the post of attorney general. At the same time, Edith Green ran the strongest race for secretary of state since Democrats had last won that office in 1874. Equally important and most satisfying, Morgan was successful in his attempt to purge Mahoney. In his bid for reelection, Mahoney finished last in a field of ten candidates for state senator in Multnomah County.[83] After his defeat Mahoney exclaimed: "Morgan and Sweetland have wrecked the Democratic Party—and they can have it."[84]

Liberal Democrats emerged from the election even more optimistic because of the developments in the Republican camp. Less than a month before the November election, Republican Senator Wayne Morse formally announced his support of Adlai Stevenson, the Democratic presidential candidate, and shortly thereafter resigned from the Republican Party. Liberal Democrats expressed elation over Morse's endorsement of Stevenson and his resignation from the G.O.P. "TO WAYNE MORSE . . . A CORDIAL WELCOME!," ran the caption on a lead editorial in the *Oregon Democrat*. After comparing Morse with such "principled liberals" as Robert M. La Follette, Gifford Pinchot, Theodore Roosevelt, and "the sainted George W. Norris," the magazine observed: "We have heard much small talk lately whether or not the Democratic Party would and should be hospitable to the ex-Republican. Of course the door is wide open, if and when he wishes to enter. Oregon

---

for Oregon school teachers, had the strong backing of labor, and supported appropriations for higher education. Portland *Oregonian*, Oct. 24, 1952, p. 18.

[82] *Ibid.*, p. 1. After achieving his purpose by publicly disavowing Mahoney, Morgan signed Mahoney's statement in the *Voter's Pamphlet*.

[83] Maure L. Goldschmidt, "The 1952 Elections In Oregon," *Western Political Quarterly* 6 (Mar. 1953), pp. 123-126.

[84] Quoted in Smith, *The Tiger in the Senate*, p. 209.

Democrats would be proud to merge behind this great liberal. When he is ready, we will welcome him to our lists."[85]

By the end of 1952, Liberal Democrats had passed a major point in their attempt to rebuild the party. Not only had they successfully concluded the battle with old-guard Democrats for control of the party, but Sweetland and Morgan had demonstrated that with attractive candidates the party could seriously threaten, if not break, the Republican hold on Oregon politics. If Senator Morse could be coaxed into the Democratic Party and other strong personalities attracted to the liberal cause, the future of the Democratic Party in Oregon appeared promising. "Democrats must prepare to resume power before long," exhorted Sweetland after the election of 1952. But, he warned, the interval before the election of 1954 "must be a period of planning, a period in which the Party itself is strengthened internally, a time to build new liberal leadership, which will itself give character and force to the Nation's oldest and greatest Party."[86] It was in this spirit of renewed hope that liberal Democrats looked forward to the election of 1954 and beyond.

[85] *Oregon Democrat* 20 (Nov. 1952), p. 5.
[86] *Ibid.* 20 (Dec. 1952-Jan. 1953), p. 4.

VII THE DEMOCRATIC PARTY AT FLOOD TIDE

Among the changes promised by the administration of Dwight D. Eisenhower in 1953 was a new natural resources policy, a matter of particular concern to the Democratic Party in Oregon. The concept of federal development and guardianship of the country's resources, a keystone of the New Deal, was threatened when the President referred to the expansion of the Tennessee Valley Authority as "creeping socialism." To Democrats in Oregon the threat became real with the selection of Governor Douglas McKay of Oregon as Secretary of the Interior.

After naming McKay to the Interior post the Republican administration proposed a new federal "partnership" formula in the development of hydroelectric power.[1] Under this plan, the government would finance flood control, irrigation, and navigational features of dams while private enterprise would underwrite power facilities and additional allocated costs. Private enterprise would then market the power.

The Eisenhower administration moved swiftly to develop its partnership program. In May 1953, McKay discarded a proposal before the federal government to build a multi-purpose dam in Hells Canyon on the Snake River. Instead, he recommended that the Idaho Power Company be permitted to construct three small dams in Hells Canyon under the partnership concept. This proposal immediately brought sharp criticism from Democrats in Oregon. "McKay's cynical knuckling down to the private power boys so soon after his assumption of office is a shock to many Oregonians," claimed the *Oregon Democrat*. Referring to McKay's plan for Hells Canyon, the magazine continued: "This is a decision to be

---

[1] Eisenhower asserted that the establishment of this new resource program "marked the close of an era. [It] liberated the Pacific Northwest from a theory which had failed." For Eisenhower's views on public power see Dwight D. Eisenhower, *The White House Years: Mandate for Change, 1953-1956* (Garden City, 1963), pp. 376-394.

made by the people and not by cowed bureaucrats! The battle lines have already been drawn!"[2] And indeed they were. The question of private vs. public power, in addition to other conservation policies supported by the Eisenhower administration and McKay, became the chief campaign issues of Democrats in 1954 and 1956. But unlike the 1930s and the years immediately following the Second World War when liberal Democrats campaigned on the issue of public power and lost, future political contests would favor them. By 1956, Democrats had drastically altered state politics and achieved their goal of giving Oregon a competitive two-party system.

Democrats knew they had a prime political issue. They also realized they needed effective spokesmen to dramatize that fact and attractive candidates to carry their standard in elections. In all of Oregon, probably in the whole country, the most talented and likely man to dramatize the issue and lead the state Democratic ticket to victory was Senator Wayne Morse. Recognizing this, one Democrat described Morse as "the most brilliant political orator in the state's history."[3]

At the time Morse bolted the Republican Party in 1952, the *Oregon Democrat* noted: "We cannot believe a realist like Wayne Morse will long remain suspended in space as an unattached 'Independent.' "[4] Morse, however, did remain officially unattached until 1955. In the interval between the fall of 1952 and Morse's decision formally to embrace the Democratic Party in February 1955, the leadership of the party engaged in a vigorous courtship of the Senator. Howard Morgan and Monroe Sweetland knew that Morse was immensely popular among the rank and file of the Democratic Party. They also believed that Morse could entice liberal Republicans into the Democratic fold, if not by change of party registration at least through support of the Democratic ticket in elections. Furthermore, because of the Senator's strong support from labor, Sweetland and Morgan saw Morse as a bridge by which labor might move to support the Democratic ticket as a whole.[5]

The drive to coax Morse into the party began at once. Through

---

[2] *Oregon Democrat* 21 (May 1953), p. 4.

[3] Richard Neuberger to Lewis Bergman, Jan. 22, 1954, Neuberger Papers.

[4] *Oregon Democrat* 20 (Dec. 1952-Jan. 1953), p. 12.

[5] Interview with Howard Morgan, Apr. 13, 1968; interview with Monroe Sweetland, Dec. 21, 1967. In 1950, conservative Republicans commissioned an opinion poll to determine Democratic and Republican support for Senators Morse and Cordon. The results showed that 89 per cent of the Democrats interviewed were satisfied with the record of Morse, whereas only 28 per cent of the Republicans interviewed approved of Morse's record. The figures for Senator Cordon were just the opposite. See Ernest G. Swigert to Robert W. Sawyer, Feb. 15, 1950, Sawyer Papers.

the pages of the *Oregon Democrat*, Sweetland showered words of praise and adulation on Morse. Referring to Morse's decision to renounce his membership in the Republican Party, Sweetland wrote: "In him the ancient ritual is performed again. A liberal Republican fights the good fight for labor, for peace, for the people against special privilege. But the barons of wealth and privilege consider the Republican Party their private club . . . So now Wayne Morse of Oregon joins the honored roll of Republicans who tried to be principled liberals within the political straight jacket."[6] Other editorials were equally glowing. Morse was declared to be "Oregon's man-of-the-year, and Number-1 national personality."[7]

While Sweetland was eulogizing Morse, Morgan set out to convince the Senator that he had enthusiastic and widespread support within the Democratic Party. In May 1953, Morgan invited Morse to speak at the annual Jefferson-Jackson banquet, an honor usually reserved for the most illustrious members of the party. Morse promptly accepted.[8] Speaking as an independent, Morse set the tone for the election of 1954. After labeling the partnership plan a "give-away" and a "sellout" to "the private utility monopoly," the Senator pointed a moral. "Some of my friends counsel me to speak softly about the political plundering of our natural resources . . . [but] when the House is being looted—do you serve the burglar cookies and cider? When you see a purse being snatched—do you calmly tell the culprit's admirers that he is a sterling fellow? No. You shout 'Stop Thief!' " Amid sustained applause, the Senator ended his speech with a promise to campaign in 1954 for those Democrats who possessed "political morality" and "humanitarian liberalism."[9]

Following Morse's rousing reception at the Jefferson-Jackson fete, Sweetland stated that the Senator "should now know . . . that he would be at home in the party of liberalism as he never has been during his former affiliation with the party of reaction. The next move is up to him."[10] Morse, however, insisted on remaining an independent.

If Morse was not yet ready to join the Democratic Party, Democrats nonetheless hoped that he would honor his pledge to support Democratic candidates actively in 1954. They recognized that the coming election would be an important test of how effective liberals had been in restructuring the party. At the same time, they believed

[6] *Oregon Democrat* 21 (Feb. 1953), p. 3.

[7] *Ibid.* 21 (May 1953), p. 1. For other complimentary editorials see *Oregon Democrat* 21 (Mar. 1953), pp. 24-26; 21 (June 1953), p. 4; 21 (Oct. 1953), p. 5.

[8] Interview with Howard Morgan, Apr. 13, 1968.

[9] *Oregon Democrat* 21 (June 1953), pp. 13-16.

[10] *Ibid.*, p. 4.

a strong Democratic showing might demonstrate to Morse the wisdom of being in the fold.

As the elections of 1954 approached, Democrats were at last solidly united. "Factional differences in Oregon Democracy are at an all-time low—in fact, there are none of the traditional splits and fissures which have enervated our Party solidarity in some past election years," announced Sweetland.[11] Proof of this fact appeared in the Democratic primary. With but one exception, Democrats had agreed on a slate of candidates before the primary, and consequently Democratic candidates ran unopposed.[12] The Democratic ticket for 1954 included State Senator Richard Neuberger as the senatorial candidate and Donnell Mitchell, Al Ullman, Edith Green, and Charles O. Porter for representatives in the First, Second, Third, and Fourth Congressional Districts. Only in their search for a gubernatorial candidate did Democrats fail to offer a formidable personality. Joseph K. Carson, Jr., an old-line Democrat who had been mayor of Portland during the New Deal (1933-1941), became the "common consent" candidate for governor because the party had a difficult time recruiting for that office. All Democratic candidates in 1954 endorsed a federal dam at Hells Canyon and attacked the conservation policies of the Eisenhower administration.

Democrats emerged from the primary united; Republicans were not so fortunate. Two races in particular seemed to demonstate that Oregon Republicans were becoming less tolerant of individual differences within the party. In one contest, Tom McCall challenged veteran representative Homer D. Angell for nomination in the Third Congressional District. A member of Congress from 1939, Angell had repeatedly won reelection in a Democratic district because of his liberal stand on labor legislation and public power. In 1954 Angell was the only member of Oregon's Republican delegation in Congress who advocated a federal dam at Hells Canyon. McCall, who defended the administration's partnership plan, defeated Angell but in the process retired one of the Republican Party's "showcase" liberals and, as subsequent events proved, ended the Republican monopoly in the Third District.

---

[11] *Ibid.* 22 (Mar. 1954), p. 3.

[12] The one exception was in the Third Congressional District. When Monroe Sweetland disclosed his decision to seek nomination in that district, it provoked a minor party crisis. Neither Howard Morgan nor Richard Neuberger wanted Sweetland to run because of his Socialist background. With McCarthyism at its peak, Neuberger and Morgan thought Sweetland's candidacy would endanger other races. Sweetland eventually withdrew, and Edith Green became the party's candidate. Interview with Monroe Sweetland, Dec. 21, 1967; interview with Howard Morgan, Apr. 13, 1968.

The second struggle in the Republican primary centered on the gubernatorial nomination. The incumbent, Paul Patterson, lined up with Eisenhower's power policy, while Secretary of State Earl T. Newbry supported a federal dam for Hells Canyon. McKay, who felt obliged to defend the partnership program, intervened in the primary and campaigned for Patterson, a circumstance that prompted Newbry's supporters to denounce McKay for "disrupting" the Oregon G.O.P. Patterson, like McCall, won nomination, but the primary struggle left a residue of resentment in Republican ranks that promised an even more serious split in 1956.[13]

With the nomination of McCall and Patterson, Republicans rounded out a slate of candidates who staunchly defended the power program of the Republican administration. Consequently, the major issue in the election of 1954 was clear-cut. Republicans prepared to do battle for the new power program while Democrats stood adamantly opposed to it.

The key political battle in 1954 centered on the contest for senator. "Both parties regarded it as the heart of the election," one political commentator has noted, and "to an unusual degree other candidates tended to cluster about the senatorial contestants."[14] The incumbent Republican Senator, Guy Cordon, seemed especially vulnerable to Democrats. First appointed to the senate in 1944 after the death of Charles McNary, Cordon over the years had served the conservative Republican cause faithfully. In 1953, he welcomed the shift in power policy and, in addition, played a major role in the enactment of an administration bill to transfer rights to offshore oil lands to various states on the Pacific Coast and the Gulf of Mexico. Cordon's conservatism and his defense of Eisenhower's conservation policies would, Democrats hoped, bring his defeat.

Richard Neuberger, the Democratic senatorial candidate, was undoubtedly the most attractive and best-known personality the party had in its ranks in 1954. As a journalist and free-lance writer, Neuberger began a literary career in the 1930s that eventually brought him national recognition as a reporter and interpreter of the Pacific Northwest. As the subject of his articles and books, Neuberger frequently selected conservation or politics. As a champion of public power, he had long supported a Columbia Valley Authority, and as a warm admirer of Franklin D. Roosevelt and

---

[13] For Republican division over the partnership plan in the primary of 1954, see Franklyn D. Mahar, "Douglas McKay and Issues of Power Development in Oregon, 1953-1956" (unpublished doctoral thesis, University of Oregon, 1968), pp. 283-287.

[14] John M. Swarthout, "The 1954 Election In Oregon," *Western Political Quarterly* 7 (Dec. 1954), p. 622.

the New Deal, he was decidedly liberal in his politics.[15] Actually, Neuberger's interest in politics extended beyond his writing. In 1934, he became an adviser to Peter Zimmerman, independent liberal candidate for governor of Oregon, and in 1936 he attempted, unsuccessfully, to win election to the Oregon state senate. Finally, in 1940, he was elected to the lower house of the state legislature but shortly thereafter resigned to enlist in the Army. After the war, he worked with liberal Democrats to rebuild the party. In 1948, he was elected to the state senate; two years later his wife, Maurine, joined him in the legislature as a member of the lower house.

An articulate speaker and skilled campaigner, Neuberger outperformed Cordon from the beginning. Neuberger took Cordon to task for his espousal of partnership and of the tidelands oil bill, both of which he described as "giveaways." Although this became the major theme of Neuberger's campaign, he also attacked Cordon's isolationist position in foreign affairs. Cordon, explained Neuberger, opposed NATO and foreign aid while favoring enactment of the Bricker amendment, a measure designed to lessen the president's power in foreign relations.[16]

The thrust of Neuberger's oratory put Cordon on the defensive for the balance of the campaign. Cordon's efforts to refute Neuberger's charges were hampered by his abhorrence of speechmaking. Cordon's so-called "passion for anonymity" was so successful that, according to one writer, he was "virtually unknown to the public at large, even in his home state of Oregon."[17]

If Cordon was reluctant to exchange vigorous political blows with Neuberger in the campaign, the national Republican Party was prepared to do battle for him, as well as defend the Eisenhower power program. During the campaign, Vice-President Nixon, Speaker of the House Joseph Martin, and eight Republican senators stumped the state for Cordon. The assertion that Cordon was virtually unknown on Capitol Hill seemed to be borne out when Martin, urging Oregonians to reelect Cordon, referred to the incumbent as "My friend, Si Gordon."[18]

Cordon's assistance from national Republican figures was balanced on the Democratic side by Senator Morse who entered the campaign on behalf of Neuberger. Morse's support of Neuberger was not altogether unexpected. The two men had maintained a

---

[15] See Richard Neuberger and Stephen B. Kahn, *Integrity: The Life of George W. Norris* (New York, 1937); Neuberger, *Adventures In Politics: We Go to the Legislature* (New York, 1954).

[16] Swarthout, "The 1954 Election In Oregon," pp. 620-625; Smith, *The Tiger in the Senate*, pp. 216-218; Mahar, "Douglas McKay and the Issues of Power Development in Oregon," pp. 287-294.

[17] Smith, *The Tiger in the Senate*, p. 211.

[18] Swarthout, "The 1954 Election In Oregon," p. 622.

long, if sometimes edgy, friendship.[19] Before and after Morse bolted the Republican Party, Neuberger wrote several articles about the Senator for national magazines, some of which, but not all, were complimentary.[20] As early as December 1953, Morse had urged Neuberger to run against Cordon.[21] Once the campaign got under way, Morse used his powerful oratory to support his protegé. According to one estimate, Morse contributed "sixty-one ripsnorting speeches" in which he characterized Cordon as "Mr. Giveaway."[22] Morse also secured campaign funds for Neuberger, both from the Democratic National Committee and from private sources in the East.[23]

Other Democratic candidates in 1954 coordinated their campaigns with Neuberger and echoed his allegation that Republicans encouraged exploitation rather than conservation by supporting partnership and the transfer of offshore oil lands. To strengthen this charge, the *Oregon Democrat* dedicated its issue of September 1954 to the memory of Republican Senator Charles McNary. "Some of our more partisan readers may wonder that a Democratic newsmagazine take time out in the midst of a heated campaign to memorialize a Republican U.S. senator of years gone by. We do this," explained the magazine, "because the Republicans have profaned the fine tradition of a liberal Republican." The main point of the *Oregon Democrat's* argument was that the Republican Party of Oregon had betrayed "the bi-partisan power policy which McNary had fathered, and which had done the Northwest great

---

[19] Neuberger first made the acquaintance of Morse as an undergraduate at the University of Oregon (1931-1934). Morse, who at that time was Dean of the School of Law, urged Neuberger to enroll as a pre-law student in the fall of 1934. Unhappily, Neuberger neglected the study of the law, so much so that Dean Morse felt obliged to fail him in a course on criminal law. On another occasion, however, Morse came to his defense when Neuberger was accused of cheating on a legal bibliography. According to one account, Morse intervened in the case and saved Neuberger from expulsion. Smith, *The Tiger in the Senate*, pp. 333-339. See also Morse to Neuberger, Apr. 13, 1933; *ibid.*, Sept. 8, 1939; *ibid.*, Nov. 26, 1940; Morse to Russ Sackett, Nov. 21, 1950, Neuberger Papers.

[20] See, for example, Richard L. Neuberger, "Wayne Morse: Republican Gadfly," *American Mercury* 65 (July 1947), pp. 16-24; Neuberger, "Morse vs. Morse," *The Nation* 170 (Jan. 14, 1950), pp. 29-30; Neuberger, "The Strange Story of Senator Morse," *American Magazine* 155 (Apr. 1953), pp. 26-27, 82-88; Neuberger, "What Will Happen To Wayne Morse?," *Frontier* 4 (June 1953), pp. 7-9, 15.

[21] Morse to Neuberger, Dec. 11, 1953, Neuberger Papers.

[22] Smith, *The Tiger in the Senate*, p. 217.

[23] Morse to Neuberger, Apr. 14, 1954; Neuberger to Morse, Apr. 17, 1954; Morse to Stephen Mitchell, June 28, 1954; Morse to Neuberger, June 30, 1954; Morse to Morris S. Novik, Nov. 22, 1954; Morse to Joseph Keenan, Nov. 22, 1954; Morse to James L. McDevitt, Nov. 22, 1954; Neuberger to Morris S. Novik, Nov. 30, 1954, Neuberger Papers.

good."[24] Republicans had thereby reversed their position on power, and now Oregon Democrats claimed the mantle of McNary's progressivism, dedication to conservation, and advocacy of power development for all the people. In the same vein, the Democratic Party inserted a rhetorical question in the *Voter's Pamphlet:* "Is there a Charles McNary, a George Joseph, a Julius Meier, a Wayne Morse left in the Republican Party? Not one. Not even an imitation of one."[25]

The balloting in November resulted in a stunning Republican defeat. Neuberger defeated Cordon by the narrow margin of 2,462 votes—one vote per precinct—to become Oregon's first Democratic senator in forty years. In the Third Congressional District, Edith Green won election over Tom McCall, recapturing a seat last won by Democrats in 1936. Democrats also elected their first Commissioner of Labor in Oregon history, and increased their representation in the lower house of the Legislative Assembly from 11 to 25 and in the state senate from 4 to 6. The Democratic gubernatorial candidate, Joseph Carson, Jr., was soundly defeated by Republican Paul Patterson, but most of the Democratic candidates for representative, while failing to unseat incumbent Republicans, lost by smaller margins than Democratic candidates had in 1952.[26]

"Years of hard work went into the day of triumph," explained Sweetland after the election. "Oregon Democrats, conditioned to alibis, explanations and 'progress reports' after each Republican victory, scarcely knew how to react to the dramatic events of November." On a serious note, Sweetland reaffirmed the party's dedication to programmatic politics: "We have never wanted victory for victory's sake. We are a Party which is in politics to achieve a program, and getting our men and women elected is only our starting point."[27]

The momentum built up by Democratic victories in 1954 carried

[24] *Oregon Democrat* 22 (Sept. 1954), pp. 3-4.

[25] *Official Voter's Pamphlet for the Regular General Election November 2, 1954* (Salem: Secretary of State, 1954) no. 1, p. 32.

[26] "Oregon Democrats owe a lot to Joe Carson in this year of victory," said Sweetland after the election. "He was an 'old-time' Democrat known and liked by the traditional Democrats now so heavily out-numbered by the new and young. On a ticket characterized by 'liberals,' Joe Carson held in line conservatives who would otherwise have been the particular object of Republican blandishments—yet Mr. Carson fought the good fight on the power issue as valiantly and forcefully as anyone." *Oregon Democrat* 22 (Nov. 1954), p. 5.

[27] *Oregon Democrat* 22 (Nov. 1954), p. 3. That programmatic politics was the central concern of Democrats in Oregon was again illustrated in 1956 when Morse ran for reelection. Governor G. Mennen Williams of Michigan campaigned for Morse in Oregon and used the "Michigan Declaration," perhaps the best statement of programmatic politics, as the theme of his addresses. See *Oregon Democrat* 24 (June 1956), pp. 8-9.

the party to a high point of political resurgence in 1956. Senator Morse, who privately decided to cast off his cloak of independence after the primary election of 1954, officially registered as a Democrat in February 1955.[28] In a speech to the Multnomah County Democratic Central Committee following his registration as a Democrat, Morse sounded the opening gun for the elections of 1956. After announcing that he would seek reelection on the Democratic ticket, the Senator assailed the Republican Party for its conservation policy and, in particular, the "sellout" at Hells Canyon.[29]

While the Democratic Party approached the election of 1956 stronger than ever before, the Republican Party showed symptoms of political paralysis. Shaken by G.O.P. reverses in 1954, Representative Harris Ellsworth noted with alarm: "I'll be darned if I know what is going to happen so far as the Republican Party of Oregon is concerned. This far about all that is happening is a lot of talk. It is a fact, however, that . . . we are going to continue taking serious defeats . . . unless there is a drastic change in the way the Republicans and the Republican organization do things."[30] Wendell Wyatt, chairman of the Republican State Central Committee, observed that because Oregon Republicans were faced "with a re-activated Democratic Party," the Central Committee found it necessary to hire professional precinct organizers. Unless the party improved its organization quickly, said Wyatt, "It will be too late and we will fail [in 1956]."[31]

It was amid such gloomy forecasts that Oregon Republicans cast about for a candidate to oppose Morse. As in 1954, Republicans and Democrats alike knew that the principal political contest in 1956 would be the senatorial race. At first it was agreed that Governor Patterson would run, but his sudden death in January 1956 left the party in a quandary. Between Patterson's death in January and the deadline for filing in March, three Republicans anounced as senatorial candidates. Among this group, the most attractive was liberal Republican Philip S. Hitchcock, former state senator and director of public relations for Lewis and Clark College. But the Eisenhower administration and conservative Republican leaders

---

[28] Although party leaders repeatedly urged Morse to become a Democrat before 1954, they decided once the election was at hand that it would be better for Morse to remain independent through the election. "Your continued exposé of the fallacies of this contradictory, reactionary Administration," wrote Sweetland to Morse, "is our strongest single trump in this campaign. I guess I'm urging that for the time being you maintain your Independent status as by far the most effective tactic—probably the soundest, too." Sweetland to Morse, Feb. 18, 1954, Neuberger Papers.

[29] *Oregon Democrat* 23 (Feb. 1955), pp. 8-9, 18-21.

[30] Harris Ellsworth to Herb Cox, Jan. 7, 1955, Ellsworth Papers.

[31] Wendell Wyatt to Ellsworth, July 20, 1955, *ibid.*

in Oregon, determined to defeat Morse for his defection from the party and his attack on the partnership plan, apparently decided that the party needed a candidate stronger than any who had announced. After consulting only a few Republicans in Oregon, the administration prevailed upon Secretary of the Interior McKay to run. At first reluctant, McKay agreed when he was assured he would face no opposition in the primary and would receive full financial support. McKay flew to Oregon on March 9, the last day for filing in the primary, and announced his candidacy.[32]

Unfortunately for McKay, and to the embarrassment of the administration, Republicans in Oregon did not greet his candidacy with unanimous enthusiasm. In spite of pressure from the Republican National Committee, Hitchcock and the other two candidates refused to withdraw from the primary. The confusion resulting from McKay's last-minute entry into the senatorial race is illustrated by the remark of former Republican Representative Lowell Stockman: "I think Mr. McKay couldn't have started out to be elected Senator on a dumber note." Observing that Oregon Republicans resented the interference of the administration in state politics, Stockman added: "The rank and file is highly confused with his method of entry into the race. Was he pushed?"[33] Charles Sprague, editor of the *Oregon Statesman*, also disapproved of the manner in which McKay entered the senatorial contest. "We think Hitchcock should stay in the race," said Sprague, "both because of his splendid qualifications and to repudiate the notion that Oregon is a province of the GOP GHQ."[34] Although McKay won nomination, it was by the surprisingly close margin of 24,000 votes, only 45 per cent of the primary vote. Hitchcock, who ran second, later endorsed McKay, but this did not restore party harmony. Many of Hitchcock's supporters remained unreconciled to McKay's candidacy, a circumstance that produced division in Republican ranks during the senatorial election.[35]

By contrast, Oregon Democrats once more enjoyed unity in 1956. With Morse leading the ticket, the party nominated its strongest group of candidates.[36] Edith Green sought reelection in

[32] A public opinion poll taken in Oregon at the direction of Thomas E. Dewey indicated that McKay could defeat Morse. For the maneuvering of national Republican leaders that led to McKay's candidacy see Sherman Adams, *Firsthand Report: The Story of the Eisenhower Administration* (New York, 1961), pp. 235-237.

[33] Lowell Stockman to Harris Ellsworth, Mar. 20, 1956, Ellsworth Papers.

[34] Salem *Oregon Statesman*, Mar. 15, 1956, p. 4.

[35] Mahar, "Douglas McKay and the Issues of Power Development in Oregon, 1953-1956," pp. 303-310.

[36] Morse encountered only token opposition in the primary, winning 80 per cent of the vote.

the Third Congressional District, while Jason Lee, Al Ullman, and Charles Porter won nomination for representative in the First, Second, and Fourth Congressional Districts. For their gubernatorial nominee, Democrats chose State Senator Robert Holmes, unquestionably the best candidate the party had advanced for that office in the postwar years. The ticket also included Robert Y. Thornton, who sought reelection as attorney general, and Monroe Sweetland, who ran for secretary of state.

The election of 1956 featured a presidential contest, but the Morse-McKay clash occupied the political spotlight in Oregon. In both the nature of the issues and the style of campaigning, the senatorial race of 1956 was a rerun of the Neuberger-Cordon contest. Morse opened his campaign early and immediately put McKay on the defensive. The policies McKay devised and carried out as Secretary of the Interior, especially partnership for Hells Canyon and the tidelands oil bill, were declared by Morse to be unadulterated "giveaways." Morse also accused McKay of allowing the Al Sarena Mining Company illegally to acquire title to 475 acres of timber in the Rogue River National Forest in southern Oregon. Morse frequently broadened his campaign by discussing foreign policy and assorted domestic issues, but the major theme of his campaign was the allegation that McKay was a tool of private utilities and special interests who sought to plunder natural resources.[37]

McKay was a poor match for Morse. A student of his career as Secretary of the Interior has evaluated his political talents as mediocre at best. "McKay was at his best being a local politician—just 'good ol' Doug,' a simple, straight-forward, conservative man who wanted to do things within the framework of the party organization."[38] As a faithful party man he answered the call of the administration to run for senator, but he failed to refute effectively Morse's charges of "giveaway." Earlier he had expressed bewilderment over opposition in Oregon to the Eisenhower power program. Writing to a friend, McKay noted, "over the United States the President's power program is overwhelmingly popular but in my home state some of the public power boys have been giving me a hard time."[39] Reducing the issue of public vs. private power to simple terms, he declared the question to be one of "collectivism on the one side versus Americanism on the other."[40]

[37] John M. Swarthout, "The 1956 Election In Oregon," *Western Political Quarterly* 10 (Mar. 1957), pp. 148-149.

[38] Mahar, "Douglas McKay and the Issues of Power Development in Oregon, 1953-1956," p. 326.

[39] Douglas McKay to Rex Ellis, May 28, 1954, Douglas McKay Papers (University of Oregon, Eugene).

[40] McKay to Cecil L. Edwards, Mar. 22, 1954, *ibid*.

Even though McKay had the active support of President Eisenhower, Vice-President Nixon, Secretary of the Interior Fred A. Seaton, and a contingent of Republican senators, he floundered in the campaign. Instead of a frank discussion of his position on the issues of the day, and most especially the Eisenhower power program, McKay focused his campaign around the personality of Morse and his defection from the Republican Party. The partnership plan for Hells Canyon was not an issue, said McKay, because on the power question "most people don't care too much about how they get it so long as they get it."[41] Speaking in Eugene, McKay asserted "The issues don't amount to anything. It's the votes that count."[42]

Following the lead of the Morse-McKay contest, Democratic congressional candidates ran a coordinated campaign in which they pinned the "giveaway" epithet on their Republican opponents. Senator Richard Neuberger and his wife, Maurine, played an active part in the campaign, appearing on behalf of Morse and other Democratic candidates over the state.[43]

On November 7, 1956, Democrats found cause to rejoice. Although Eisenhower carried the state in the presidential election and Democrats lost the races for secretary of state and state treasurer, the party won an unprecedented victory. Morse defeated McKay by over 61,000 votes, winning almost as great a per cent of the total vote as Eisenhower. Democrats won three of the four races for representative, Robert Holmes was elected governor, Robert Thornton was reelected as attorney general, and Democrats won control of the state legislature for the first time since 1878.

Democratic victories in 1954 and 1956 reflect both short-term partisan forces and larger trends in Oregon politics. Central to both were the character of the issues, the caliber of candidates, the state of party organization, and the nature of Republican opposition. All of these elements, in varying degrees, contributed to the party's success.

The question of hydroelectric development, an issue in most Oregon elections since the New Deal, was undoubtedly a significant factor in Democratic success. Whatever the merits of the partnership plan, Republicans, and especially Douglas McKay, did a poor job in refuting Democratic allegations that the new power policy represented a surrender to special interests. And, in a more

---

[41] Mahar, "Douglas McKay and the Issues of Power Development in Oregon, 1953-1956," p. 317.

[42] Eugene *Register-Guard*, Sept. 22, 1956, p. 1.

[43] For a discussion of congressional and state races in 1956 see Swarthout, "The 1956 Election In Oregon," pp. 142-150; Burton, "Charles O. Porter: Embattled Liberal," pp. 43-48.

general sense, there was more than political propaganda in Democratic assertions that Oregon Republicans of the mid-1950s had abandoned Charles McNary's bipartisan approach to power development. That Republican leaders came to realize this was demonstrated in 1958 when Republican Governor Mark Hatfield joined Democratic Senator Richard Neuberger in a show of bipartisan support for creation of a regional power corporation to replace the Bonneville Power Administration. In that same year Herbert Lundy, political columnist for the Portland *Oregonian,* announced that the Republican Party "is going to stand by its guns and make it clear, at long last, that the privately owned utilities no longer have a dominant voice in Oregon Republican campaign policies. This stand may cost candidates and the party some contributions. But it is the best thing that has happened to the Oregon GOP in modern times."[44]

By casting themselves in the role of nonpartisan champions of power development for all the people, Neuberger in 1954 and Morse in 1956, as well as other Democratic candidates, resurrected the style of politics Democrats had practiced during the progressive era. But it was not only on the power issue that Democrats made such appeals. Through the adoption of programmatic politics, Democrats argued that such things as the creation of a junior college for Portland, federal aid to education, reapportionment of the state legislature, and the establishment of a permanent F.E.P.C. were in the interest of the community. This approach to politics, in a state conditioned to nonpartisanship through the progressive heritage, was an essential ingredient to Democratic success.

The impact of issues often depends on the effectiveness of the spokesmen who develop them. In Wayne Morse, Richard Neuberger, Edith Green, Robert Holmes and others, Democrats found a group of candidates who were more articulate and attractive than any the party had advanced since the progressive era. Sometimes their appeal was strengthened by the relative weakness of their Republican opponents. Certainly the contrast was sharp between Neuberger and Cordon, Morse and McKay, and Charles Porter and Harris Ellsworth. To the extent that personality plays a role in determining votes, Democrats were clearly favored.

In addition to effective issues and good candidates, the Democratic victories of 1954 and 1956 were the result of work at the grass roots, both in organizing the party and registering eligible

---

[44] Portland *Oregonian,* June 6, 1958, p. 26. In 1956 Oran Bronson, public relations officer for Portland Gas and Electric Company, joined McKay's campaign staff. His appointment, however, was not widely known nor announced to the press. See Bob Grant to Harris Ellsworth, Aug. 12, 1956, Ellsworth Papers.

voters. By 1954, the party had well organized Central Committees in 32 of the state's 36 counties, and beyond that a network of efficient precinct organizations.[45] In 1950, the Democratic registration, for the first time in the state's history, exceeded that of Republicans. In 1954, Democrats claimed a majority in registration in half of Oregon's counties, and by 1956 the party had increased that ratio to almost two-thirds.[46]

A further and perhaps more fundamental explanation for Democratic ascendancy in state politics by 1956 is found in the larger political trends in Oregon history. The fact that Republicans had dominated state politics for most of the twentieth century has led some political commentators to describe Oregon as "The Vermont of the West." But the Republican Party of Oregon never possessed ideological or organizational unity. As was the case in the Democratic Party of the South, a two- and sometimes three-party system existed under the Republican label. A rough division between what might be termed conservatives and progressives was clearly evident on such issues as reform at the turn of the century and public power in the twenties and thirties. Democrats were sometimes aided by Republican divisions, as in the progressive era, but as the minority party in state politics they were unable to change Oregon's so-called one-party system. During the New Deal, of course, they were presented with an unprecedented opportunity to reshape state politics, but internal divisions prevented their success.

After the Second World War, however, a group of young Democrats set out to make the party. Building on the economic and demographic changes that occurred during the war, they overthrew the party's conservative leadership and transformed the Democratic Party into a vigorous spokesman for liberalism. Having done that, they created a political organization in which liberal Republicans could be at home. Responding to the postwar reorientation of the Democratic Party, the Republican leadership moved to the right, at least temporarily, and widened the ideological gap between the two parties.[47] Consequently, just as Senator

---

[45] *Oregon Democrat* 22 (June 1954), p. 22; 22 (July 1954), pp. 12-13.

[46] Between 1950 and 1956 party registration fluctuated a good deal. The figures are as follows: 1950, 378,357 D to 361,158 R; 1952, 416,589 D to 421,681 R; 1954, 402,283 D to 404,694 R; 1956, 450,122 D to 413,220 R. See *Oregon Democrat* 22 (Oct. 1954), p. 15; 24 (Oct. 1956), pp. 12-13; Swarthout, "The 1956 Election In Oregon," p. 143.

[47] By purging Homer Angell in 1954 because of his position on hydroelectric development, for example, Republican leaders deprived the party of labor support in the Third Congressional District. "There is no question but that Oregon Republicanism has come dangerously close in late years to control by a few men," argued one political analyst in 1956. "Sometimes known as the

Morse moved from the Republican to the Democratic Party, his two conservative Democratic opponents in the senatorial elections of 1944 and 1950 moved to the Republican Party. Transfer of party allegiance also took place among the rank and file. Earlier, when liberals fought with conservatives for control of the Democratic Party, most shifts in registration involved Democrats who became Republicans. But by 1954, this trend had been reversed. In that year, 62 per cent of those changing party affiliation moved from the Republican to the Democratic Party.[48]

Democrats altered the Oregon political scene by advantageous use of local and regional issues, selection of attractive candidates, and detailed party organization; but their success in 1956 was also the result, in part, of a retreat of the Republican Party to conservatism. This move polarized the position of the two parties, and led to widespread realignment of individual allegiances. The combination of these positive and negative forces brought the political fortunes of the Oregon Democratic Party to flood tide in 1956.

'Arlington Club Crowd,' less than a dozen of them have succeeded with some regularity in dictating party policy and hand-picking the party's candidates for major office." See Swarthout, "The 1956 Election In Oregon," p. 143.

[48] *Oregon Democrat* 22 (Oct. 1954), p. 12.

Epilogue

Following the election of 1956, political commentators in Oregon were agreed that the state had undergone decided political change. Dramatizing their conclusions were not only the unprecedented victories of the Democratic Party, but also the pronounced pessimism of the G.O.P. Almost visibly shaken by defeat, the councils of the Republican Party were marked by confusion and dissension. Seriously divided, and virtually without leadership, the once dominant G.O.P. was momentarily afflicted with political atrophy.

By contrast, Democrats were sanguine about continued victories in Oregon politics. Some were even euphoric, believing that a political millennium had come into being. After several decades as Oregon's minority party, Democrats had demonstrated that state politics was no longer the special preserve of Republicans. United in victory, they assumed that this happy state of party affairs would continue.

Yet the years after 1956 brought Democrats neither unqualified political success nor a durable unity. By the late 1960s, it was obvious that the Democratic flood tide of 1956 had ebbed considerably; some argued it had ebbed to the point of no return, at least in the predictable future. There was ample, if not conclusive, evidence to support this gloomy forecast.

Since the early 1950s, the Democratic Party had steadily increased its majority of registered voters, so that by 1969 the favorable margin stood at over 100,000. Nevertheless, Democrats lost the three gubernatorial elections between 1958 and 1966, and suffered a general erosion of electoral support in other contests. In 1969, Republicans held most major national and state offices, including both of Oregon's Senate seats and two of the state's four congressional positions.

To some, such a decline in relative power reflected the permanent reestablishment of Republican hegemony in Oregon. This view, however plausible in the late 1960s, ignored the fact that the diminution of Democratic power occurred gradually and may have been the product of short-term partisan trends which favored the Republicans, trends that do not necessarily foretell the shape of the future. Democrats, for example, retained control of the State Legislative Assembly until 1964, and held a numerical majority in the senate between 1958 and 1969.[1] On the national level, Democrats remained in possession of both Senate seats until 1966 and did not lose control to Republicans until the defeat of Senator Wayne Morse in 1968. There were also some victories. In 1964 Democrat Robert Straub won the office of state treasurer, last won by his party in 1948, and was reelected in 1968. Moreover, Democrats held the office of attorney general until 1968, and two of the three Democrats elected as representatives in 1956 still held office in 1969.

The most striking aspect of Oregon politics after 1956 was the persistence of traditional patterns. This was true regardless of the long-range significance of political trends of the 1960s. The most enduring and recognizable of these Oregon patterns in the twentieth century was the political independence of both Republican and Democratic candidates and the weakness of formal party organization. In reconstructing their party after the Second World War, Democrats appeared to depart from this pattern. Through teamwork born of programmatic politics, liberal Democrats overthrew the party's old guard, built party organization at the local and state level, and successfully challenged the Oregon G.O.P. Ironically, once victory was achieved, the Democrats almost immediately fell to quarreling among themselves, and allowed party organization to wither. In fact, at the heart of Democratic difficulties in the first few years after 1956 were a number of bitter and open disputes among the coterie of leaders who had reshaped the party after the war. Some of these Democrats—most notably those elected to high state and national office in 1956—exhibited a political independence more appropriate for members of a minority party. Unaccustomed to their new role as representatives of the party in power, they seemed unable to operate within the framework of a party or make a permanent break with Oregon's tradition of political independence. Such recidivistic behavior frequently caused divisions which led to the formation of personal followings within the party. This had a demoralizing influence on organization and on unity of purpose.

---

[1] Although Democrats maintained control of the senate, that body was dominated by a coalition of conservative Democrats and Republicans. In 1960 Walter Pearson and Thomas Mahoney, old-guard Democrats who opposed the building of a liberal party, won election to the state senate from Multnomah County. See John M. Swarthout, "The 1960 Election In Oregon," *Western Political Quarterly*, 14, part 2 (Mar. 1961), pp. 355-364; Swarthout and Gervais, "Oregon: Political Experiment Station," p. 319.

It seems incongruous that a group of men motivated by programmatic politics, even in victory, became victims of what often appeared to be petty bickering and vindictive character assassination. But when the cast of characters is considered, the collapse of party solidarity is more easily understood. The leaders of the revived Democratic Party were combative, aggressive, politically independent individuals, a volatile set who found cooperation in opposition to a common foe necessary and desirable. In the heat of political battle with old-guard Democrats and Republicans, liberal Democrats had little time to examine their own differences. But differences of opinion on party policy and other matters did exist and later found expression in intraparty quarrels.

The fact that Monroe Sweetland, Howard Morgan, Richard Neuberger, and Wayne Morse surrendered to common suspicions that apparently ignored or denied programmatic values did not invalidate their agreement on the general goals of this approach to politics, though it obviously complicated any such agreement. Between 1946 and 1956, programmatic objectives on the state level were easily defined. After 1956 they were less obvious. In the case of Senators Morse and Neuberger, the view from Washington added a new dimension. Even though charges of self-aggrandizement and egocentrism were leveled at Morse in his celebrated quarrel with Neuberger between 1958 and 1960, it may be that their dispute partly followed on different views of how best to practice programmatic politics on the national level. In the Senate, as one historian noted, "Neuberger moved increasingly toward nonpartisan support of the Eisenhower administration, whereas Morse emphasized his new Democratic loyalties."[2] There were other issues, perhaps more important, which led to the final break between Morse and Neuberger, but these issues did not turn on a denial of programmatic politics on the part of either man.[3]

Intraparty feuds after 1956 did not immediately result in widespread Democratic losses at the polls, but they eventually tended to discredit the party. By the time Democrats began to suffer political reversals, the party faced additional problems, chief among which were financial insolvency and a shortage of appealing candidates.

---

[2] Pomeroy, *The Pacific Slope*, p. 328.

[3] The Morse-Neuberger feud had the effect of dividing the party into two separate camps. Just as the Democratic congressional delegation divided their loyalties between Morse or Neuberger, so too did party officials and rank-and-file Democrats in Oregon. In 1959, Morse announced he would campaign against Neuberger in the senatorial election of 1960. What promised to be a most divisive party battle never took place; Neuberger died shortly before the primary. His widow, Maurine, was elected to the Senate in 1960. For a partisan discussion of the relationship between Morse and Neuberger and their quarrel, see Smith, *The Tiger in the Senate*, pp. 333-370.

Democratic troubles following 1956 were paralleled by the emergence of new leadership in Republican circles which began the process of refurbishing the G.O.P. through the adoption of nonpartisan politics, a strategy long practiced by Democrats as a minority party. Rejecting the reputation of conservatism bestowed on the party in the late 1940s and early 1950s by Douglas McKay and Guy Cordon, Republican figures like Mark Hatfield and Robert Packwood remodeled state Republicanism along moderate, if not always clearly liberal, lines. With studied disregard of formal party organization and the Republican label, Hatfield's ecumenical approach to politics enabled him to defeat Democrat Robert Holmes in the gubernatorial election of 1958. In his campaign, Hatfield stressed the nonpartisan nature of the governorship and sounded pleas much like those of Democrat George Chamberlain at the turn of the century.[4] Assuming the same political posture, Hatfield won reelection to the governorship in 1962, and was elected to the United States Senate in 1966.[5]

Like Hatfield, Robert Packwood emphasized youth and liberalism in revitalizing the G.O.P. Working independently of the Republican State Central Committee, he inaugurated the "Dorchester Conferences" in 1965 to organize the moderate and liberal wings of the Republican Party. Using these meetings as a sounding board for liberalism, Packwood called for a new Republican coalition constituted of organized labor, minorities, and "campus intellectuals."[6] The Portland *Oregonian*, impressed with the "intelligent, articulate and enthusiastic young people" who attended the first Dorchester Conference, observed that "Oregon's old elephant . . . [had] taken a dip in the Fountain of Youth.'[7] Packwood's efforts to rebuild

---

[4] Hatfield first adopted nonpartisanship in a state-wide campaign in 1956 when he defeated Monroe Sweetland for the office of secretary of state. During the campaign, Sweetland tried to counter this tack by advertising the fact that Hatfield was a Republican. Noting that Hatfield's campaign literature made scant reference to his party affiliation, Sweetland wrote in the *Oregon Democrats:* "As a public service we now release exclusively for our readers that . . . Mark Hatfield [is] running on the Republican Ticket." *Oregon Democrat,* 24 (Oct. 1956), p. 3. See also John M. Swarthout, "The 1958 Election In Oregon," *Western Political Quarterly,* 12, part 2 (Mar. 1959), pp. 328-344. For Hatfield's comments on his campaign strategy, see Mark O. Hatfield, *Not Quite So Simple* (New York, 1968), pp. 21-25, 29-34.

[5] Donald G. Balmer, "The 1962 Election In Oregon," *Western Political Quarterly,* 16 (June, 1963), pp. 453-459; Balmer, "The 1966 Election in Oregon," *Western Political Quarterly,* 20, part 2 (June, 1967), pp. 593-601.

[6] Portland *Oregonian,* Apr. 12, 1965, p. 18.

[7] *Ibid.* Apr. 13, 1965, p. 18. In 1969, a group of young liberal Democrats called a meeting similar to the Dorchester Conferences. Known as the "Democforum," this meeting, and a second in 1970, were conducted independently of the regular party machinery. See Portland *Oregonian,* May 29, 1969, p. 32; June 22, 1970, p. 1.

the G.O.P. paid handsome dividends in 1968 when he was elected to the United States Senate.[8]

Emulating the style of politics practiced by Hatfield and Packwood, other Republicans also won elections despite a rising majority of registered Democratic voters. The personal, nonpartisan campaigns of some Republicans in the 1960s was so reminiscent of Oregon's earlier politics that one political analyst referred to the practitioners as the " 'new Progressives.' "[9] And, like the old progressives, at least one of the "new progressives," Republican Senator Mark Hatfield, demonstrated an independence of party in Washington. Hatfield proved to be as independent of Republican President Richard Nixon as Senator Wayne Morse was of Democratic President Lyndon Johnson. In this, Hatfield and Morse were not unlike Senators George Chamberlain and Harry Lane, who acted independently of President Woodrow Wilson.

In general, Democrats stressed the party label in campaigns against Republicans who emphasized nonpartisanship, often with unsatisfactory results. Perhaps complacent because of advantages in party registration, and not sufficiently aware that exhortations to party loyalty were ineffective in a party no longer united, Democrats unwittingly allowed certain Republicans to claim nonpartisanship as their principal campaign appeal.

Politics in Oregon after 1956 proved remarkably similar to traditional political patterns. While Democrats had once capitalized on nonpartisanship, independence of party organization, and the politics of personality, Republicans appropriated this strategy in the 1960s. All of this recalled a political system conceived and born in the first decade of the twentieth century.

---

[8] The senatorial election of 1968 came at a time when the Oregon Democratic Party was split over American foreign policy in Vietnam. Packwood's victory over Senator Morse stemmed as much from Democratic division as his political image. See Joseph M. Allman, "The 1968 Elections In Oregon," *Western Political Quarterly*, 22 (Sept., 1969), pp. 517-525.

[9] Swarthout and Gervais, "Oregon: Political Experiment Station," p. 312.

Note on Sources

Very little has appeared in print on twentieth-century Oregon politics, and virtually nothing on the history of the Democratic Party in Oregon during this period. There are a few articles and general histories of the Pacific Northwest, but the only detailed studies are unpublished master's theses and doctoral dissertations. Most of the theses and dissertations are focused on the progressive era of Oregon politics. The chief source for this study, therefore, was original records and manuscripts. Listed below are some, but not all, of the most significant sources; others are cited in the footnotes.

This book could not have been written without access to the rich collection of manuscripts at the University of Oregon Library in Eugene. Among the most useful collections were the papers of Sam H. Brown, Henry M. Hanzen, Robert A. Miller, Richard L. Neuberger, Thomas B. Neuhausen, and Walter M. Pierce. All of these men were active in Oregon politics, either as politicians or campaign strategists. The Neuberger papers were especially valuable because they contained correspondence of Senator Harry Lane for whom only scattered letters exist. The Hanzen papers include an unpublished manuscript, "The Joseph-Meier Political Revolution," which is an interesting, informative, first-hand account of the gubernatorial election of 1930. The Thomas B. Neuhausen manuscripts were an extremely valuable source for Oregon poltics and the Democratic Party from the Republican point of view between the progressive period and the early 1930s.

Also consulted at the University of Oregon Library were the papers of Homer D. Angell, Harris Ellsworth, Nina Lane Faubion, Thomas G. Green, Nan Wood Honeyman, Claude R. Lester, Douglas McKay, Robert Sawyer, Oswald West, and the records of the Oregon Commonwealth Federation.

The private correspondence of George E. Chamberlain and Charles H. Martin at the Oregon Historical Society in Portland were rich in political comment. The Chamberlain manuscripts were an informative source on the progressive era of Oregon politics and Governor Martin's letters were a colorful and indispensable guide to the New Deal years. The papers of Milton A. Miller at the Oregon State Library in Salem shed some light on Democratic politics during the early 1930s.

Among the unpublished doctoral dissertations the most informative were Warren M. Blankenship, "Progressives and the Progressive Party in Oregon, 1906-1916" (University of Oregon, 1966); Franklyn D. Mahar, "Douglas McKay and the Issues of Power Development in Oregon, 1953-1956" (University of Oregon, 1968); Albert H. Pike, Jr., "Jonathan Bourne, Jr., Progressive" (University of Oregon, 1957); and Herman C. Voeltz, "Proposals for a Columbia Valley Authority: A History of Political Controversy" (University of Oregon, 1960). Several master's theses were helpful, but most especially the following: Maude D. Chapman, "Sylvester Pennoyer, Governor of Oregon, 1887-1896" (University of Oregon, 1943); Russell G. Hendricks, "The Effect of the Direct Primary Upon Senatorial Elections in Oregon, 1900-1909" (University of Oregon, 1951); John D. Phillips, 'Charles L. McNary: Progressive Ideology and Minority Politics During the New Deal" (University of Oregon, 1963); and Robert C. Woodward, "William Simon U'Ren: In An Age of Protest" (University of Oregon, 1956). Two undergraduate theses at Reed College in Portland merit special acknowledgment: George M. Joseph, "George W. Joseph and the Oregon Progressive Tradition" (Reed College, 1952) and Harold Swayze, "Party Politics in Oregon" (Reed College, 1952).

Newspapers and contemporary periodicals were of considerable value. Of most general use were the Portland *Oregonian*, *Oregon Journal*, Salem *Capital Journal*, Salem *Capital Press*, and the Salem *Oregon Statesman*. Two contemporary periodicals, the *Oregon Voter* and the *Oregon Democrat*, contained a great deal of information on state politics. Established in 1915, the *Oregon Voter* was an unofficial voice for the Republican Party. The *Oregon Democrat*, which began continuous publication in 1933, was the official magazine of the Democratic Party.

Although not specifically cited in footnotes, state election results for the years between 1906 and 1956 were drawn from *Abstract of Votes* (Salem: Secretary of State). Registration figures for the Republican and the Democratic parties betwen 1909 and 1970 were based on reports in the annual *Oregon Blue Book* (Salem: Secretary of State). *Trends in Oregon Voting, 1858-1960* (Salem: Secretary of State, 1962) was important in calculating voting trends over the twentieth century.

Because of the paucity of books and articles on Oregon politics, secondary sources were of limited value. Some secondary material, however, offered general information which was valuable in suggesting contrasts between Democratic politics in Oregon and Democratic politics in other states and the national scene. Particularly instructive were David Burner, *The Politics of Provincialism: The Democratic Party in Transition, 1918-1932* (New York: Alfred A. Knopf, 1968); Daniel J. Elazar, *American Federalism: A View from the States* (New York: Thomas Y. Crowell Company, 1966); Leon D. Epstein, *Politics In Wisconsin* (Madison: University of Wisconsin Press, 1958); John H. Fenton, *Midwest Politics* (New York: Holt, Rinehart and Winston, 1966); Frank H. Jonas, ed. *Politics in the American West* (Salt Lake City: University of Utah Press, 1969); V. O. Key, Jr., *American State Politics: An Introduction* (New York: Alfred A. Knopf, 1956); James T. Patterson, *The New Deal and the States: Federalism In Transition* (Princeton: Princeton University Press, 1969); and Earl Pomeroy, *The Pacific Slope: A History of California, Oregon, Washington, Idaho, Utah, and Nevada* (New York: Alfred A. Knopf, 1965).

Also useful in a comparative assessment of Democratic politics in Oregon were Samuel J. Eldersveld, "The Influence of Metropolitan Pluralities in Presidential Elections Since 1920: A Study of Twelve Key Cities," *American Political Science Review*, 43 (Dec., 1949), pp. 1189-1206; V. O. Key, Jr., "A Theory of Critical Elections," *Journal of Politics*, 17 (Feb., 1955), pp. 3-18; Samuel C. Patterson, "The Political Cultures of the American States," *Journal of Politics*, 30 (Sept., 1968), pp. 187-209; and the articles on elections in Western states which appeared in the *Western Political Quarterly* beginning in 1948.

Interviews with Monroe Sweetland, Howard Morgan, James Goodsell, and Edward F. Bailey, Democrats active in politics before and after the Second World War, provided an essential and useful background to this study.

Appendices

APPENDIX I

Party Registration For General Elections In Oregon, 1908-1956

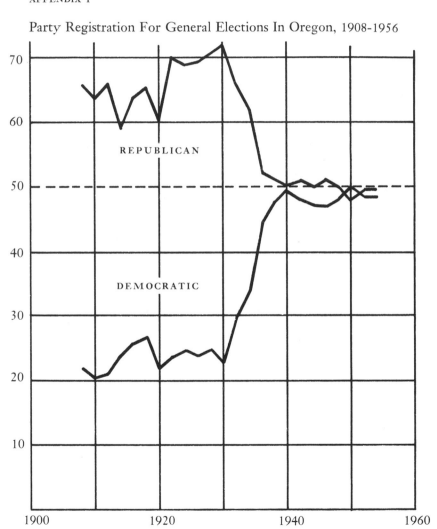

SOURCE: *Trends In Oregon Voting, 1858-1960* (Salem: Secretary of State, 1962).

APPENDIX II

Major Party Vote In Percentages of Total Votes Cast,
Presidential Elections In Oregon, 1900-1956

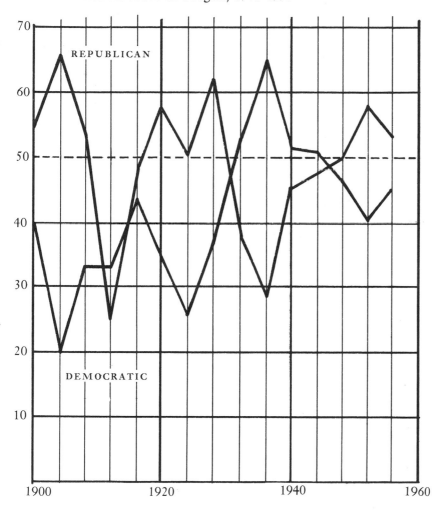

SOURCE: *Trends In Oregon Voting, 1858-1960* (Salem: Secretary of State, 1962).

APPENDIX III

Percentage Point Change In Democratic Per Cent of Two-Party Vote, Presidential Elections 1920-1956

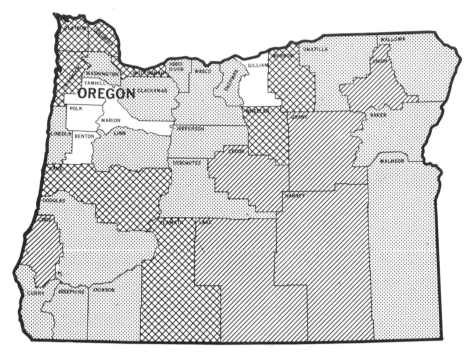

15 Per Cent or more Increase:	14 to 10 Per Cent Increase:	9 to 0 Per Cent Increase:	1 Per Cent or more Decrease
CLATSOP	COOS	BAKER	BENTON
COLUMBIA	CROOK	CLACKAMAS	GILLIAM
KLAMATH	GRANT	CURRY	MARION
LANE	HARNEY	DESCHUTES	POLK
MORROW	LAKE	DOUGLAS	YAMHILL
MULTNOMAH	UNION	HOOD RIVER	
TILLAMOOK		JACKSON	
WHEELER		JEFFERSON	
		JOSEPHINE	
		LINCOLN	
		LINN	
		MALHEUR	
		SHERMAN	
		UMATILLA	
		WALLOWA	
		WASCO	
		WASHINGTON	

NOTE: Political change for the period 1920 to 1956 is measured by computing a line of regression (or secular trend line) for each of the counties of the state. Consequently, the measure of change is a product of all elections of the series and not the first and last election.

Index

Aiken, Henry C., 108
Aldrich, E. B., 59
Al Sarena Mining Company, 135
American Federation of Labor (AFL), 68-69, 84, 100
American Protective Association, 46
Americans For Democratic Action (ADA), 106, 109
Angell, Homer D., 69, 88n111, 100, 128, 138n47
Anti-Saloon League, 55
Arlington Club, 55
Association Against the Prohibition Amendment, 62

Bacon, Keith, 106
Bailey, Edward F., 12n26, 41n6, 47, 72, 74
Bonneville Dam, 75, 76, 78n68, 82, 83
Bonneville Power Administration, 137
Booth, Robert A., 36
Bourne, Jonathan, Jr., 23, 28, 32, 33, 34, 35
Bowerman, Jay, 31, 32, 32n46
Brannan Farm Plan, 104, 105
Bridges, Harry, 69
Brown, Sam H., 76, 77, 78-80
Bryan, William J., 20, 21
Bull, Vernon D., 110, 115n47
Bureau of Reclamation, 75
Burke, W. E., 83
Burner, David, 40n4

Cake, H. M., 28
Carll, William E., 20
Carney, Byron F., 83, 88, 107, 110
Carson, Joseph K., Jr., 83, 128, 132
Chamberlain, George E.: early career of, 25-27; independence of party, 12, 37, 41, 145; and presidential campaign of 1904 and 1908, 22; gubernatorial election of 1902, 25-26; as governor, 27; senatorial campaign

of 1908, 29-30; friendship with Theodore Roosevelt, 30n38; supports West, 32; senatorial campaign of 1914, 36; senatorial campaign of 1920, 42-46; appointed to U.S. Shipping Board, 46; and Haney, 52-53; see also Nonpartisanship
Chapman, C. C.: on Democrats and nonpartisanship, 12; on Pierce, 48; on Ku Klux Klan, 49n30; on Haney, 52; on anti-Haney Democrats, 56; on Zimmerman, 79
Civil Works Administration (CWA), 67
Clark, Alfred E., 32, 34
Cleveland, Grover, 19
Columbia Valley Authority (CVA): as political issue in 1930s, 75; Oregon Grange supports, 75; State Federation of Labor supports, 75; Portland Chamber of Commerce opposes, 75; Martin opposes, 82; Pierce supports, 83; OCF supports, 84; as political issue in 1950, 105, 113-114, 115-120
Compulsory School Bill (1922), 47, 48, 49
Congress of Industrial Organizations (CIO), 68-69, 100, 114
Coolidge, Calvin, 52, 98
Corbett, Henry, 23
Cordon, Guy, 129, 130, 131, 135, 144
Cox, James M., 46, 58n61
Culbertson, William C., 74

Dana, Marshall, 53
Daniels, Josephus, 43
Davidson, C. Girard, 114
Davis, John W., 39, 50, 51
DeCicco, Mike, 108, 110, 111, 112, 121
Democratic Party, in Oregon: history of before 1890, 2; areas of strength, 96-97; finances of, 11, 22, 23, 59, 105,

143; organization, 7, 10, 11, 12, 18, 22, 23, 36, 59, 64, 71, 101, 105, 107, 139, 142, 143; and labor, 13, 14, 64, 68-69, 75-76, 85, 100, 101, 105, 114, 120, 128; rural-urban antagonisms in 1920s, 40-41; and New Deal, 66; compared with Democratic parties of Minnesota, Wisconsin, and Michigan, 65, 103; see also Patronage, Nonpartisanship, Prohibition, and Voting trends
Democratic Party, national: composition of in 1930s, 63; Oregon Democrats subordinate identification with, 45, 100; rural-urban antagonisms in 1920s, 40-41; finances in presidential elections of 1900, 1904, and 1908 in Oregon, 22-23
Democratic-Progressive coalition of 1924, 50
Demoforum, 144n7
Dever, Lem A., 55n50
Dewey, Thomas E., 109, 134
Donaldson, C. M., 21
Donaugh, Carl C., 61, 62, 66, 81n81, 115n47
Dorchester Conference, 144
Dreyer, Phil, 115n47
Dunne, Joe E., 76, 79, 80, 81

Earl, Stanley, 114
Eisenhower, Dwight D., 98n12, 125, 126, 129, 133, 136
Elections:
Primary, of 1903, 27; of 1906, 28; of 1910, 30; of 1912, 32; of 1918, 41n5; of 1920, 42, 43-44; of 1922, 47; of 1926, 52-55; of 1928, 56-58; of 1930, 71-72; of 1932, 62; of 1934, 76-79; of 1938, 84-87; of 1942, 101; of 1948, 108; of 1950, 114-117; of 1952, 121-122; of 1954, 128-129; of 1956, 135-136; of 1960, 143n3; see also Voting trends
General, of 1890, 18; of 1892, 18; of 1894, 19; of 1896, 20; of 1898, 20; of 1902, 26, 27; of 1904, 28; of 1906, 28; of 1908, 29; of 1910, 30, 31; of 1912, 32, 33; of 1914, 35, 36; of 1916, 36, 39; of 1918, 36; of 1920, 39, 43-44; of 1922, 46, 48-50; of 1924, 39, 50-51; of 1926, 55-56; of 1928, 39, 58; of 1930, 71-74; of 1932, 63, 64, 65; of 1934, 79-80; of 1936, 65, 69; of 1938, 65, 68, 87; of 1940, 88; of 1942, 88; of 1944, 100; of 1948, 109, 110; of 1950, 117-120; of 1952, 123-124; of 1954, 128, 129-132; of 1956, 134, 135-136, 138-139, 141, 144n4; of 1958, 144; of 1960, 143n3; of 1962, 144; of 1964, 142; of 1966, 142, 144; of

1968, 144-145; see also Voting trends
Ellingson, A. L., 106
Elliott, Marion L. "Mike," 111, 112
Ellsworth, Harris, 118, 119, 121, 133, 137

Fair Deal, 104-118
Fair Employment Practices Commission (FEPC), 104, 137
Federation of Patriotic Societies, 46, 49
Fisk, Fred, 101
Flegel, Austin F., 35n60, 47, 114, 115, 116, 120
Fulton, Charles J., 28
Furnish, William J., 26

Garner, John Nance, 62
Gearin, John, 28
Geer, T. T., 27
Goodsell, James, 105, 106, 111
Grand Coulee Dam, 75
Grange Power Bill (1930), 71, 72, 73, 75
Great Depression: political effect in nation, 61; political effect in Oregon, 63, 92, 93, 96, 97, 98, 99
Green, Edith, 122, 123, 128, 134, 137

Hall, Charles, 47
Hamaker, Gilbert, 41, 43, 44, 57
Haney, Bert E.: early career of, 52n38; appointed U.S. Shipping Board, 52; as senatorial candidate in 1926, 52, 53, 54, 55; supports Meier, 74; and Martin, 79
Hanley, William, 36
Harding, Warren G., 46, 98
Hatfield, Mark O., 137, 144, 145
Hells Canyon, 125, 129, 133, 136
Hess, Henry, 83, 86, 87
Hitchcock, Philip S., 134, 135
Hoff, O. P., 50
Holman, Rufus, 76, 77
Holmes, Robert D., 106, 110, 122, 136, 137, 144
Honeyman, Nan Wood, 65, 68-69, 83, 85, 87, 107
Hoover, "Deadwood" Dave, 119
Hoover, Herbert, 59, 98
Hosch, J. F., 83
Hughes, Charles E., 36
Humphrey, Hubert, 108, 109
Humphreys, Lester W., 107
Hydroelectric power: public development of as a political issue, 15, 50n33, 62, 71-72ff, 113-114ff, 125-126ff, 136-137; failure of Democratic leadership to support in 1930s, 73-74ff; liberal Democrats support, 106, 113-114ff, 125-126ff;

OCF supports, 83-84, 104-105; Oregon Grange supports, 75; Oregon State Federation of Labor supports, 75; *see also* Hells Canyon, Grange Power Bill (1930), and Partnership

Ickes, Harold, 86, 87

Jackson, C. S., 42
"Jeffersonian Democrats For Dewey," 109
Johnson, Lyndon, 145
Joseph, George W., 50n33, 71-73, 132
Josslin, William, 110, 110n26, 116, 121

Kelly, John W., 42
Key, V. O., Jr., 58n65, 91, 92
King, Will R., 20, 21, 41, 44, 51, 53, 59
Knights of Labor, 18
Ku Klux Klan, in Oregon: 39, 46-49, 51n35, 55n50, 99
Korell, Franklin F., 48, 74

La Follette, Robert M., 39, 50, 51
Lane, Harry: early career of, 35; elected mayor of Portland, 25; campaigns for West, 32; senatorial campaign of 1912, 33-35; on Chamberlain and patronage, 43; independence of Wilson, 145
Latourette, Earl C., 112
Latourette, Howard, as National Committeeman, 83, 88; as conservative Democrat, 100n13; and senatorial campaign of 1950, 115, 116, 118-119
Laurion, Mrs. Ramona, 111
League For CVA, 114
Lee, Jason, 135
Lessard, Dellmore, 109
Lundy, Herbert, 137

McAdoo, William G., 42, 56, 62
McArthur, Clifton N., 36n60, 48
McCall, Tom, 117, 128, 129, 132
McCarthyism, in election of 1950, 117-119
McGrath, J. Howard, 108
McKay, Douglas, 10, 114, 125, 129, 134-136, 144
McNary, Charles L.: in senatorial campaign of 1918, 37; in senatorial campaign of 1924, 51; and Pierce, 53; and nonpartisanship during 1930s, 67; and senatorial campaign of 1936, 72; position on public power, 73, 132, 137; and senatorial campaign of 1942, 101; death of, 129
Maddron, William F., 106

Mahoney, Thomas R., 69, 104, 111, 112, 122, 123, 142n1
Mahoney, Willis, 67, 69, 78, 79, 80, 81, 83
Marr, James T., 114
"Martin-For-Governor" Club, 86
Martin, Charles H.: early career of, 69-70; and congressional elections of 1930 and 1932, 62-63, 64; and gubernatorial election campaign of 1934, 77-82; on prohibition, 62, 63n7; on relief, 70, 82n86; on law and order, 70-71, 85; on OCF, 84n 92; on labor, 85; on public power, 73, 78, 79, 81, 82, 83, 86; and opposition to New Deal, 70, 82-83, 86-87; opposed by New Deal Democrats, 82-83; denounced by *Oregon Democrat*, 85; and gubernatorial primary of 1938, 85-87; campaigns for Republicans, 87, 88n111
Martin, Joseph, 130
Martin, Volney, 122
Matthews, Francis P., 108
May, Walter W. R., 78
Mays Law, 27
Meier, Julius, 72, 73, 74, 76, 132
Metschan, Phil, 72, 73, 74n53
Miller, Robert A., 43
Mitchell, Donnell, 128
Mitchell, John H., 24
Morgan, Howard: and Sweetland in WWII, 91; elected to state legislature, 110; supports New Deal, 91n1; opposes DeCicco, 110-111; opposes Mahoney, 122-123; as candidate for Commissioner of Labor, 116; supports Flegel, 116, 120; on CVA, 120; as chairman of State Central Committee, 121-123; and Morse, 126-127; opposes Sweetland, 128n12; and party schism after 1956, 143
Morse, Wayne L.: and senatorial campaign of 1944, 100; and labor, 100, 126; conservative Republicans oppose, 100, 126n5; bolts Republican Party, 16, 123-124; in senatorial campaign of 1950, 114, 117, 119; wins Democratic support, 118-119, 126-127; campaigns for Neuberger, 131; becomes Democrat, 133; and senatorial campaign of 1956, 133, 134-136; defeat by Packwood, 142, 145n8; quarrel with Neuberger, 143; as nonpartisan, 137; independence of party, 16, 145
Murphy, Daniel, 19
Murray, William "Alfalfa Bill," 62
Myers, Frank S., 43

Myers, Jefferson, 31, 50, 51

National Recovery Act (NRA), 85
Neuberger, Maurine, 130, 136, 143*n*3
Neuberger, Richard L.: early career of, 129-131; on public power, 71; on Zimmerman, 80*n*74; on Morse as politician, 131*n*20, 126, 118*n*63; on CVA, 114, 116; elected to state senate, 110; senatorial campaign of 1954, 128, 129-131; campaigns for Morse, 136; quarrel with Morse, 143; as nonpartisan, 137, 143
Neuhausen, Thomas, 44, 45*n*16, 48, 50, 54, 73*n*50
Newbry, Earl T., 129
New Deal: Oregon Democrats fail to profit from, 64-65, 91, 100, 138; and public power policies, 71, 75-76, 82-83; and Charles McNary, 67; and political coalition of, 13, 63
Nixon, Richard M., 130, 136, 145
Nonpartisanship: in Oregon politics, 14-16, 66-67, 99, 137, 144-145; and Democrats, 11, 12, 18, 21, 23, 25, 26, 35, 41, 63, 99, 137, 144; and Republicans, 15-16, 35, 137, 144; and Chamberlain, 15, 21-23, 25-29, 41, 42-46, 52, 145; and West, 31, 36, 41; and Lane, 32-34, 145; and Haney, 52-56; and McNary, 37, 66-67, 132, 137; and Angell, 100*n*14; and Hatfield, 144-145; and Morse, 16, 138-139; and Neuberger, 130, 137, 143; *see also* Political culture and Programmatic politics
Norris, George, 87

Olcott, Ben, 47
Oregon: economy of, 4-5, 94-95, 103; demography of, 2-4, 92-93; geography of, 4-5; religion in, 4; as "Vermont of the West," 108, 138; political change in, 1-2, 3, 89, 93-97, 137, 141-143
Oregon Automobile Dealers Association, 10
Oregon Commonwealth Federation (OCF), 84, 86, 88, 104, 106, 107, 112
Oregon Democrat: begins publication, 63; Sweetland purchases, 109
Oregon Democratic League, 81
Oregon Grange, 13, 18, 64, 71, 72, 75, 76, 80, 82, 84, 86, 105, 120
Oregon State Federation of Labor, 64, 68, 69, 71, 72, 80, 83, 100, 105, 120
Oregon System, 21, 27, 30, 31, 34
Oregon Tammany Society, 57, 58
Oregon Voter: see Chapman, C. C.
Osborne, Ben T., 84

Packwood, Robert, 144, 145
Partnership plan, 125, 126, 128
Patronage: used by Democrats, 12-13, 12*n*28, 23, 27, 32*n*46, 33, 36, 49; as source of Democratic schism in 1920s, 41, 42-43, 44, 46, 52; in 1930s, 67-68, 71, 88; in 1940s, 104, 108, 110, 112; used by Republicans, 104
Patterson, James T., 66
Patterson, Paul, 129, 132, 133
Pearson, Walter J., 104, 109, 112, 115-116, 120, 121, 142*n*1
Perkins, Frances, 86
Pierce, Cornelia, 74
Pierce, Nathan, 19
Pierce, Walter M.: early career of, 47*n*24; gubernatorial election campaign of 1922, 47-51; support of La Follette in 1924, 50-51; and gubernatorial election of 1926, 56; on state of party, 52; on prohibition, 57-58; on public power, 51, 72-73, 78, 83; elected to Congress in 1932, 63; reelected to Congress, 65, 78; elected National Committeeman, 73; sides with Meier, 74; opposes Martin, 83, 85; defeat in election of 1942, 88
Political culture, 14-16
Political parties, in Oregon: general nature of, 7, 10, 11, 12, 13, 137-138, 142; statutory provisions for, 10; effect of direct primary upon, 10-11, 17, 27, 28, 29; tests of competitiveness, 6-9; effect of intrastate cohesiveness upon, 6, 13-14
Populist (People's) Party, in Oregon: 18-21
Porter, Charles O., 106, 128, 135, 137
Portland Chamber of Commerce, 52, 75, 77
Pratt, Martin, 112
Programmatic politics, 103, 104, 132, 137, 138, 142
Progressive Party (1912), 32-35
Prohibition: impact upon Oregon Democrats, 40-41; impact upon Oregon Republicans, 55; as issue in senatorial election of 1926, 54-56; in presidential election of 1928, 56-58
Public-utility districts, 73, 74, 84
Public Works Administration (PWA), 75
Putnam, George, 57

Reames, Alfred E., 86
Reed, James, 57, 58
Republican Assembly, 30, 31
Republican Party, in Oregon: as ma-

jority party, 1, 6, 7; effect of immigration upon, 3; lack of organizational unity, 7, 10, 12, 13, 138; division within during Progressive era, 23-25; effect of Great Depression upon, 93, 96; conservatism of during 1950s, 138; revitalization of in 1960s, 144-145; and Arlington Club, 138n47; compared with Republican Party of Wisconsin, 7n17; compared with Democratic Party system of South, 7n17, 138; *see also* Voting trends

Republican Party, national: and economic collapse of 1929, 64-65; and urban vote in 1920s, 97-98; and conservation policies under Eisenhower, 125

Rogers, Will, 1

Roosevelt, Franklin D.: presidential vote for in Oregon, 65; McNary cooperates with, 66-67; and patronage for OCF, 88; and Martin, 81-82

Roosevelt, Theodore, 30n38, 32

Schenck, Rosemary, 67
Scott, Harvey W., 19, 30-31
Seaton, Fred A., 136
Selling, Ben, 32, 34
Shaw, Dave C., 115, 119, 120-121
Shouse, Jouett, 62
Simon, Joseph, 23
Skelton, Keith, 106
Smith, Alfred E., 41, 56, 57, 58
Smith, Charles J., 35, 53, 74
Smith, Edgar W., 100, 101
Snell, Earl, 10, 101
Solomon, Gus J., 112
Sprague, Charles A., 10, 87, 120, 134
Stanton, Charles V., 117
Stanfield, Robert N., 44, 45, 54, 55, 56
Starkweather, Harvey, 41, 43, 44, 53, 59, 69
Statement Number One, 28, 29, 30
Statement Number Two, 28
Steffens, Lincoln, 30
Steiwer, Frederick, 55, 86
Sterling, Donald J., 79
Stockman, Lowell, 134
Story, J. L., 21
Straub, Robert, 142
Swanson, Walter A., 115
Sweetland, Monroe: as organizer of OCF, 84; as New Deal Democrat, 88; and Morgan in WWII, 91; on party organization, 104, 124; on role of OCF in rebuilding party, 106, 107; as publicity chairman of party, 107; campaign for National Committeeman, 108; as National Committeeman, 108-109; and presidential campaign of 1948, 109; and DeCicco, 111-112; and Solomon, 112; on CVA, 113, 120; on Flegel, 115; victim of McCarthyism, 117; dispute with Latourette, 118; supports Morse, 118; reelection as National Committeeman, 121; and recruitment of candidates, 122, 123; on Morgan, 121; and praise of Morse, 126-127; on party unity, 128; plans to run for Congress, 128n12; on Carson, 132n26; on programmatic politics, 132; advice to Morse, 133n28; candidate for Secretary of State, 135, 144n4; and party schism after 1956, 143

Taft-Hartley Act, 104, 105, 114, 118
Taft, William H., 34, 35
Teal, Joseph N., 19
Tennessee Valley Authority (TVA), 75, 125
Tierney, Frank, 83, 87n106, 88
Thiessen, G. W., 75n56, 83
Thompson, D. P., 18
Thornton, Robert Y., 122, 123, 136
Tompkins, Morton, 77, 107, 114
Truman, Harry S., 97, 98, 104, 109, 112, 113, 118, 120

Ullman, Al, 106, 128, 135
Union Party, 18
United States Army Corps of Engineers, 75
United States Shipping Board, 46, 52
U'Ren, William S., 21, 24

Veatch, R. M., 21
Versailles, Treaty of, 42, 44, 45
Voting trends, in Oregon: for president, 97, 151; for governor, 98-99; for senator, 98-99; change in Democratic per cent of two-party vote for president, 152; Republican primary vote for governor, 7, 8-9; 1928 as critical election, 58n65

Wallace, Lew, 100n13, 101, 104, 107, 108, 109, 111, 112, 115, 116, 120
Walsh, Thomas J., 57, 58
Ward, L. T., 115
Watkins, Elton, 48, 52, 53, 55, 73, 81
Weatherford, Mark V., 83
Weaver, James B., 19
West, Oswald: on Chamberlain and Theodore Roosevelt, 30n38; gubernatorial campaign of 1910, 31-32; and gubernatorial campaign of 1914, 35; and senatorial campaign

of 1918, 36-37, 41n5; center of controversy in 1920s, 41-42; supports Chamberlain in 1920, 43-44; elected National Committeeman in 1926, 56; opposition to Smith in 1928, 56-58; as champion of prohibition, 57, 57-62; on Democratic leadership, 59, and FDR, 62; and Martin, 62; on public power, 72-73; defeated for National Committeeman, 73; as utility lobbyist, 41-42, 72n43, 77; role in Martin campaign of 1934, 77; criticized by Mahoney, 78; campaign strategist for Martin in 1938, 83, 86, 87n105; on OCF, 88; on Sweetland, 103; on liberal Democrats, 117-119
Whedon, Daniel D., 84

Whitbeck, Walter, 67, 101
Wilbur, George R., 72, 73, 79
Wilkins, W. E., 108
Williams, G. Mennen, 132n27
Williams, Ralph E., 35
Williams, Vernon, 66, 83, 85
Wilson, Manley J., 109, 110
Wilson, Woodrow, 35, 39, 44, 98n12
Withycombe, James, 27, 35
Wood, C. E. S., 19, 27, 34n53, 36, 41
Wood, Louis A., 115, 116
Wyatt, Wendell, 133

Young Democratic Clubs of America, 62
Young Democratic League, 62

Zimmerman, Peter, 64, 79, 80, 81, 82n 84, 84, 130

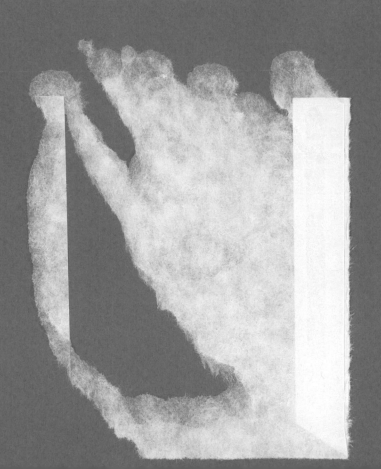